Ann Rule worked the all-night shift at a suicide hotline with a handsome, whip-smart psychology major who became her close friend. Soon the world would know him: serial killer Ted Bundy . . .

THE STRANGER BESIDE ME

Now in an updated edition!

"Shattering . . . written with compassion but also with professional objectivity."

—*The Seattle Times*

"Overwhelming!"

—*Houston Post*

"Rule has an extraordinary angle on the most fascinating killer in modern American history. . . . As dramatic and chilling as a bedroom window shattering at midnight."

—*The New York Times*

And praise for one of Ann Rule's classics of true crime!

DEAD BY SUNSET

"Fascinating. . . . A labyrinthine tale."
—*The New York Times Book Review*

"A chilling, haunting portrait. . . . Rule provides a perceptive character analysis of a malignant, self-centered, charismatic con artist."

—*Publishers Weekly*

BOOKS BY ANN RULE

ANN RULE

PRACTICE TO DECEIVE

POCKET BOOKS

New York   London   Toronto   Sydney   New Delhi

Pocket Books
A Division of Simon & Schuster, Inc.
1230 Avenue of the Americas
New York, NY 10020

All names in this book that are marked with an asterisk are pseudonyms.

First Pocket Books paperback edition November 2014

POCKET and colophon are registered trademarks of Simon & Schuster, Inc.

For information about special discounts for bulk purchases,please contact Simon & Schuster Special Sales at 1-866-506-1949 or business@simonandschuster.com.

The Simon & Schuster Speakers Bureau can bring authors to your live event. For more information or to book an event, contact the Simon & Schuster Speakers Bureau at 1-866-248-3049 or visit our website at www.simonspeakers.com.

Manufactured in the United States of America

10   9   8   7   6   5

ISBN 978-1-4165-4463-0
ISBN 978-1-4516-8737-8 (ebook)

To good cops everywhere who never give up, even when they are investigating the most difficult cases imaginable. The public will never really know the overtime they put in, the emotional toll they often pay, or how much it matters to them that justice will one day be served.

Oh what a tangled web we weave
    when first we practice to deceive.
        —Sir Walter Scott, *Marmion*,
        Canto VI, XVII

CONTENTS

FOREWORD

THIS STORY OF MURDER has as many facets as an intricately cut diamond, far too many to seem believable as either fiction or nonfiction. Either way, as the bizarre scenarios blaze a path through encounters between people who would not be expected to know one another, this saga might well seem contrived. As nonfiction—which it is—it is a murky sea of reality with myriad characters who seem larger than life. They are infinitely different from one another in personalities, lifestyles, and possible motivations.

I have wondered if their machinations can be reconstructed here in any orderly fashion. Where do I jump in and build a foundation of sentences and paragraphs strong enough to bear the weight of everything that must be told? There are no locks that my author's keys will open easily, just as there are few threads that might be woven into a pattern that makes sense.

The denouement of this baffling case took a decade. The entire story traverses fifty years. Even now, there are shadowy corners where secrets still hide.

Many innocents have died violent deaths in unlikely places. Over time, the motives behind *why* these particular human beings were singled out for death are more obscure.

IN THE SIXTIES, A group of authors decided to write a rather silly book where each writer penned a chapter. New additions didn't necessarily have to have anything to do with the story line that came before. The provocative title and book jacket drew potential buyers, and *Naked Came the Stranger* became a bizarre bestseller.

Some years later, I belonged to a similar social organization of a dozen or so Seattle best-selling authors. We called it the Bitch and Moan Society. It was a venue to air our disappointments, complaints, and anxieties about our profession. Eventually, we decided to write a book similar to *Naked Came the Stranger,* where we, too, took turns writing disconnected chapters.

Our manuscript, *Deadly Obsession, Possession, and Depression Revisited,* was packed with implausible plots and wacky characters. A reader could start at the beginning, the end, or the middle and none of it fit together, which isn't surprising, because each of us wrote in a different genre: romance, horror, military espionage, true crime, psychological suspense, teenage love stories, humor, and historical sagas. We never intended to publish it, which was just as well, but we all laughed hysterically when each segment was read aloud.

One of our rules demanded that we always had to "put the action on an island!"

In many ways *Practice to Deceive* has challenged me to cover murderous plots with players as diverse as our mythical *Deadly Obsession*. And, ironically, many of the nefarious plots in this book *did* take place on an island.

CAST OF CHARACTERS

JAMES STACKHOUSE
First wife: Mary Ellen
          Children:
Thomas Stackhouse
Michael Stackhouse
Lana Stackhouse Galbraith
Brenda Stackhouse Gard
Rhonda Stackhouse Vogl
Robby Stackhouse

Second wife: Doris
          Children:
Peggy Sue Stackhouse
Amy (stepdaughter)
Sue "Sweet Sue" Mahoney (stepdaughter)

Third wife: Terry
(three stepchildren)

GAIL DOUGLAS O'NEAL

First husband: Jim Douglas
Children:
Matthew Douglas
Russel Douglas
Holly Douglas Hunsicker

Second husband: Bob O'Neal

RUSSEL DOUGLAS

First and only wife: Brenna

Mistress: Fran Lester*
Children:
Jack Douglas
Hannah Douglas

PEGGY SUE STACKHOUSE

First husband: Reverend Tony Harris

Second husband: Kelvin Thomas
Children:
Mariah Thomas
Taylor Thomas

Third husband: Mark Allen

JIM HUDEN

First wife: Patti Lewandowski

Second wife: Jean Huden

Mistress: Peggy Sue Stackhouse Harris
Thomas Allen

Vickie Boyer, best friend of Peggy Sue Thomas for seven years

Cindy Francisco, good friend of Peggy Sue Thomas

Bill Hill, Buck Naked and the X-hibitionists band member and close friend of Jim Huden in Florida

Dick Deposit, Lloyd Jackson, Bill Marlow, Ken Kramer, Ron Young, all longtime friends of Jim Huden on Whidbey Island

INVESTIGATORS, ISLAND COUNTY SHERIFF'S OFFICE

Detective Mike Birchfield

Detective Sergeant Mike Beech

Sergeant Mark Plumberg

Detective Shawn Warwick

Detective Sue Quandt

Detective Ed Wallace

Island County Coroner Robert Bishop

Mine That Bird, Kentucky Derby winner, 2009

PART ONE

The Body in the Woods

Chapter One

WHIDBEY ISLAND, WASHINGTON, is one of the largest islands in the continental United States, a vacation spot for some, home to sixty thousand residents, and a massive duty station for navy personnel. Ferries and the Deception Pass Bridge transport visitors and residents alike to this idyllic body of land that floats on Puget Sound with any number of passages, inlets, bays, and other waterways.

Whidbey is a study in contrasts. The sprawling Whidbey Island Naval Air Station is in the town of Oak Harbor at the northern tip of the forty-seven-mile-long island. It is the premier naval aviation installation in the Pacific Northwest and the location of all electronic attack squadrons flying the EA-6B Prowler and the EA-18G Growler. It is also home to four P-3 Orion Maritime Patrol squadrons and two Fleet Reconnaissance squadrons that fly the EP-3E Aries.

South of Oak Harbor along Highway 520, there are smaller, homier towns: Coupeville, the Island County seat, Greenbank, Langley, Freeland, and Clinton. Although supermarkets and a few modest malls have opened in the last several years, much of Whidbey Island is composed of hamlets, bucolic pastures, evergreen forests, marinas, and a good number of lavish waterfront estates built by people from the mainland.

Visiting much of Coupeville is akin to stepping back in time; the tree-shaded streets are lined with any number of restored houses more than a hundred years old.

From some island locations, there are views of Seattle rising out of a fog-smudged mist, but mostly Whidbey Island is still a place to get away from the stresses of city life. With so much waterfront and so many parks, Whidbey draws tourists in every season. And it is a great place to raise a family with good schools, friendly neighbors, and a true sense of community.

A number of high school graduates move off-island as they search for a quicker-paced world, but they almost always come back for reunions and holidays to catch up with family and old friends.

There isn't a lot of crime on Whidbey; bank robbers prefer spots where they don't have to wait for a ferry to make a clean getaway. There are, of course, some sex crimes, and a murder from time to time. When law enforcement officers *do* have a homicide to investigate, it tends to be out of the ordinary, even grotesque. Island County detectives have investigated explosive cases that made headlines in Seattle, and sometimes nationwide. Colton Harris Moore, "the Barefoot Bandit," a brilliant teenage lawbreaker who went from robbing cabins to stealing airplanes and boats, began his crimes on Camano Island where he grew up—but he was tried on Whidbey Island.

Like all insular areas, Whidbey Island has active gossip chains of communication. Illicit liaisons seldom remain secret for long. There aren't many "No-Tell Motels" or discreet cocktail lounges where lovers can hope to escape prying eyes. Frankly, some of the posher restaurants and health clubs have been headquarters for swingers and "key clubs," and they aren't all that secretive. With the advent of the Internet, gossip spreads more rapidly with every year that goes by.

During the last days of 2003, the chains were buzzing. Some residents were fascinated with a violent mystery and some were just plain frightened.

CHAPTER TWO

WAHL ROAD IS ABOUT four miles from the small Whidbey Island town of Freeland, and a hodgepodge of homes and buildings line the narrow roadway. Some are sparsely furnished old cabins with few luxuries, and then there are newer cabins, upscale houses, and even a few lodges worth a million dollars or more where access to those walking to the beach is cut off by iron gates and impenetrable shrubbery. As Wahl Road wends its way parallel to the part of Puget Sound known as "Double Bluff," it passes everything from a monastery to trailers tucked far off into the woods.

Many of the residences are getaway retreats for people who live in Seattle, Everett, or Bellingham, Washington—or even in Vancouver, British Columbia. Since many of the places are vacant during the winter months, neighbors who are full-time residents keep an eye out for strangers or any sign of suspicious activity.

Nicole Lua and a woman friend—Janet Hall— left Lua's Wahl Road home at about three in the afternoon on the day after Christmas 2003, and headed toward the Double Bluff beach area where winter sunsets are often spectacular. There was a narrow parklike area they could access via the road or by cutting through neighbors' yards.

It was raining and threatening to rain more, but it wasn't that cold for December, about forty degrees, which would drop to just above freezing during the night. Many of the homes in their neighborhood had already turned on their Christmas lights, and beams and shards of color sliced through the rain and fog. As always, the day after Christmas didn't seem nearly as joyful as the day *before* Christmas.

As the two women cut across the thickly forested property at 6665 Wahl Road, Nicole noticed a bright yellow SUV parked in a small cleared space at right angles to the dirt driveway leading back to a cabin. She knew that her neighbors who lived there—the Black family—had gone to Costa Rica for the Christmas holiday, and she was a little surprised to see a strange vehicle there. It was an idle curiosity, however, since nothing seemed to be amiss, and there was a light on in the cottage kitchen. The Blacks sometimes invited friends to stay at their vacation spot.

The two women didn't walk near the yellow car. When they headed back from the beachfront, it was four thirty and full dark during this week of the shortest days of the year. Now they could see that the yellow Tracker was still there, and its pale dome light was on. Caution told them not to walk closer to a strange car in the dark on their own. If the car had a mechanical problem or was out of gas, the driver had probably called for help or walked up Wahl Road toward town.

They decided they would look for it the next day—if it was still there. If it was, they would call the Island County Sheriff's Office and ask that a deputy check it out.

Before they did that, however, someone else noticed the yellow car that was almost hidden by the fir trees beside the long driveway. On the early Saturday afternoon of December 27, 2003, Joseph Doucette, who was a schoolteacher in Bellingham, Washington, left one of the cabins on the Blacks' property with his sons to take a walk.

One of the Blacks' sons was Doucette's pupil, and the teacher, his wife, their two sons, and her sister had happily accepted an invitation to spend Christmas in the cozy cabin.

With all the excitement of Christmas and the somewhat close quarters of a cottage, the little boys were bouncing off the walls. Doucette rounded them up and they headed out for a hike with their dog, hoping they could get rid of some of the pent-up energy.

The Bellingham teacher saw the yellow SUV backed into a grassy spot between two fir trees. Its dome light was still on. His oldest son noticed that the passenger door was open.

"I thought I should go up and shut the door," Doucette recalled. "To keep the battery from draining and rain from getting in. I called out to anyone who might be in the car, but no one answered."

With an eerie sense that there might be something really wrong, Doucette quickly led his boys back to their cabin and told them to stay inside while he checked on something. Once his sons were safely out of the way, the teacher jogged back to the SUV.

As he moved to shut the car door, he glanced in and froze in shock. There *was* someone inside the Tracker. The man behind the steering wheel appeared to be asleep, drunk—or perhaps even dead. Half hoping he might only be imagining the worst, Joe Doucette looked closer. The silent figure appeared to be buckled into a seat belt. He saw that the man was slumped over with his head down and his fists tightly clenched.

Backing away, Doucette knew he shouldn't touch anything, and he hurried back to his cabin to call 911.

He told the Island County dispatcher that he'd noticed something that looked "like goo" coming out of the man's forehead. That led him to believe that the stranger might be dead.

Doucette had no idea who the man was or what had happened. He stayed beside the yellow vehicle, waiting for the ICOM (Island Communications) operator to dispatch someone who might know how to determine that.

*   *   *

ISLAND COUNTY SHERIFF'S SERGEANT Rick Norrie was working the 1 P.M. to 8 P.M. shift that Saturday afternoon, the supervisor of patrol duties in
the south sector of Island County. At 4:26, ICOM
dispatched him to investigate a "possible death"
at 6665 Wahl Road in Freeland. He arrived at the
scene eight minutes later, the first of many sheriff's
officers and emergency responders to head for the
"unexplained/possible death."

He didn't know what he would find. As with
any call concerning a body, neither Norrie nor anyone else knew exactly what might have occurred.
He could have responded to a heart attack victim, to someone who had suffered an accident, to
a drunk sleeping it off, or to a suicide. The latter
was the most likely; the holiday season is depressing
for many people, and anyone who staffs crisis lines
or works in public safety knows that suicides peak
around Christmas and New Year's.

To get to Wahl Road from the shopping center
in Freeland, most drivers take Fish Road from Freeland's shopping center, turning left on Woodard to
its end, left on Lancaster Road, and then right on
Wahl. Double Bluff beach was on the same side as
the address given, and Mutiny Bay was across the
road beyond a row of houses there.

Sergeant Norrie drove slowly down the narrow
dirt driveway. He spotted the vehicle in question
and saw that it was a yellow GEO Tracker, license
number 128-NXQ. As he got out of his patrol
unit fifteen feet away, Norrie immediately saw

that the GEO's front passenger door was open, and the dome light illuminated the front seat area. He could see a white male with short brown hair slumped over the steering wheel.

As he approached the open door, Norrie saw that the driver had apparently suffered serious head trauma. His forehead bulged with some kind of matter and large globules of blood. The man's flannel shirt was soaked with drying red stains and Norrie noted that the driver's-side door panel was also splattered with what appeared to be blood.

Still, Norrie wasn't sure yet if the man was alive and unconscious or deceased. He moved to the driver's window, which was lowered about four inches. Not really expecting a response, he spoke aloud, identifying himself as a sheriff's deputy, as he reached in to touch the silent man's right shoulder.

He felt no life at all; rigor mortis was well established, leaving the dead man frozen in his position behind the wheel.

Paramedics Darren Reid and William Brooks from Whidbey Island Fire Station 3 arrived a minute or so after Norrie did.

"I think he's gone," Norrie told Reid. "He's in almost full rigor."

Reid checked and confirmed what Norrie said.

The obvious expectation was that this violent death would prove to be a suicide.

The bleak spot in the woods was soon crowded with responders. A few minutes later, Officer Leif

Haugen of the Langley Police Department and Deputy Laura Price of the sheriff's office joined Norrie. They had passed some EMT rigs and an ambulance leaving the address given, but there were no sirens. That probably meant that whoever was down the driveway was dead.

Haugen and Norrie began to seal off a crime-scene area with yellow crime-scene tape while Price started taking photographs.

She saw that the dead man was probably in his early to midthirties. He had sandy-blond hair, and he obviously hadn't shaved for a few days. The coagulated mass of blood seemed to be from a wound right in the center of his forehead at the bridge of his nose. Oddly, he had fragments of blue glass in his hair. Wondering at first what they were, Laura Price found the lens from sunglasses on the passenger side resting near the seat. Then she spotted the blue frame from the sunglasses on the driver's-side floor.

It had been a gloomy few days and she wondered why anyone would be wearing sunglasses.

She saw that rain and some tree debris had blown into the passenger side, and noticed an envelope and other mail lying on the floor there, along with cans and paper cups. She looked in the backseat of the GEO; she saw no blood—only clothing, shoes, and trash—but she couldn't see exactly what was there because of the dim light, and she didn't want to disturb them.

Looking through the back window, Deputy

Price observed a snow sled with coats lying on top of it.

The dead man had bled heavily and his plaid shirt, crotch, and thighs were drenched with it. The seat belt had blood on it, but it wasn't latched.

His hands were also covered with blood and the steering wheel had grip imprints from his stained fingers. Price saw that he wore white socks with flip-flops, but the left-foot sandal was missing.

Moving around the vehicle, Laura Price took many photographs with 35-millimeter film.

Once the scene was contained and preliminary photos were taken, Rick Norrie asked Haugen and Price to begin a tentative canvass of nearby houses to see if anyone had heard anything unusual coming from the Blacks' property in the past few days.

WHEN NICOLE LUA SAW blue lights whirling atop several deputy sheriffs' cars a few doors down, she walked over to see what was going on. She hadn't called the sheriff after all, but now she felt a sense of dread. She had probably been correct in assuming that there was something eerie about the parked car.

Whoever the dead person was, Nicole explained that she thought the body probably had been there the day before, too. She and her friend had noticed the SUV there almost exactly twenty-four hours earlier. It didn't belong to anyone that she knew on Wahl Road, nor had she seen it before.

Who *was* the dead man? And why had he ended

up in a small parking area off a narrow road that was shadowed by towering trees? No one driving by on Wahl Road would have seen the yellow Tracker. It seemed that he, or someone else perhaps, had chosen this hidden spot for just that reason.

The vehicle's glove box was open. Later, neither officer could recall which of them had opened it. With extreme care, they removed the vehicle's registration that lay on top of papers there. With a flashlight, they looked at the registered owner's name.

It read Russel Douglas, age thirty-three, with an address at the Mission Ridge Apartments in Renton, Washington, a city southeast of Seattle. Norrie wondered what could have been so bad that a man this young would have shot himself.

It would take a postmortem exam to be sure, but it appeared that Douglas had sustained only that one wound—right in the middle of his forehead, just above the bridge of his nose. The bullet must have penetrated his sunglasses at that point, sending the broken glass all over.

Norrie noted a shell casing between the driver's seat and the door. It looked to be from a .380 caliber bullet. The bronze casing would at least tell them what kind of gun they were looking for, although it was unlikely they would find it in the dark, even with the mass of auxiliary lighting the sheriff's department was bringing in.

In the driver's door itself, he saw a green and yellow sealed box of 30/30 caliber rounds. Maybe there were *two* weapons. Norrie didn't open the box, but waited for detectives to arrive.

He did, however, continue to look for a gun that had fired the fatal shot into Russel's forehead.

He couldn't find it. Depending on the ejection recoil pattern, it might be in the dark rear seat of the Tracker, or it might even have flown out the passenger door, only to be swallowed up in the undergrowth of salal, sword ferns, kinnikinnick, and huckleberries.

Rick Norrie called Island County's detective commander, Sergeant Mike Beech, advising that he was standing by on what appeared to be a suicide. He asked that one of the county's detectives respond, as well as County Coroner Robert Bishop.

At 5:35 P.M., Detective Mike Birchfield pulled up to the scene and the death investigation was turned over to him. Less than an hour had passed since Sergeant Norrie first arrived at the death scene, but it seemed so much longer.

Soon, the pullout beside the driveway was almost as bright as day as the auxiliary lighting showed up and was turned on.

Lieutenant Harry Uncapher, an evidence technician, and Deputy Scott Davis joined the investigators working in the rain. Uncapher bagged the shell casing, papers, documents, and everything that might become vital physical evidence, and he sealed and labeled everything so the chain of evidence would be sacrosanct. He recovered a Nextel cell phone from the left visor, a black fanny pack with a checkbook, more personal papers, and identification documents.

Scott Davis took measurements to triangulate points that would show the precise spot where the Tracker sat. Later, he would draw the scene to scale.

Detective Birchfield asked Rick Norrie and Leif Haugen to extend the crime scene by roping off both an inner and outer circle around the Tracker to be sure that no one could accidentally step on items of possible evidence. He asked Laura Price to start a log that would show the names of anyone who might come inside the tapes, along with the times they arrived.

This wasn't the first unattended death any of the officers had encountered, but it was still shocking. The sheer amount of blood on the dead man and in his car was appalling.

Detective Mark Plumberg, who was even more of a detail man than Birchfield, arrived at the scene. He had never had occasion to go to Wahl Road before. The two seasoned investigators would work this strange case together, although Birchfield would be the lead investigator in the beginning. They had no idea just how long the trail would be before they found out the baffling story behind the body in the woods.

It was probably better that they could not see what lay ahead, how long it would take to solve the puzzle of Russel Douglas's death, or the tragedies the future would bring.

Indeed, one of them would not live to see the final denouement.

The two detectives saw that the Tracker's keys were still in the ignition. They measured the driver's window and saw it was lowered by 6.5 inches. Although it had been unhooked, the driver's seat belt was still partially wound around his torso. It looked as if the dead man had rolled down his window to speak to someone. He might have been in the process of removing his seat belt before getting out of the car. More likely, Plumberg felt, someone had unbuckled the belt after he was shot.

Rick Norrie said he had looked for the gun to no avail. As they searched for the missing gun and failed to find it, Birchfield and Plumberg regretted that any of the first patrol officers on the scene had touched the yellow SUV. Although the sodden grass around the car probably wouldn't have given up much in the way of footprints, they would never know, because several people had walked there by now.

And it was definitely beginning to look as if this might not be a suicide after all. Unless they found the gun within a reasonable distance from the Tracker, this could very well turn out to be a homicide. People who shoot themselves in the forehead cannot then fling the weapon many feet away.

Experienced detectives know that the manner of death should be viewed first as homicide, second as suicide, then accidental, natural, and finally, as undetermined. Because this had seemed to scream suicide, the scene wasn't as untouched as Birchfield and Plumberg would have liked.

Mark Plumberg remembers standing on the edge of Wahl Road, and looking all around him. Something niggled at him.

"I saw how deserted it was. Totally out of easy access except for the few families who lived there in the winter. I said to myself 'This is ridiculous! Why would the victim have come way out here—he had to have been lured out here by someone.'

"Mike Birchfield said he had that sense from the beginning, too."

Even on that first night, Mark Plumberg was curious about something he noted. A small, partially coagulated pool of blood was next to the dead man's hand, and that hand would have been directly below the gunshot wound on the bridge of his nose. It seemed to him that that odd stain should still have been on the victim's hand if he had remained in the same position since the time of the shooting.

"But it wasn't," Plumberg said. "I thought then—and I still do—that someone had attempted to move the body for some reason—possibly looking for the bullet casing. That made me doubt even more that we were looking at a suicide."

Still, working with only artificial light, the two detectives couldn't say for sure where the casing was.

They would have to look for it in the morning.

PART TWO

Russ and Brenna

CHAPTER THREE

CORONER DR. ROBERT BISHOP released the body and it was taken to Burley's Funeral Chapel to await autopsy. The Tracker would be towed to the Island County Criminal Justice Center to be stored in a locked sally port until the Washington State Patrol Crime Lab criminalists could process it.

It was after ten when Mark Plumberg and Mike Birchfield cleared the scene, leaving reserve deputies Bill Carpenter and Jay Geiler to provide security in case anyone—a killer or merely someone curious—should try to get inside the crime-scene tapes.

The detective team had their suspicions and their gut reactions, but the probe was embryonic at this point; the two uniformed officers who had done the initial canvass of nearby houses *had* located one possible witness who sounded as if she had seen the dead man's car the day before.

Diane Bailey, who lived a short distance from

the Blacks' property where Russel Douglas was shot, gave a statement about a "boxy, small, bright yellow SUV" that was driving west along Wahl Road, as if the driver was searching for an address. That had been sometime between 11:30 A.M. and 1 P.M. on the twenty-sixth. She hadn't paid that much attention to it until she saw the same vehicle backing out of her own driveway.

"It looked as though he'd seen my red Volvo parked there and realized he had the wrong address," she said.

Ms. Bailey hadn't had a clear view of the driver, but her recall did help to place the Tracker in the Double Bluff neighborhood sometime around noon on Friday.

MARK PLUMBERG AND MIKE BIRCHFIELD weren't through for the night. They still faced one of the tasks that any cop hates—notifying the deceased's next of kin. There is no easy way to break such awful news; police know that they will hear sobs and see tears or the shocked, frozen reaction on the faces of those the dead have loved and who have loved them.

Mike Birchfield knew of Russel Douglas; his wife, Brenna Douglas, had babysat with the detective's children. Several deputies' wives went to her beauty shop—Just B's—to have her do their hair. That was one semilucky thing for the detectives; most residents on Whidbey Island knew each other, or they had mutual acquaintances.

And then there was the gossip line that they knew would begin beating jungle drums with both solid and mythical information within hours. They had to find Brenna soon and tell her what had happened before someone called her and bluntly gave her the news that her husband was dead of a gunshot wound to the head.

Russel Douglas might have been living in an apartment off-island, but his driver's license gave his address on Furman Avenue in the Whidbey Island town of Langley. Mike Birchfield knew that that was Brenna's current address. There had been rumors for months that Russel and Brenna were estranged and living apart; that could explain why Douglas had two addresses.

But they weren't divorced.

IT WAS ABOUT A quarter after ten when Mike Birchfield and Mark Plumberg pulled into the driveway of Brenna Douglas's home in Langley. There was a maroon van parked in the driveway, but there were no lights on in the house. Plumberg stayed back in the yard while Birchfield approached the front door. A large dog was in the yard, barking at him.

Birchfield shone his flashlight through the living room window, and saw a woman in a robe walking toward the front door.

"That's Brenna," Birchfield said.

She opened the door without hesitation. Squinting in the porch light, she asked, "Can I help you?"

Mike Birchfield showed her his identification as

a sheriff's detective and introduced her to Plumberg. As they walked into the living room, it appeared that she was ready for bed.

"Could you talk to us?" Plumberg asked, wondering why she would open the door so readily when she saw two strange men in her yard.

"Come on in," she said, opening the door wider. "What's going on?"

"We want to talk with you about your husband," Mike Birchfield said as they walked in. They stood awkwardly for a minute or two before he gestured toward the dining room: "Could we sit down at that table?"

Brenna Douglas seemed at ease as she led them toward the dining room. She asked no questions. Mark Plumberg pulled out a legal pad. He would take notes while Birchfield interviewed Brenna Douglas.

As they passed a chair near the front door, he saw a note on lined tablet paper there. It was addressed to "Russ," and read: "The kids and I went out and we'll be back later."

It was a strange tableau. Even though it was fairly late at night and there were two detectives sitting with her, Brenna showed no curiosity about why they were there.

Birchfield began easily, asking about Russel Douglas's hobbies, habits, and how her relationship with him was going. She answered with a tumble of words, and the sheriff's men noted that she often spoke negatively of her husband.

"When did you see your husband last?" Birch-field asked.

"It was before noon yesterday," Brenna Douglas said. "I called him several times on his cell phone yesterday—but he didn't answer. I slept with my phone beside me, but he never called. I know he planned to go surfing."

That didn't seem strange. Mark Plumberg was a scuba diver himself, and he knew that the waters surrounding Whidbey Island drew surfers and div-ers any time of year as long as they had adequate protection from the cold. He wondered if she was concerned that Russel might have drowned—or disappeared in the dark water.

Brenna explained that she and Russel were still married, but that they had separated seven months before and he was living in Renton. Christmas weekend also happened to be his time to see their two children—Jack, eight, and Han-nah, five.

Her words continued to burst out, almost as if she was trying to delay learning whatever the two detectives were there to tell her. Even so, she had little positive to say about Russel. She said they were separated because Russel had had a couple of affairs, one of them homosexual.

"I just couldn't accept his deviant lifestyle," Brenna said.

According to his wife, Russel Douglas had been cruel and brutally open about sharing that lifestyle with her. She knew about an older woman who lived in Tacoma, Washington, twenty-six miles south of Seattle.

"Her first name is Fran* and she's around fifty years old. I think she works for a telecom company. Russel sometimes tries to tell me about how he parties and has sex with her. I think he does that just to get to me . . ."

"Where do you think he is now?" Birchfield asked. "What do you think has happened to him?"

"I don't know. I talked to him on Christmas Day and he told me he had a promotion at work. He was happy about that.

"I talked to his sister, Holly Hunziker, the next day; she lives in Everett. She and I are good friends, and I wanted to take her a birthday present because her birthday's so close to Christmas, and she kind of gets left out. She said she was going out, so we just spoke on the phone. Then the kids and I went shopping and to see a movie—*Hook*."

Still, Brenna Douglas didn't ask why they were there close to 11 P.M., wanting to talk about her husband.

Mike Birchfield asked about Russel's friends and who his doctor was. She said she didn't know. She had no idea who his friends were. He might have friends at his job, but she didn't know any of them. If he knew anyone on Whidbey Island, he would have had to meet them through her. She stressed that point over and over. Russel had no friends on the island unless it was someone he might have met because *she* had many friends.

"Are you surprised that we're here tonight?" Birchfield finally asked bluntly.

"Yes . . . and no. I don't know where he is. He just came back into my life a couple of weeks ago."

Brenna didn't seem to be very happy about that. She described Russel as very controlling, a man who cheated on her callously and mentally "abused" her.

"Is he physically abusive?"

"Not so much, but he does—did—some pushing."

"Does Russel own any firearms?"

"A .22 rifle, and some knives," she said. "No handguns."

"Do *you* own any guns?"

Brenna Douglas didn't blink or seem frightened by this line of questioning. "I have a .22 caliber pistol."

"Could we see it?"

She walked to her bedroom and came back with the pistol. She explained that her home had been burglarized recently, and she thought it might have been Russel who broke in. She didn't say why she thought that.

"My stepfather gave me this gun after that happened. I only fired it once."

The two detectives exchanged a glance. They had been in the house for almost half an hour, and Brenna had yet to ask them why they were there, or why they were asking about her husband.

Her behavior wasn't as uncommon as it might

seem on the surface; some people, dreading terrible news, try to stall because they don't want to know. Brenna was placid, even stoic. As much as she denigrated her husband, he *was* the father of her children, and she had allowed him to stay with her over Christmas. It was even possible they had been partially reconciled.

"Do you know why we're here, Brenna?" Birchfield asked quietly.

"No—not really."

"Russel was found dead in his car this afternoon."

"Oh . . ."

That was all she said. Was she in shock? They waited, but she didn't ask why her husband was dead, how he died, or where he was when he died. She seemed so composed that she was almost aloof.

Or was she stunned into silence, shocked to her core?

While Mike Birchfield continued to question the new widow for another five minutes or so, asking about the couple's relationship, Russel's lifestyle—even touching on his sexual habits—Brenna answered woodenly.

But she still didn't ask how her husband had been killed, so Birchfield kept talking.

"He was shot in the head."

Brenna sat like stone, completely void of reaction. Was she in deep shock?

Or was she not surprised?

Now she began to speak, breathlessly running

one sentence into another. She certainly didn't avoid speaking ill of the dead. Brenna repeated that Russel had "rubbed in her face" his clubbing, partying, and cheating. She thought he might be a sadomasochist, although she said he had never tried anything like that with her.

"I just couldn't accept his sexual ideas—he thought whatever he saw on the Internet was 'normal.'"

"Did you ever participate in any of those sexual activities?"

"*No!*"

"Why do you think he wanted to get back together with you?"

"Control. He liked to play control games with me. Like on Thanksgiving. He was supposed to meet me at the ferry about seven in the morning. But he didn't show up. I finally called him at ten thirty and he was just then leaving Tacoma. He did things like that as his way of controlling me."

"Did he build you up and then let you down when he treated you bad?"

"Yes."

"How did that make you feel?"

"Sad."

"Did he ever make you angry?"

"Yes! When he treated me bad."

When Mike Birchfield asked her if she thought Russel Douglas had mental problems, she nodded. Now she recalled the names of two counselors he had been seeing.

Once again, Brenna stated that Russel had "run off before," only to come back and try to get her to make their relationship work.

"Russel started divorce papers but he never went ahead with them," she said.

"Why didn't you file for divorce?"

"I guess I was hoping we could work it out. Russel and I have owned Just B's salon in Langley for about a year. Our business is pretty successful. I'm the one who works there, but he was going to do our taxes this year."

"Do you know where his current address is?"

"No—but I know how to get to his apartment. I know he runs—ran—and went to Gold's Gym that's near his apartment. He used to work out at Ken's Korner in Clinton about eight years ago—when we were first married."

But Brenna added that Russel wasn't exactly a health freak—he drank a lot. It was very common for him to get drunk.

"Drugs?" Birchfield asked.

"I don't know."

Mark Plumberg asked Brenna about the note he'd seen near the front door.

"I wrote it this morning. He's been staying here since Christmas Eve. I left him a note that me and the kids were going off-island. We took the one o'clock ferry to Mukilteo."

At that point, Brenna's phone rang. She left the room to answer it. When she came back, she explained that two of her friends—sisters—had called, and that they often called her late at night because it was a good time to talk after her children went to sleep.

Within about fifteen minutes, the two women arrived at her door to comfort Brenna in her loss.

Mike Birchfield asked her if she would be willing to come to the precinct office in Coupeville the next day for a further interview.

Finally, she looked stricken. "What do I do?" she asked. "What do I do with his family?"

There was no way to answer that. Birchfield studied her face before he commented casually that she hadn't been very emotional or surprised when he told her that her husband—albeit an estranged husband—was dead.

"Why is that?"

Brenna sighed. "When my mom died, Russel told me I was not allowed to cry. Now, I guess I've learned to just suppress my emotions."

"Do you know what your husband had in his car?" Mark Plumberg asked.

"Tons of stuff—sleds for the kids, files from his work, some clothes."

"Have you been in his vehicle since he arrived here on Christmas Eve?"

She nodded. "I drove it to the Star Store on Christmas Day to buy some pies, and then Russel drove me to our salon so I could hide a key for one of my girls to open the shop the day after Christmas."

"When your husband left here on the twenty-

sixth," Mike Birchfield began, "what did he do—
or say?"

"It was about a quarter to eleven. He kissed me
and the kids, and he said he'd be back in a few
hours. He said he had to get some things done.

"But he never came back."

It was late, and it seemed wise to end this first
interview. Mike Birchfield and Mark Plumberg had
many more questions they wanted to ask Brenna
Douglas, but they could wait until morning.

As they left, one of Brenna's friends asked if
she should bring an attorney with her for the next
day's interview.

"That's up to her," Birchfield answered.

This was the beginning of one of the most challenging investigations the Island County Sheriff's
Office and the Island County Prosecuting Attorney's Office had ever faced. It was not what
it seemed to be; just when they pieced together
part of the deadly foundation of a murder case, it
would tear loose of another section. Their probe
would involve Oregon, Idaho, Nevada, New Mexico, Florida, Texas, Alaska, and Mexico.

And it would take years.

CHAPTER FOUR

THE ONE PERSON A homicide investigator needs to interview the most is forever out of reach. The victim can no longer speak, and yet superior detectives find ways to know that person more thoroughly than anyone they know in life. They must weigh everything they learn about the dead, balancing what one witness says against what other witnesses assure them is the truth. At times, when the victim has lived an uncomplicated life, that can be a fairly simple exercise. With someone like Russel Douglas, the challenge from the beginning was overwhelming.

Beyond losing their very lives, homicide victims lose their privacy. Their hopes, dreams, flaws, sins, accomplishments—*everything*—become public knowledge. In a sense, their very innards are spread out for public viewing to be picked over, criticized, and exploited. The media does that, of course, and detectives have to explore every facet of the dead person's life if they hope to find who might have had a motive, opportunity, or means to destroy him—or her.

Who was Russel Douglas? His semi-estranged wife had made him sound monstrous even as she learned he was dead—murdered.

But that was only one person's opinion. Russel *did* have friends, coworkers, even a lover who would speak positively about him.

Mark Plumberg and Mike Birchfield had to examine physical evidence and study forensic results. They also had to seek out dozens of people whose paths had crossed Douglas's.

As they returned to 6665 Wahl Road the next morning, they found that daylight wasn't going to reveal much. The gun simply wasn't there, nor was there any other ballistic evidence. There were some tire marks in the soft dirt of the driveway that indicated that a vehicle had turned around near the cottage. But the details of the tires were blurred, not nearly distinctive enough to compare to exemplars of other tire imprints.

By noon, Plumberg and Birchfield met Brenna Douglas in the South Precinct office for a second interview. She brought Russel's "work computer," a laptop, with her. They learned that he was employed by the Tetra Tech Corporation, near Redmond. He was a zone manager and was highly skilled with computers. Brenna said he was working toward his master's degree in the University of Phoenix's distance education program, and had an email account with the school, along with several other accounts.

Indeed, he was within only a few credits before he got his MA.

Mark Plumberg interviewed Brenna in one room, while Mike Birchfield talked to Russel's sister, Holly Hunziker, in another.

Plumberg asked Brenna if she had thought of anything since they last talked that might help the investigation. She mentioned that some of her clients at Just B's had told her they had seen her husband a few times on the ferry as it docked at Whidbey.

"That was odd, because during some of those times, he didn't come to see me—or our children. I don't know who he was meeting."

For some reason, Brenna had concluded that Russ might be having a homosexual affair with some man on the island.

It wasn't long before Brenna began talking again about Russel's lifestyle. She was convinced he was into "swinging" and bizarre sexual exploration. She had seen his body piercings, and said he even had his nipples pierced.

"He wanted to get more piercings, but I just could not deal with that!"

She spoke in an oddly matter-of-fact manner. Nevertheless, she had let Russel back into her life in the past few weeks to see if he had changed. She didn't really want him back, and she said she had discussed it with their very young children, and they didn't want him living with them, either.

"We were doing very well since he left us last May."

Mark Plumberg noticed how relaxed and comfortable the recent widow appeared to be. She sipped from a cup of coffee she'd brought with her. She was almost inappropriately animated as he talked to her.

It seemed that she could not say enough bad things about the man who had been found dead less than twenty-four hours earlier. Brenna repeated that she thought he was having an affair with a man she named. Her suspicions had been fueled by pornography she found on his computer in September.

"For Christmas, do you know what he gave me? Lingerie, flavored condoms, and a sex swing! We agreed to take it slow, and I asked him if that was his idea of 'slow.'"

Plumberg asked her if Russel had tried to get her to engage in any unusual sex since he'd been home for Christmas, and she shook her head.

"No, he's been on his best behavior. We did have *very* protected sex. I guess I just wanted to feel loved."

Brenna was a study in ambivalence. One minute she characterized her late husband as gay, and the next she talked about his lust for her and other women.

More confusing, the Christmas she described sounded like any happy family's, although Russel was a "little upset" because she changed their usual Christmas morning. He had wanted their children to wait while he had breakfast before they opened their presents.

"I told him that now the kids were coming first, and he could just wait for his breakfast."

Brenna's stepfather, who had been widowed a year earlier, came over to have dinner with them and left between five and six. Then Russel had played Xbox with Jack, while she and Hannah watched a movie in her room.

"Russel came into my bedroom later and we watched *Bad Boys II* and then we went to sleep."

On December 26, she had stayed at home after Russel left, although she was upset because she had wanted to go to the "eye doctor." She had called Russel's cell phone a few times to see where he was, but he didn't answer.

"Were you worried about your husband?" Plumberg asked.

"A little—because we hadn't been fighting or anything so I didn't know why he wouldn't come back. Then I got mad because I thought he was back to his 'old routine' of only being concerned about himself."

With no word from him, she had gone to the mainland—as she said before—eaten at the Red Robin restaurant, shopped at Penney's and some "video game place," and then gone to the movie. She had receipts and ticket stubs that verified this.

Brenna Douglas's description of Russel's alleged "abuse" indicated that it was more verbal than physical. He had taken their children to visit his lover, Fran, at Thanksgiving and unplugged the phone there so she couldn't talk to them.

"He never went places with me. Oh, once we went to a game and there were these two women sitting in front of us. I simply commented about how 'trashy' they were dressed, and he turned on me and in a real loud voice, he said I was just jealous because I was the 'fattest woman in a stadium of thirty thousand people!'"

Brenna's complaints might have been justified in other circumstances, but they sounded weak and selfish when compared to the unsolved homicide of her husband who had a bullet in his brain.

She *was* a big woman, but in an attractive, buxom way, and she was also pretty with long, luxuriant hair. And there was no way she could have been the "fattest woman" in the stadium. She appeared somehow stronger than the photos Plumberg had seen of Russel Douglas. In a physical fight—if, indeed, they ever engaged in one—Brenna would have had a good chance of winning.

Plumberg tried again to get any information Brenna might have on who hated Russel enough to kill him. Was there anyone he seemed afraid of?

She had no idea. Then she remembered that he had told her about a man who was a "headhunter" who was looking for him the week before Christmas. She hadn't known what a headhunter was until Russel told her they were people who tried to steal employees away from other companies and offer them jobs.

"This guy told Russel he would have to sign a secrecy thing. They had to meet at night and no one was supposed to know. We were having dinner at his mother's house just before Christmas when he said that. Gail will remember that, too."

Gail O'Neal, Russ's mother, *did* recall a discussion about a "headhunter." That holiday dinner in 2003 was the last time she saw her son alive.

Brenna seemed to be on good terms with her mother-in-law, even though Russel had told any number of people that he disliked his mother because of the strict and punitive way she had raised him.

Asked about that later, Gail O'Neal, who has a PhD in nursing and teaches at Washington State University, nodded. She knew that Russ had blamed her for some of his misfortunes.

"He always blamed someone else for the unhappiness in his life," she said. "He was a grown man and he was still complaining that he had a miserable childhood. He felt he had missed out on so much in his life, and he looked for someone he could hold responsible."

When her ex-husband, Jim Douglas, left Whidbey Island and moved to Alaska, Gail and her second husband—Bob O'Neal—raised her two sons.

NOW, AS HE CONTINUED talking with Brenna Douglas, Mark Plumberg saw that if Russ intended to hide anything from his wife, he hadn't done a very good job of it. Brenna knew all of the passwords on his email accounts. And she said she checked on them regularly.

Once more, Mark Plumberg asked for the names of Russel's friends—someone the detective could talk to.

She shook her head. She didn't know of any friends who might know much about him. She was quite sure he'd been trying to get into a swingers' club at an island restaurant.

"I know they meet on Saturday nights and it's called a 'key club.'"

That sounded like something out of the seventies.

Detective Plumberg looked straight into Brenna's eyes and held her gaze. She didn't look away.

"I'm going to have to ask you some tough questions," he began.

Instantly, she became very still and her body was rigid as she folded her hands in her lap.

"Does anyone in your family have any reason to kill Russel?"

"No."

"Did *you* have any reason to kill him?"

"No," she answered in a flat voice.

Plumberg moved on to other questions, and she seemed to know he was getting ready to close the interview. Now, where she had been tense, her voice tight, Brenna relaxed, returning to her former casual mien.

The detective didn't know what that meant. He

didn't know her—not yet—or anyone she might be close to, either someone she wanted to protect or who might possibly know hidden things about her.

He closed his notepad and smiled. "You can call me anytime if you remember anything—or if you have questions or need to talk to me."

CHAPTER FIVE

MIKE BIRCHFIELD TALKED TO Douglas's sister, Holly Hunziker. She seemed to have been close to Brenna, and she recalled that Brenna had phoned her on the twenty-sixth and asked to bring a birthday present to her. Her niece and nephew had sung "Happy Birthday" to Holly over the phone. Her sister-in-law usually made a point to recognize her birthday, Holly said, because it came hard on the heels of Christmas Day. But this year, it hadn't worked out as Holly wasn't going to be home.

Holly's opinion of her brother was surprisingly negative. She spoke of the verbal and psychological abuse he had heaped on Brenna, and about the sexual scenarios he also forced on her. Holly, too, mentioned that Russel had had affairs with both women and men.

"He had weird ideas when it came to sex, and he was always trying to get Brenna to join in."

What Holly was saying was much like the information Brenna had given the two detectives the night before, and Birchfield asked Holly if she had firsthand knowledge of her brother's erotic obsessions, and she admitted that she didn't; she only knew what Brenna had told her.

She recalled hearing that a few years earlier, Russel and Brenna had a business for a while where they gave "parties" in other people's homes where they sold sex toys. Brenna had told her that they had to put on a show, demonstrating the bizarre condoms, bondage items, and phallic substitutes and she hated it. They had soon quit that business.

Despite Brenna's apparent distaste for her husband's alleged proclivities, Holly said Brenna was very jealous. She had tried to keep tabs on him and who he was seeing. She particularly resented Fran, the older woman he was supposed to be dating during their estrangement.

Mike Birchfield studied Holly. "I have to tell you that I find it strange that all I've been hearing about Russel is mostly negative—and he hasn't been dead more than two days."

"Holly looked sheepish," he wrote in his follow-up report later, "but she didn't say anything."

The Island County investigators knew *how* Russel Douglas had died, but they were a long way from knowing *why*. Although his widow and his own sister had said virtually nothing positive about him, what they described didn't seem bad enough to mark him for murder. And murders without a motive are not easy to solve.

The Island County investigators learned that Russ and Brenna had dated since they were in high school. Russ went solo to a club where teenagers were allowed and one of his sister's friends introduced him to Brenna.

When Holly and their mother, Gail, realized that the couple was getting serious, they were appalled. They seemed to have nothing in common, both had short fuses, and they always seemed to be fighting.

"It was a horrible, *horrible* relationship," Holly remembers. "Brenna didn't get along with her mother, and she was completely on her own by the time she was twenty-one; she had an apartment, a job, a car."

Russ wasn't sure where he was going, but he did believe in education. Brenna scoffed at higher education, and was adamant that she didn't want her children to go to college.

"They might have gone on to better lives *separately*," Holly said later. "But they just didn't belong together."

When Brenna became pregnant in 1994, she and Russ talked to Gail about it.

"What are you going to do?" she asked.

"Have the baby," Brenna said.

"Good. That's good," Gail said, "but don't get married. You don't need to get married to have a child. Give yourselves some time."

His mother's advice got through to Russ Douglas enough that they waited about finalizing their union. Gail hoped that they would see what everyone who knew them felt about their chances for a happy marriage.

"They waited awhile," Gail said sadly, "but they eventually got married during the late summer of 1995. Their baby, Jack, was one at the time."

Brenna regretted all the arguments she had had with her mother, and tried to effect reconciliation. They talked many times a day on the phone, and that made Russ jealous.

Brenna thought that Gail was controlling Russ. And vice versa.

Gail raised briards, and she offered one of the puppies to Russ and Brenna. Russ was trying to make everyone happy in the vain hope that his wife and his family could get along—and he accepted the active pup, whose breed grows to between seventy-five and a hundred pounds. They are wonderful dogs, but they need daily exercise, exacting training because they can be stubborn, and their luxurious coats have to be brushed at least every other day. Gail used her dogs to herd sheep, an activity that these French sheepdogs were born to perform. Briards love children and they protect their owners' home and family.

Of course, it was not a good choice for a couple already dealing with a baby, and Brenna railed at Russ that their dog was way too much for her to handle and clean up after.

Seeing that the match wasn't a good one, Gail offered to take the puppy back and keep it until they were ready.

"I knew they would never be ready, but it seemed like a good way to get the poor pup out of there," Gail said, "and hopefully, to stop some of their fights. Finally, Russ agreed to let me take the puppy. And, of course, they never asked for it back."

Brenna's favorite pastime was shopping.

"I would have to call her a shopaholic," Gail O'Neal said. "She could easily spend a thousand dollars on one trip to Costco. I helped her unload after a visit to the grocery store once, and was surprised to see that she had two large freezers *and* a refrigerator and I could hardly find room in any of them to store her new purchases! And she still fed her kids junk food all the time."

It was more than just the expected bickering between a wife and her mother-in-law. Both Russ and Brenna called Gail O'Neal for advice, and she did her best to remain neutral. She knew her son was immature and sometimes hard to deal with, but so was Brenna—only in a different way.

When Russel Douglas complained about something—even something as childish as not being able to find his favorite soda pop—his mother told him, "You're an adult. You want a Mountain Dew, and your store doesn't have it. You are grown up—just go find a store that carries it, and get your Mountain Dew yourself."

WHILE MIKE BIRCHFIELD SEARCHED for a financial reason behind the homicide, Mark Plumberg prepared to find out as much about Douglas as he possibly could. The picture on his driver's license showed a bland-looking man with an almost shy smile. He certainly didn't appear to be a sex-obsessed fiend, but then few sex offenders do. He apparently had a good job and was a devoted father to his two small children, supporting them financially and visiting them whenever Brenna allowed him to see them.

On the evening of December 28, Plumberg and Birchfield executed a search warrant on Russel Douglas's apartment in Renton. The now-dead man had left a radio on, and the sound of soft jazz in the background made their visit a little eerie.

The place was sparsely furnished. It was little more than a studio unit, but it did have one bedroom and one bathroom on the second floor of a building with many apartments. It looked like a temporary place where a man might live while he tried to salvage a marriage gone sour—or while he was making plans for a divorce. A bachelor's apartment in every sense of the term.

The investigators found a surfboard in its carrying case leaning against a bedroom wall, so Russ obviously hadn't gone surfing. According to Brenna, Russel had told her that he had a number of errands to run that day after Christmas. One of them was apparently a present for her; she thought it might be a tablecloth she wanted.

His closet was stuffed with clothing, books, and various papers. There was also a .22 rifle there, and two plastic garbage bags with adult sex toys—nothing very shocking or different than a lot of men had. Outside of those objects, the two detectives found nothing that smacked of pornography or sexual perversion.

There were two computer cases, but when they looked inside, neither had a computer in it. Among the myriad papers, they found a number of notes that appeared to be in Douglas's handwriting. An initial glance at them showed they were introspective, written by a man who asked himself questions about how he should be managing his life, a man wondering how he could achieve happiness.

Mark Plumberg set those aside to study in depth later; they might let him understand who Russel Douglas had been.

The next morning, Plumberg attended Russel Douglas's postmortem examination. Dr. Daniel Selove, a forensic pathologist who often travels around Washington State to do autopsies in sparsely populated counties, performed this after-death exploration while Island County Coroner Dr. Robert Bishop stood by.

There were no surprises. Douglas had died of that single bullet fired into the bridge of his nose, and the slug had plowed into his head, forcing out a large amount of brain matter that dangled grotesquely from his forehead.

He would have died instantly. When the bullet was removed, Plumberg logged it into evidence, along with plastic bags that held hair and nail clippings, a loose hair from the victim's lower lip, and anal and oral swabs.

Even the fragment of blue plastic from his broken sunglasses was saved. If the hair on his lip wasn't his, it would only be probable evidence. Unless its follicle is attached to a hair, it is impossible to tell anything beyond class and characteristics.

Plumberg was aware once again that it would surely take a motive or, he hoped, a match to the bullet casing and slug to the gun that fired it. And that gun seemed to be as lost as if it had been flung into Puget Sound.

Perhaps it had been.

Douglas's clothing was bagged and sent to the Washington State Police lab to be tested by criminalists. They found semen on the victim's underwear, but DNA results weeks later indicated the fluid was his own.

On New Year's Eve 2003 Mark Plumberg took the slug and the shell casing, labeled C-1, to Evan Thompson at the Seattle Police Department's Crime Lab. If possible, they needed to know what brand of gun might have fired it. If they ever found the gun, that could be a vital link between the murder and the murderer. Less likely, the shooter's DNA might be on the casing, but Plumberg would take the casing to the Washington State Police Lab in Marysville, Washington, to test for that only after Thompson examined the bullet and casing.

The Seattle criminalist saw immediately that the missing gun was definitely a cheap .380 automatic weapon. The brand of guns that came to his mind were possibly a Llama, a Grendel, or a Bersa.

Immediately after the tests, Mark Plumberg took possession of the bullet/slug and casing again.

NICOLE LUA AND HER friend Janet Hall were interviewed for a second time. The women who had first noticed the yellow Tracker on their late-afternoon walk the day after Christmas had told Mike Birchfield that they hadn't seen that either of its doors were open at that time.

On reflection, they now told Plumberg they believed that they had seen the *driver's door* open. If their recall was accurate, that would mean that the shooter was probably still at the scene when they passed by.

And it was fortunate that they hadn't approached the vehicle. Perhaps the killer had subsequently shut the door next to the steering wheel, gone around the SUV to search for something on the passenger side, and left that door open when he left.

If so, what was he—or she—looking for? And had he found and removed it?

Russel Douglas's father, Jim, flew down from Juneau, Alaska, and he and other members of his family met with Mike Birchfield on December 30 at Brenna's house in Langley. Birchfield's interviews with the Douglas side of the family were private.

Jim said he and Russel were as close as a father and son could be, considering that Jim lived far away in Alaska. "We would talk on the phone about once a month."

Jim Douglas was aware of his son's bouts with depression; Russ had suffered with periods of sadness for most of his life. He was probably bipolar. When he was up, he was way up—but when he was down, he sometimes threatened suicide.

"Russel was a loner," Jim said. "He never seemed to have a lot of friends."

"Did he like his job? How about his marriage?" Birchfield asked.

"Yeah, I think he did like his job. He was really excited about getting his master's degree in business."

As for Russel and Brenna's marriage, his father acknowledged that they were having trouble, but he didn't know the specifics beyond arguments over money.

"You know of any physical abuse?"

"No—I wasn't aware of anything like that."

Jim Douglas knew that Russ and Brenna had split up for a while, but he had never heard anything about Russel having a girlfriend. He hadn't known anything about a divorce—but his ex-wife, Gail, said that Brenna told her they were going to start divorce filing as soon as she could get health insurance.

"Brenna told my ex-wife they were trying to stay friends, but that they were getting a divorce as soon as they could."

"Did he ever talk to you about someone being mad at him, or who he might be having trouble with?"

Douglas shook his head.

He had sent his son a hundred-dollar check for Christmas, and his bank said that it had been cashed at the Bank of America in Renton on December 23.

Matthew Douglas, Russel's brother, was a U.S. Army captain stationed at Fort Bliss in El Paso, Texas. He and his fiancée, Tracy Harvey, had been in Washington State during the Christmas holidays. On the weekend his brother was killed, Matthew and Tracy were in British Columbia, Canada. Now, they, too, were at Brenna's house to talk to Mike Birchfield.

Captain Douglas told the detective that he and Russel weren't close, mostly because Russel kept to himself, especially while they were growing up in Coupeville on Whidbey Island. He agreed that sometimes his brother and his mother, Gail, didn't get along very well.

"He resented what he considered very strict rules in our house."

Matthew recalled Russel as a good student, a man who had strived to get a superior education. He was also into physical fitness and worked out three or four days a week.

When Russ was born, he had severely crossed eyes, and it took several operations to fix the problem. As an adult, his eyes could still seem off kilter when he was tired. That may have had something to do with his overweening desire to succeed.

"He could be eccentric in his lifestyle and the way he dressed," Matthew said. "When he began a hobby, he would immediately go to extremes. Like learning to play the guitar or surfing. He wasn't very good at either, but he spent a lot of his time and money trying."

Captain Douglas said he'd never known his brother to have a drug or drinking problem, allowing that if he had, he would be more likely to go to their dad to talk about it.

"I don't think Russel liked being married," Matthew said. "But he was a good father. He and Brenna argued a lot, and she kicked him out of the house last May sometime."

"Was he ever abusive to her—or the kids?"

"No, not that I ever heard of. I knew he had a girlfriend who was a lot older than he was."

"He into anything weird—or could he have been gay?"

Matthew shook his head. "I'd have a hard time believing any of that."

WHILE BRENNA TOLD DETECTIVES about all of Russ's faults, she said the opposite to her friends and acquaintances. "Russ was my best friend. How am I going to go on without him?"

Which was it? Brenna was all over the emotional map.

Neither Mike Birchfield nor Mark Plumberg

had located another witness who had disparaged
Russel Douglas the way his estranged wife had.
Russel's brother, who would keep in close touch
with Birchfield for months as he hoped to hear
that the person who shot Russel had been arrested,
would be back and forth about whether Brenna
was sincere in her protestations of grief.

"After staying with Brenna," Matthew wrote,
"and watching her fear and frustration, I ultimately can't find anything that would have me
question her grief as anything other than genuine."

ON JANUARY 2, 2004, a memorial service for Russel
Douglas was held at St. Peter's Lutheran Church in
Clinton, the small town on the south end of Whid-
bey Island where the Mukilteo ferry docks.

Most savvy detectives attend the funerals and
memorials held for the victims of the crimes they
are working on. Both Mark Plumberg and Mike
Birchfield were at the church. As mourners and
the curious arrived, Birchfield sat in his car in the
church parking lot, while Plumberg parked in the
driveway of an apartment complex that was right
across the street from the church entrance. They
observed people and vehicles, jotting down license
numbers.

It is not at all unusual for killers to go to the funerals of their victims. They may mimic arsonists
who mingle with the crowd at buildings they have
torched; it is an extra element of the thrills they
seek, gloating in their belief that they have fooled

everyone. And then again, in some cases, murderers close to the deceased may risk waving red flags if they stay *away* from memorials and funerals.

Plumberg observed two white males who drove up in green pickup trucks, one brand-new and one somewhat battered. As he watched, the driver of the older truck retrieved something from the new truck, put it into his vehicle, and drove away.

Did this mean anything? Birchfield said no. He had seen that the cargo consisted only of fishing poles.

Birchfield went into the church, while Mark Plumberg stayed outside, taking pictures of vehicles in the parking lot and watching for any activity or emotional outbursts that might be significant.

As people left St. Peter's after the memorial service, he walked over to a group of men and asked if they might be Russel Douglas's coworkers.

They nodded, but turned away. One man glared at the sheriff's detective and said, "Yeah—but I don't want to talk to you!"

"Why is that?" Plumberg asked.

"I think it's really inconsiderate of you to approach us at our friend's memorial service."

"I'm only trying to identify people who may have known Russel so we can do a better job of investigating this homicide."

"Well, we still don't want to talk to you!"

The man beside him nodded in agreement and they hurriedly got into the same car and drove away. Later, Russ's coworkers would be more agreeable to the detectives' questioning.

Aside from the shock and grief Russel Douglas's mother, father, stepfather, and brother had displayed when they were told he had been killed, his coworkers were the first people who seemed truly saddened.

Still, the investigators had met very few of the many people with whom the dead man had interacted. They soon learned that despite his widow's insistence that he had few friends, that wasn't true. Not at all.

CHAPTER SIX

ONE OF THE PEOPLE who was rumored to have been closest to Russel Douglas in recent months was Fran Lester.* Fran *was* old enough to be his mother, but Brenna and others close to Russel thought he and Fran had had an intimate relationship. Russel apparently told his wife that he had broken off the affair three weeks before Christmas. It might have ended or it might have continued to the day of his death.

Fran Lester was a genuine person, not some nameless man or woman he was seeing secretly, or a member of a swingers' group. Mark Plumberg and Mike Birchfield had no trouble finding her address in Tacoma, and they went there after Douglas's services, arriving about 4:30. She was quite willing to talk with them, and asked only that her friend Cynthia Corning* be allowed to sit in.

"Cynthia knew Russel, too," she explained.

Fran Lester was earthy, frank, and she was

clearly a nice woman. She appeared to understand Russel Douglas well, and had wanted the best for him—even if he did succeed in mending the gaping holes in his marriage. She knew her romance with him would run its course, but she was happy while it lasted. Indeed, she said, she was ultimately the one who sent him away weeks before Christmas.

Fran said that she had met Russel in a cocktail lounge at the resort town of Ocean Shores on the Washington coast. She had been on vacation from her telecommunications job in Tacoma at TESINC and he was there to surf. He was sitting at the bar by himself, and Fran said she had approached him. They hit it off right away.

"He told me he had children, but they weren't with him that first weekend," she added. "He told me that he was divorced. We were having dinner once after we'd been dating for six or eight weeks, and he confessed that he was still married—but that he'd moved out of his house in April 2003. I didn't meet his kids until about three months ago.

"We talked that first night until five in the morning. We came to have mutual trust for each other."

Once again, Mike Birchfield was asking the questions, while Mark Plumberg took copious notes.

"Tell us about Russel," Mike Birchfield asked.

"He was very shy, very quiet," Cynthia cut in.

"But he was open to anything and everything," Fran finished. "I guess maybe you've been to his apartment and seen some of his wild clothes?"

Russel's heritage was Scottish, and she recalled

that she had told him once that her fantasy was having sex with a man wearing a kilt. Sure enough, the next week he had come to her place wearing a kilt.

Still, most of Russel's own fantasies were fairly tame, even unimaginative.

"He wanted to be naked on the beach," she said with a shrug. "That's not really weird."

The sex toys in his apartment? Fran dismissed that with a shake of her head. "He and his wife had a business where they sold those things at home parties. And they were the 'entertainment' at some of those parties."

According to Fran, Russel didn't have very good relationships with the women in his life. There were the problems with Brenna, of course, and he hadn't gotten along with his own mother, Gail O'Neal. He told Fran that she was very strict when he was a child, and his early years weren't happy.

"He hasn't even talked to his mother for a year."

That, of course, wasn't true.

Russ Douglas's tendency to blame his mother for things she had no control over probably was behind that lie.

And his perceived problems with his mother may have been why Russel was attracted to Fran. Fran had been both his lover *and* an older woman who told them that she had "loved him unconditionally."

"I think he loved me in the way he could—but not in the way I loved him. He could relax around me, and I loved him even though he had a 'dark side.'"

"What do you mean by that?" Birchfield asked.

"Russ had a lot of anxiety and emotional pain. He thought people had betrayed him. He was trying to find himself."

"Was he stable?"

"Russ? No—oh no—but he was trying. He was in therapy for depression. I knew he took some prescription drugs. It might have been Prozac."

Just as his father had said, the man Fran Lester was describing sounded bipolar, with the strongest pull toward depression. Indeed, Fran said she'd been stunned when she heard he was dead. *Murdered.*

"Frankly, I thought it would have been a suicide. When I thought of his being killed, it was a shock."

Russ had been very careful to maintain his privacy when the two first met. He wouldn't tell Fran his address or even consider giving her a key to his apartment. After a while, they saw each other "four or five" times a week, and exchanged keys.

"After we broke up, I mailed his key back to him and he mailed the key to my house to me."

His lover characterized Douglas as very insecure.

"He was afraid of most women," she said. "He developed physically late in life. He was smart enough, but he was naive. People who think sex is a game are very naive.

"Russel wasn't really very good at anything," Fran added with a sigh. "He couldn't throw darts, dance, play the guitar, or surf. I guess his only real talent was that he had a lot of endurance in bed."

"But you told me he was insecure," Mike Birch-field reminded her.

"Well, he wasn't insecure during sex."

He was not, however, as uninhibited as Brenna Douglas had suggested.

"Did he ever try to get you into S and M?" Birchfield asked.

"*No!* He was very sensitive emotionally. He would never be physically or sexually aggressive. He wouldn't even do minor playful, physical stuff during sex."

Fran's view of Russel Douglas seemed diametrically opposed to his widow's. As far as Fran knew, he wasn't into pornography, swinging, or heavy drinking. She had once offered to get some porno movies, but he turned down her offer.

She had never seen him intoxicated, but she had suspected that he'd done drugs one night when he kissed her and she had a metallic taste in her mouth.

Russel had told her that he and Brenna sometimes fought physically, although he was the one who got hit. Brenna could defend herself.

Fran Lester said that she knew Russel was still sleeping with Brenna. "Every time he got his hair cut."

That didn't seem to bother Fran. Nor was she disturbed about how he spoke of Brenna. She knew he was proud of his wife, and how well she ran their beauty salon, Just B's.

As long as he did the books.

"The worst thing he ever said about her was

that she was not good with money," Fran said. "He said that Brenna was 'the one' for him, and he called his kids at least every other day."

Birchfield asked a vital question: "Was Russel bisexual?"

"I don't think so. He told me about a guy at Gold's Gym who hit on him. He told the guy that he was 'taken,' by a girlfriend. I guess that would be me.

"I asked him once if he was ever interested in homosexual relations, and he said he'd thought about it—but he hadn't done it."

Russel had also thought about a threesome, but that never happened. Indeed, his most adventurous lovemaking had been with his wife. He told Fran that he and Brenna had "done it" on the ferry, and almost everywhere else, tantalized by the danger of getting caught.

"Could you trust him?"

"Yes!" she answered emphatically, but then quickly added, "but I wouldn't trust him to be faithful."

Russel had told Fran once that "some woman" was stalking him, but she had no details about who that woman might be. He hadn't mentioned anything about a "headhunter" to her.

Fran Lester pondered Birchfield's question about what might have gotten Russ into a position of vulnerability.

"His mouth—his mouth could get him into trouble because he didn't think about what he said before he said it."

Russ Douglas had never had a problem with

strangers, she said, because he was a "hermit" who avoided strangers. But she said he was a "whiner" and a "spoiled brat" who sometimes made a big fuss about nothing. Once, he'd even thrown a hissy fit because a store didn't have the kind of pop he wanted, an incident his mother had also referred to.

"He was a 'whiner'?" Birchfield repeated.

"All men are," she said with a laugh.

Fran was not a shrinking violet, either, in what she said or what words she used to say something. Although she loved Russel Douglas, she had grown tired of how spoiled he acted at times. They had tried to preserve the feeling of fun they had on the night they met, but it was hard for her to ignore his pettiness.

"We broke up on December 6," she said. "I was upset with him and I did call him a spoiled brat, and I hurt his feelings. That ended our relationship."

Fran wasn't aware that his own mother and sister had often told him the same thing—that she had hit a tender nerve. Of all things, Russ Douglas didn't want to be seen as a "spoiled brat," although his very behavior at times showed that he was.

Fran Lester said she had last heard from Russ on Christmas Eve. He was trying to decide if he should spend Christmas with his wife and children. She told him he had to make up his own mind about that. The Friday *after* Christmas, she opened a last email from him that he had sent on Christmas Eve.

"I sent him an answer," she said. "It's probably in his computer, but I don't think he ever got it."

The two women with whom Russel Douglas had been involved had given such different opinions. Fran Lester had pooh-poohed the idea that he was ever drawn into swinging with strangers, assuring both detectives he was much too shy and anxious to do that.

And yet his wife described him as almost maniacally involved in aberrant sex.

Was it possible he was both personalities? He seemed to be bipolar, but it was doubtful that he was a true Jekyll and Hyde combination.

Surprisingly, Russ's mother, Gail, and his sister, Holly, felt no ill will toward Fran Lester. While Russ could be annoying and immature, Brenna was the one who had always seemed to be manipulating in the background.

Brenna would agree to attend holiday celebrations or family reunions, and invariably back out at the last minute. When she and Russ did attend such functions, Brenna made a point of sitting far apart from the rest of the family.

"We felt that Brenna was controlling Russ," Gail said. "He wasn't the one that was deliberately avoiding us."

One Thanksgiving, the family all went to Kalispell, Montana, to Gail's sister's home. The next day, Brenna and Russ went shopping and left baby Jack with Gail.

They were gone long enough for Jack to start getting hungry. Gail warmed a jar of baby food and was feeding it to him when Brenna walked in the door.

"What are you *doing*?" Brenna shrieked.

"He was so hungry—" Gail began.

Brenna grabbed the baby food jar out of Gail's hand and threw it into the sink.

"We *never* warm his food," she screamed. "He eats cold food!"

Baffled, Gail stared at her daughter-in-law. She didn't know of anyone who didn't warm their small babies' food.

Clearly, Brenna was trying to control Russ *and* his family. She and his sister, Holly, had been close, but she drew away from Holly after Russ's murder, and she refused to even discuss the details of the insurance policies he had.

She derided Russ and his family for thinking education was important. Brenna was by no means dumb, but she hated schools and colleges.

At another Montana family reunion, Brenna insisted that she and her family wouldn't stay in the homes relatives had prepared for sleepovers. Instead, she insisted on staying in the RV she and Russ owned, and then she made him park far away from the group.

That was not a good trip. They were all going to meet at a campground, and someone inadvertently gave Russ the wrong directions. When Gail discovered that, she tried to get in touch with them, but their cell phone was turned off. By retracing the turns along the way, the Douglases finally arrived—but they were forty-five minutes late.

Brenna was furious. She screamed at Gail.

"How dare you give me the wrong directions! I know you did it on purpose!"

Brenna's diabetic mother had surgery—a gastric bypass—but complications set in, and she died suddenly of a pulmonary embolism and heart failure.

"Russ took some of his 401(k) money to pay for his mother-in-law's funeral," Gail O'Neal said. "That was why he agreed to buy the second insurance policy on his own life. He told Brenna, 'I don't want that to happen to you. I want you taken care of.'"

Brenna's chaotic emotions and bad business sense weren't positive influences in Russ's life, but he was apparently doing his best at the time he was murdered. And his mother thanked his mistress for that.

"Fran was key to helping my son grow up," Gail said. "He did act like a self-indulgent kid sometimes, and Fran let him have it. When he whined about his miserable marriage, she told him, 'Either get a divorce, or get into counseling.'

"And he was beginning to change and stop feeling so sorry for himself. Before, he would call Brenna and threaten suicide if she wouldn't take him back. Poor 'Eeyore.' All of a sudden, I said, 'Oh my God—Russ has grown up.'

"He was finally happy, but Brenna wasn't. He was responsible—he paid child support and he paid spousal support, too. But I don't think Brenna wanted him back."

Initially, Gail tried to help Brenna out of the financial mess her beauty salon books were in, and recommended a CPA who could help her. That annoyed her newly widowed daughter-in-law.

Two remarks that Brenna Douglas made to Gail still disturb her. She doesn't know what Brenna was trying to say. At first, Gail couldn't believe that Brenna had anything at all to do with Russ's murder, but as the circumstantial evidence piled up, she wondered.

"I asked her a direct question once. And she was very snotty when she answered me. I asked her: 'Have you ever thought—when you were working with your friend—Peggy Sue—that Russ was worth more dead to you than alive?'"

Peggy Sue Thomas often worked at Just B's as a hairdresser; she was Brenna's landlady, and the two were close friends.

"She said, 'Well . . . I *might have.*'"

Later, Brenna suddenly burst out with an inscrutable remark:

"If push comes to shove, I have a bomb that will devastate the family . . ."

What did she mean?

BOTH BRENNA AND FRAN could account for their whereabouts on the afternoon of December 26. And their stories checked out.

But someone had shot Russ during that time. So far, Detectives Mark Plumberg and Mike Birchfield were as puzzled about the actual killer as they were when they first walked up to the yellow Tracker in the woods.

They had to spread their net wider and find more people who might have been involved with the dead man. The worst possible outcome of their probe would be that this was a stranger-to-stranger murder, the cold act of someone who had *no* connection at all to Russel Douglas, someone who simply wanted to feel what it was like to kill someone.

And that is the kind of homicide that frightens everyone who lives in the area of the crime, and makes people lock their doors and cars when they usually don't.

Wherever shocking crimes happen, television news crews invariably film footage of residents who seem to read from the same script. As the interviewees face the camera, they shake their heads and say, "Something like this just doesn't happen here. We can't understand why Russ was murdered. I guess it happens in a big city or a bad neighborhood—but not *here.*"

But, of course, it does happen *there.*

And it invariably shakes bystanders hard. With the first news bulletin, they have to acknowledge their own mortality. And, yes, wonder if they might be next.

When the killer isn't caught, they grow more afraid as time passes.

PART THREE

The Investigation

CHAPTER SEVEN

ONE OF THE MAIN questions that needed to be answered was how Russ Douglas had ended up on Wahl Road, an area where no one had ever known him to be.

The investigating team studied the placement of homes along Wahl Road. Diane Bailey, the only witness who had seen the yellow Tracker and its driver *before* he was shot, lived just west of a rather impressive residence closer to Admiralty Way. The place had stone pillars and a heavy gate across its driveway. As the detectives walked farther west, they passed the Baileys' driveway, another narrow road leading in, and finally the dirt road where Douglas's body was discovered.

Interestingly, there was another expensive-looking home on the other end of the street where Wahl Road turned into Ebb Tide. It was almost a mirror image of the first estate; it, too, had stone pillars and fortresslike iron gates. It was difficult to see the large house beyond because of an over-growth of landscaping. It was right next door to the property where Russ was found dead.

If Douglas was unfamiliar with the Double Bluff region and had been summoned or directed to "a long driveway next to a large estate with stone pillars and heavy gates," he might very well have first turned into Diane Bailey's driveway in error. Fir trees hid almost all of the homes on the street, so giving the color of the house or any other defining characteristic would have been useless. The person giving directions would have been much more likely to describe the fenced-off estates with impressive landscaping as landmarks for him to watch for.

The victim must have realized he was in the wrong place and quickly backed out when he saw the Baileys' red Volvo. He had to pass only two more lots to get to 6665 Wahl Road. And just beyond was the entrance to the next lavish grounds.

So far, Mark Plumberg and Mike Birchfield had only tenuous leads to follow, many of which would turn out to be gossip or from someone with an active imagination. They hoped that they might find some links that would hook with other links if they meshed. They talked with present and former residents west of the Blacks' land. They figured that they might find someone who had a connection to the second estate—someone who had included it in the directions given to Russ Douglas.

But first they had to search the Chevy Tracker

thoroughly. They went to the Armory, where it had been stored awaiting Washington State Patrol criminalists who would process it for prints, blood, and any other human secretions.

Russel Douglas had traveled a lot for his job with Tetra Tech, and his car looked as though he had practically lived in it. It was a hot mess. Apparently, he had just dropped things on the floor rather than keeping a litter bag handy. There were many papers, slips, and receipts inside, along with fast food wrappers and paper cups, most of the trash discolored by dried blood. The receipts were the kind everyone has—from grocery stores and restaurants. The murder victim had patronized 7-Eleven, Applebee's, Starbucks, Fred Meyer, Chevron, Barnes & Noble, Sleepwater Surf, and a number of clothing stores, including one company that advertised clothes and accessories specifically designed for transvestites.

There was a Washington State Ferry receipt from Clinton to Mukilteo from December 13, and some bank slips. It didn't appear that someone had rifled through the Tracker searching for something. Rather, Douglas's SUV was cluttered by someone who wasn't concerned with neatness. They found nothing that might be of much evidentiary interest. Still, they bagged and labeled into evidence everything they found.

The two detectives located a fanny pack in the Tracker. It contained a book of thirteen unused ferry tickets, two bank ATM cards, a checkbook with Russel Douglas's name, many assorted condoms in flavors ranging from mint to chocolate, a Nextel ID card, receipts from Amour on the Boulevard in a shopping mall, a business card from Las Vegas Limousines, and seventy-six dollars in paper currency in various denominations from twenties to ones.

One dollar bill had writing on the back: the name "Francisco C." It did not resemble Douglas's handwriting. Francisco was probably someone who had signed the bill before Russ Douglas ever got it.

Mark Plumberg and Mike Birchfield saved even the most infinitesimal items because one day they might be priceless to the investigation. They had to find some connection between the killer(s) and his/their victim. Something as simple as a matchbook might make that link possible.

They did locate Russ's missing laptop computer. Tracy Harvey, his brother's fiancée, said it had come from his apartment. Matthew agreed that it had been in his custody since then, most of the time in the trunk of his car. He had intended to give it to the investigators at his brother's memorial service.

Brenna Douglas had voluntarily brought one of her husband's computers to her first interview at the Island County Sheriff's South Precinct. If she knew where his work computer was, why didn't she tell detectives about it then?

At her mother-in-law's suggestion, Brenna hired

a lawyer—Jessie Valentine. Ms. Valentine advised her client to participate in no more interviews with detectives unless she was present.

Mike Birchfield asked Lieutenant Harry Uncapher to examine the computer and its case for latent fingerprints. He was puzzled when he learned that there *were* no fingerprints to be found. How odd. The computer had to have been taken out of its case innumerable times; it and the case should have more than a sprinkling of prints. But neither the mouse nor the keyboard gave up any obvious or latent fingerprints.

"It's my opinion," Birchfield said, "that someone wiped the computer clean of any prints."

Was it possible that Russ Douglas had been murdered because of something he knew that was part of a high-tech war? There are many high-profile electronic device companies around Seattle. In most of them, visitors have to clear security and sign agreements that they won't disclose what they might see beyond the security-monitored doors.

It seemed hardly likely that Douglas had high-security clearance or knew any high-tech secrets. But then his murder itself was hardly likely.

BY SERVING A SEARCH warrant on the Bank of America where Russel Douglas kept his account, Mark Plumberg was able to get a glimpse at his lifestyle, to know where he went on certain days, when he made deposits and withdrawals, where he made regular payments. Ever since he moved away from his home in the spring of 2003, he had been dependable with support checks for his children.

Russ's job with Tetra Tech paid well, but he was far from wealthy. He paid rent on his apartment, monthly payments on his new GEO Tracker, and he spent quite a lot of money on his hobbies and on sports and fitness.

Russ had no mortgage payments; the house in Langley where Brenna and their children lived was rented from a woman named Peggy Sue Thomas. Peggy had worked for Brenna at Just B's Beauty Salon for a while, but she had moved away from Whidbey Island sometime before, and the house was up for sale. Reportedly, Brenna hoped to buy it but didn't have enough for a down payment. This was the second mention of "Peggy" that had surfaced in the early part of the investigation.

MIKE BIRCHFIELD TALKED TO the manager of the Gold's Gym franchise in Renton. The logbook there showed that Russ's last workout ended at 9 P.M. on December 23. He asked if it was true that Douglas had been at the gym so often, lifting weights in particular, because he was going to enter a bodybuilding contest.

The manager said he doubted that.

"We have two members who may be doing that, but he wasn't one of them. You have to follow a very strict routine to do that, and the club usually gets involved. Russ's workout routine was nowhere near the competitive level."

Even at Gold's Gym, the homicide victim had been a loner; he had no workout partners, and only casual acquaintances there.

"He was very friendly and outgoing with our staff," the manager said, "but the interesting thing about him was how flamboyantly he dressed. I'm talking pink spandex stretch shorts, gold chains, and wild shirts."

Birchfield asked if Douglas had ever mentioned that someone was stalking him or trying to hurt him.

"No way."

Even though each day's detective work was filling in the profile of Russel Douglas, changing it from a "stick drawing" to the image of a man of many facets, Mark Plumberg was aware that his investigation had a ways to go. Just as he had with other cases, he expected to come to know Russel Douglas, a man he had never met and *would* never meet, far more than most people the investigator knew in his own life.

That wasn't going to be easy, given the indications that the victim of a case that grew colder as the days passed hadn't appeared to know *himself*. Russel Douglas had frantically plunged from one activity into another, seen at least two women during the same period, sought therapy, and spent much time in introspection.

Mark Plumberg studied the series of scratchy notes that Russ had written to himself, possibly as a part of his therapy. Most of the sentences were in question form. He'd clearly been a man consumed with angst. Indeed, if they *had* found a gun near the death car at the Wahl Road crime scene, Plumberg realized that they almost certainly would have written off the case as a suicide and never second-guessed their conclusions.

But the gun was missing. With a sinking feeling, the detective believed that this case might turn out to be the perfect murder—if the shooter had already pitched it off a ferry on his or her trip off-island.

Once again, he read Russ's notes, which began with his sense that his troubles had started with his childhood:

> "Question: Where is your focus? Why is your focus?"
>
> Weight of world and past constantly on your shoulders. Bear this enormous burden. Feel others "got away w/life" and you got caught/trapped. Feel you settled by settling down. Marriage feels like a mistake because of your past. Past feels like a mistake—memory/observation.

He wrote of his upbringing by his mother:

> ENVIRONMENT—Self righteousness
> —Perfection
>   Ultimate Restriction
> —No Risk—absolute safety
> (FEAR BASED)

What makes you uncomfortable and angry feeds off itself. Left feeling *lost, insecure, unfulfilled, different, rejected, broken, bitter/anger* → *depression*.

You want the impossible! Because you were given contradictory upbringing and standards—even within yourself. If you don't somehow conquer this, you'll lose what you have. You'll continue on the path of negativity in thoughts, words, and actions.

Russ Douglas's current dilemma appeared to be over his marriage to Brenna:

Why are you so afraid to just be w/o Brenna and take off? Why are you holding yourself and them back? Are you afraid to leave? Are you afraid this isn't what you really want? Are you afraid this is what you want but you also didn't get what you wanted at all and always regret it?

Perception? Judgment? Rejection? Humiliation—from a divorce?

Afraid if you leave, it won't get better?

Afraid to leave and end up where you were when you were alone and still not get "it"?

Afraid of lifestyle change?

Good. Responsibility and Commitment—w/o you what will your kids do?

Plumberg shook his head. It was sadly ironic to read Douglas's questions to himself about how he could find happiness and overcome what he perceived he had suffered in the first three decades of his life.

Now, he had no future and his decisions wouldn't matter at all.

But Russ Douglas didn't know that as he'd scribbled his jumbled thoughts, trying to winnow out some magic formula for a better life.

One conclusion kept appearing.

Who provided you with the most happiness? *Brenna. This is true!*

With only a very short time to live, Russel Douglas seemed to have made up his mind. He didn't want a divorce; he wanted to move back into the house on Furman Road with his wife and children.

What, then, had drawn him to Wahl Road in Freeland? Where he would die instantly? Plumberg guessed that the victim was ambushed—lured to his murder by some sort of ruse.

CHAPTER EIGHT

ON JANUARY 13, 2004, the detective team from Island County drove to the Redmond offices of Tetra Tech, hoping they might find out more about the people with whom Russel Douglas had interacted. Harry Turpin, the Tetra Tech supervisor, spoke with them first, and he described Russel as a "good employee" who had been with the company since July 2003.

Asked if he had observed anything out of the norm about Russel, he nodded.

"Well, once he came to work in a kilt, and another time he wore a kind of sarong—maybe you'd call it a long loincloth. We're casual here—but not that casual. I took him aside and explained to him that basically we're employed by Nextel, and they're right next door. We have to dress the way Nextel staff dresses.

"He apologized and said he wouldn't do that again."

And he hadn't. Turpin said he'd never had any disciplinary problems with Russel. He knew that he and his wife were getting divorced and that he had a girlfriend, but learned later that the lovers had broken up and Russ was getting back together with his wife.

"I heard that just before the, ah, end."

Turpin recalled a three-day business trip with several of his employees, including Russ Douglas. They had gone to Klamath Falls, Oregon. Nothing unusual happened on the trip.

Some of Tetra Tech's employees had worked with Douglas at his former job with the city of Mukilteo, and they occasionally "razzed" him about his less-than-stellar performance there, but Turpin felt he was doing very well in his new job. In fact, he had been assigned—beginning in January 2004—to the "leasing side" of Tetra. It wasn't a big promotion, but it would have put him in a position with the likelihood of more upward mobility. He would scout out locations where his company could erect cell phone towers.

Systematically, Mike Birchfield and Mark Plumberg met with many of the Tetra Tech workers. He had been well liked by his coworkers.

"He liked his job and everyone at work loved him," one woman said. "His kids meant a lot to him. He didn't come to our Christmas party because his wife wouldn't let him bring them with him."

She confided that Russ had always wanted to

be "best" at everything he did and wasn't always successful. But, on the job, he was fine "once he got rolling."

Asked about drug or alcohol use, the woman looked shocked. "I'm telling you that I would be blown away if I found out Russ had a problem with either one!"

The Island County investigators found that Russel Douglas *had* confided his marital difficulties to many of his coworkers. Some knew that he'd had a girlfriend for a while, and others didn't. Most described him as "happy" and "friendly," although they didn't know where he spent his time after work hours. And no one described him as a druggie or drinker.

He was a hard worker, a man excited about his new job in the company and his MBA, both of which would come true in the early months of 2004.

Although he admitted that he and his wife, Brenna, often argued, his fellow workers believed he was doing everything he could to pick up his marriage again and make it work. They had married young, when they already had a one-year-old son. But it wasn't a "shotgun wedding" in any real sense. Russ loved Brenna and she seemed to love him.

PART FOUR

Likely and
Unlikely Suspects

CHAPTER NINE

MANY OF THE RESIDENTS of Island County tried to help in the investigation of Russel Douglas's murder, most of them well intentioned. Mike Birchfield and Mark Plumberg listened to every lead that came in. Some sounded plausible, and others were a combination of gossip, rumor, and wild imagining. The two detectives were trying to locate patterns and connections, and listening to the lay public could very well net something that established those.

Viola Peckinpaugh* called Plumberg on January 6, 2004. Her friends had urged her to come forward. She was acquainted with Brenna Douglas and she was concerned that her ex-husband, Floyd Peckinpaugh,* might somehow be involved in Russel's murder.

"I know that Floyd was angry with some company that didn't pay him for a concrete job—and I'm pretty sure it was a telecom company. He was making threats, and he would sit in his truck making phone calls to that company. He owns a gun."

During Viola's marriage to Floyd, she said he had lived a "secret life," where he had affairs and did drugs. She was worried that Floyd might have shot Douglas because he was angry that Russ's employer hadn't paid him.

When Plumberg checked with Russ's coworkers at Tetra Tech, they said it was highly unlikely that he had been involved in any operations on Whidbey Island that dealt with concrete. It seemed a far reach to connect him to Floyd Peckinpaugh.

This was one of the early leads that ended nowhere. And there were to be many of them.

Another tip came to Mike Birchfield that same week. A man named Dirk Kenwell* brought a friend of his—Sandra Malle*—to the South Precinct. Sandra was concerned about an acquaintance who had recently moved to Whidbey Island. She explained that she had known Eddie Navarre* since the early eighties, and that he was a peculiar man with a criminal history, a heroin user, and possessed of a very nasty temper.

Navarre currently sold orange juice franchises.

Sandra was an artist on the island, and the last person she ever wanted to run into again was Navarre. When nearly two decades had passed, she didn't expect to. He was part of a different world, a self-styled "hippie." They had never been romantically involved and, as far as she knew, he'd never been very interested in women.

Sandra was afraid of him and also sorry for him, as he appeared to be living in his van. She had invited him to stay with Kenwell and herself for a few nights. But they had to ask him to leave after the second night.

"He got very pushy and we had no privacy."

Eddie Navarre became one of the first "persons of interest" in the probe of Russ Douglas's murder. But the Island County investigators couldn't interview him; he had disappeared.

Russ Douglas had led a scattered, compartmentalized life. Very few of his friends knew one another, and few groups truly knew him. There were people who had worked for the city of Mukilteo with him, coworkers at Tetra Tech, members of Gold's Gym, Fran Lester, his girlfriend in Tacoma, Brenna and her family, *his* family, even strangers who had met him in a bar or on the beach when he was surfing.

The one constant that he talked about to almost everyone was his estranged wife, their constant arguments, and his back-and-forth feelings on whether he should go back home and try again.

If she would have him.

CHAPTER TEN

ON JANUARY 26, 2004, Mike Birchfield received a phone call from a private investigator—John Blaine*—who had been hired by Farmers' New World Life Insurance Company to do a follow-up on a claim made by Mrs. Brenna Douglas. Blaine wanted to set up a meeting.

Birchfield agreed to talk with him, and told Blaine that he had asked Brenna about any insurance policies her late husband might have had.

"She said the only one she was aware of was a policy that came with his job at Tetra Tech."

"What did Douglas do for a living?" the PI asked.

"He was a zone manager for a company called Tetra Tech."

"Our application shows him as an unemployed hairdresser."

That application was made in the autumn of 2002. Birchfield found that Russ had worked for the city of Mukilteo at that time. He *was*, technically, also a hairdresser because he and Brenna were partners at Just B's. Why he didn't list his employment with the city of Mukilteo, too, was puzzling.

The payoff value of this second policy was three hundred thousand dollars.

Brenna Douglas had filed claims to release information regarding the claim on January 3, 2004—nine days after Russ's death—and again on January 12.

The insurance investigator traveled to Whidbey Island on February 4 to talk with Mike Birchfield and, he hoped, to Brenna. Blaine had phoned her and found her "evasive," although she did agree to meet with him.

Blaine asked the Island County detective about the way Russel Douglas had died, and how Brenna had reacted. Birchfield recalled how stoic she had been, and her apparent lack of shock or emotion when she heard she was a widow.

"We haven't ruled her out as a suspect at this time," he said. "But we can't really include her in, either."

John Blaine met with Brenna and it was an emotional interview. He felt that she was holding some information back, although he wasn't sure what it might be. She wept often. When he mentioned that she and Russel had been on the verge of a divorce, she was vehement in denying that— insisting that they were *not* considering that when her husband was shot.

"We were working things out," she insisted.

"While we were apart, Russ was writing a novel for me."

"Would you agree to take a polygraph exam?" Blaine asked.

"No," she answered. "I don't want to take one."

With Blaine's help, Birchfield learned that Russel had had somewhere between four hundred thousand dollars and seven hundred thousand dollars in life insurance when he died. The last policies he bought in 2002 insured both himself and Brenna. Whether he knew that his wife went back soon after and lowered the amount on her life is moot.

The insurance underwriters involved continued their probes to see if there were any reasons that the policies should not be honored.

If this was a scenario for a film noir in the forties where Barbara Stanwyck or Bette Davis plotted to do away with her movie husband for an insurance payoff, a real-life *Double Indemnity,* the murder of Russ Douglas probably would have been solved.

But it wasn't. One has to consider how a young mother who had lived through months of marital discord and indecision, with two children to raise, might react to the news that her estranged husband had been murdered. Brenna's flat response and inappropriate attitude could very well have been a result of shock. How humans react to profoundly bad news isn't predictable.

The question was: was Russ's death *really* profoundly bad news for Brenna Douglas?

Brenna couldn't handle money; Russ had said

that often enough, and she had counted on him to do the books at their beauty salon. His mother—Gail O'Neal—verified that.

"Russ was going to do their income tax," O'Neal said. "But she hadn't kept any records, bank statements, and other supportive information on the beauty salon's profit and loss. And he found they owed a lot of back taxes."

Brenna Douglas didn't have much money; she didn't even own her house. She might have filed a claim for insurance so rapidly because she was afraid she wouldn't be able to support her children and herself.

Insurance adjusters for AIG were leery about payoffs to a beneficiary who was a probable suspect in the murder of the insured, and Brenna was in that category. They were more willing to set up trust funds for Jack and Hannah than to write a check for four hundred thousand dollars to Brenna.

She would have none of that. She wrote out her statement. "The proceeds are rightfully mine, and while I intend to invest the money and it will ultimately go to benefit my children, it is inappropriate to hold the money or award it to my children on the unsupported allegation of the prosecutor.

"Again, I categorically state that I was not involved in the death of my husband in any way!"

Joan McPherson, an attorney appointed to represent Jack and Hannah, said she didn't think that Brenna had any part in Russ's homicide, but she still recommended that insurance money should be withheld until there was no question at all of Brenna's innocence.

Brenna was in debt; she hadn't waited for the insurance money. By the late spring of 2004, she had bought a house, a Suburban, and an RV. In August of that year, she lost the house because she wasn't making payments.

In December 2005, Island County Superior Court Judge Vickie Churchill ordered that since there was no solid proof that Brenna was a part of any plot against her late husband, AIG should give her the proceeds of the first policy. It was believed to be around four hundred thousand dollars, with twelve hundred dollars in interest added.

A year later, she sued Farmers New World Life Insurance for three hundred thousand dollars on December 26, the third anniversary of Russ's murder.

Brenna Douglas didn't win this claim. Although she asked for a waiver of Russel's medical information, the company refused. Russ had lied on his application and failed to mention some slight irregularities with his heart and his treatment for depression.

CHAPTER ELEVEN

I HAVE NEVER WRITTEN ABOUT a case where the investigating detectives interviewed as many possible witnesses or informants as this one. That they hadn't come up with a prime suspect by February 2004 wasn't from lack of trying. Now, Mark Plumberg and Mike Birchfield enlarged their search for the Christmas killer. At the same time, there were other less compelling crimes to respond to on an island so large in area with relatively few residents.

They asked for information from the public about anyone who might have visited Whidbey Island during the holidays in 2003.

They had searched computers for email correspondence, and now they scanned telephone records of calls that Russel Douglas had made and received.

On May 12, 2004, the two detectives went over the Nextel records for Russel. It would be ironic if there was any kind of solid clue in them that could lead to a killer who had by now gotten away with murder for almost five months.

They found one number that they didn't recognize; there weren't that many calls from that area code. It had a 702 prefix, which meant it had emanated from the Las Vegas area, or from a cell phone listed to that area.

Whoever had the phone with the Las Vegas number had called Russ Douglas three times on December 23, 2003. And *he* had called that number twice on that same day. If it was a cell phone, the calls from the Nevada number could have been made in that state—or from anywhere in America, for that matter.

Mike Birchfield picked up his phone and dialed the number. It rang a few times, and then a recording of a female voice came on, saying her name was "Peggy" and asking callers to leave a message.

He didn't do that. Only a few moments passed before the detective's phone rang. A woman named Peggy was calling.

"I just got a call from your number," she said.

Mark Plumberg answered and identified himself.

"We called you because your number came up in an investigation here—on the murder of a man named Russel Douglas."

"Peggy" was quite forthcoming.

"You called my cell phone," she said. "I'll give you my home phone number, too. I used to live up there, but I'm a limousine driver in Las Vegas now."

Peggy, who was using the last name "Thomas," said she knew both Russ and his wife, Brenna. She owned their rental house on Furman Avenue in Langley. They were supposed to buy the house from her—but that hadn't occurred yet.

"I'm an unwilling landlord," she said. "I know—knew—them both, but I'm closer to Brenna."

Plumberg asked about the five calls between her cell phone and Russel's two days before Christmas.

That was simple enough for her to explain. Peggy Sue Thomas said she had been "in the area" visiting her family for the holidays, and she had wanted to meet with Russ to give him a Christmas present she'd bought for Brenna.

"We kept playing phone tag."

"Did you see Russel?"

"No, I was supposed to get together with Russ and Brenna during the holidays, but that never happened."

A moment later, she corrected herself. She hadn't seen the couple per se, but she *had* seen Russ at his apartment about nine on the night of the twenty-third and she gave him the present for Brenna then.

"Do you remember what he was wearing?"

"I can't really recall—wait—I think he had on spandex shorts and a bandanna that covered his whole head."

Peggy said that she had only talked to Russ

for about five minutes, but she remembered how happy he was and excited about spending time with Brenna and his kids over the holidays.

"He felt pretty good and thought he and Brenna could get back together, and get past his affair."

"What do you know about that affair?" Plumberg asked.

"I just knew it was in another state—I don't know if it was with a woman or what. I know Brenna was crushed about an affair he had with a man."

Peggy seemed to know the couple very well. Before the twenty-third, Russ and his girlfriend had come to Las Vegas in October. Peggy hadn't seen him during that visit, but she'd talked to him when he called her.

"Did he talk about his girlfriend?"

"Only a story he told me about them getting thrown out of a bar for dancing on the table."

Plumberg asked Peggy if she could tell the investigators about Russel or if she knew anyone who could help them.

"Well, Russ sometimes wears kilts," she said, "and he likes to explore sexually."

It occurred to Mark Plumberg that Peggy was following a story line that was very like what Brenna had told him back on December 28.

"Do you have any *personal* knowledge of his activities?"

"Well, I've personally seen him in a kilt," she said. "And once at a meeting at the salon he told me he would like to 'party' with me. The way he said it, it really had sexual undertones."

Asked if she knew anything about Russel and a "swinging lifestyle" in Las Vegas, she laughed.

"He'd probably be more likely to find that on Whidbey Island than he would in Vegas."

She mentioned rumors she'd heard about spots on the island—clubs and gyms—where that could have happened.

Peggy said she would call if she thought of anything more about Russ that might have led to his murder. She didn't seem at all concerned that she had been contacted by detectives investigating a murder. In fact she spoke with great confidence.

More tips continued to come into the sheriff's detectives, but Peggy Sue Thomas remained on the "interview again" list.

CHAPTER TWELVE

IN LATE DECEMBER 2003, Mark Plumberg couldn't know that he would one day become the lead investigator in the most intense—and frustrating—homicide probe he has ever known. Almost a decade later, he still wakes in the darkest hours of the night and thinks about it.

In June 2004, he revisited the Russel Douglas murder investigation from scratch, reading over the stacks of follow-up reports and statements he and Mike Birchfield had gathered.

After he had reinterviewed Sandra Malle, the glass artisan in Freeland, Plumberg's chosen person of interest was Eddie Navarre. Almost everything Sandra Malle said about the juice entrepreneur made him a very plausible suspect.

Mark Plumberg listened carefully as she added more about Navarre. She had known him in the eighties in Sarasota, Florida. She worked in a health food store at the time, and he had been into nutrition, even though he had always been overweight. At that time, they had been casual friends—"hanging out and partying" together.

"He used heroin," Sandra said. "He also used to hang out at health clubs and he picked up prostitutes."

"Was he homosexual or bisexual?"

"I wasn't aware of that, but I wouldn't put it past him. I stopped hanging around with him because of his temper. It was scary and we suspected that he sometimes carried guns."

Sandra Malle didn't know how Navarre had found her in 2003, all the way across the country and after such a long time. She guessed that she might have known that she moved to the Seattle area, but was mystified how he could have found her on Whidbey Island.

"My phone number isn't listed," she said. "I sometimes advertise in the local papers here, but I haven't since early autumn. And then I didn't use my name—only my glass business name."

"Did he know any of your friends on the island?"

She shook her head. She had talked with the small circle of friends who knew where she lived and none of them had ever heard of Navarre.

"I just don't know. He told me he drove by my house many times. He even used the term 'stalked' when he talked about finding me. He said he had to be convinced that I lived here before he knocked on my door. I remember he said that I had 'no idea' what he went through to find me."

Eddie Navarre had always told stories about his life that Sandra doubted. After Christmas 2003, he explained that he had come up the West Coast from California, looking for someplace to live that was "laid back," where there would be "no hassles."

He told her he had been living with an older woman in California who was "in the movie business."

She could not tell Mark Plumberg any details on crimes Navarre might have committed, but she did know that he'd had "minor brushes" with police. That didn't matter; he had already obtained Eddie Navarre's rap sheet.

"So you moved out here and you hadn't heard from him before?"

"Not until November. He called me out of the blue on Thanksgiving—this last Thanksgiving. I talked to him for a while, but I made sure he knew I wasn't interested in seeing or hearing from him again."

Sandra thought she had succeeded in blowing Navarre off.

At that time, he lived a good distance away in Redmond (the town where Russel Douglas had worked for Tetra Tech), and then in a penthouse suite in a hotel in Lynnwood, Washington, which wasn't far from the Mukilteo ferry dock.

"He told me he left Redmond because he had an argument with his landlady."

"Did Eddie Navarre have a gun?"

"I'm not sure, but he told me several times that he was 'protected—because you never know.' He may have actually told me he had a gun—but I never saw one."

Eddie Navarre had always seemed paranoid about the police. And he used very bigoted terms for minorities.

"Black people, gay people, cops, and basically everyone who wasn't white like him."

Although Navarre had purported to be a hippie, Sandra had seen that he coveted a lavish lifestyle and put a price on almost everything.

His current occupation was with some company that sold healthy juice bar franchises for twenty-five thousand dollars. He said his boss was located in Arizona, and the 2001 van he was driving was a company car.

It was a nice Chrysler van that was silver and gold. Sandra had written down the license number, and Birchfield had checked it out the first time she reported how strange Eddie Navarre was. It was legally owned by a man who lived in Scottsdale.

"Eddie said he was very angry with his boss because he wasn't paying him on time."

The thing that brought Sandra Malle to the South Precinct in the first place, however, was that Navarre had come to Whidbey Island on the weekend of December 26 to 29. He appeared at her house in Freeland on the twenty-ninth. He probably was down on his luck because he said he'd been sleeping in his van in a state park for two nights, and she found it strange that he had gone from a penthouse suite to sleeping in his van.

"He showed me how he had blacked out the van's windows so the police couldn't look in on him. He had a TV, computer, feather bed, clothes, and a large black 'Tupperware-style' tote in there," Sandra recalled. "He was proud of the way he had it all set up so the van could run his computer and TV. He said he found the feather bed in a bag beside the road someplace."

Plumberg wondered if Russel Douglas might have had a feather bed in his Tracker—since he traveled so much for his job.

Eddie Navarre wove many good stories, including his tale of owning a huge marijuana farm in Gainesville, Florida, his promise of a twenty-thousand-dollar investment from an elderly man in Canada who wanted to help him republish a book/pamphlet he'd written in the eighties called *Layman's Guide to Fasting,* and the fact that he had to work only two or three hours a day selling the juice franchises that were making him wealthy.

And yet Mark Plumberg felt he was a shadow man. Sandra didn't know where he lived, only that it was supposed to be a garage apartment with "new tile."

He asked Sandra if Navarre had ever mentioned a watch to her. She suddenly looked surprised.

"Yeah—a watch. How did you know—?"

And then she shook her head as if she'd been about to say something and then stopped.

"I've forgotten the conversation," she said, "but sometime during the first week of spring this year—March 21—Eddie called me to tell me he'd found a ring and asked if I wanted it. I wasn't interested, and I never saw the ring.

"During that conversation, he mentioned a watch that he had that he was very proud of."

"What kind of watch did he wear?" Plumberg asked.

She pointed to his Timex "Ironman" black sport watch, and said, "Like yours—a simple black watch like yours."

Sandra Malle regretted ever having let Navarre back into her life, and she was frightened that he still might hurt her. He was angry when she and her boyfriend kicked him out.

"He wasn't very happy."

"Did you ever threaten to call the police?"

"No, we didn't. He made it very clear that he didn't like police and he wanted to avoid them— you—at all costs."

Now, Navarre was stalking Sandra Malle, and she was frightened. He was acting weirder and weirder.

"After Dirk and I asked him to leave, he kept calling my phone. I wouldn't answer and he'd let it ring off the hook. I've seen his van drive by my house several times a day. Once, he came over to my house and sat in the driveway and honked the horn. He sat there for over an hour. I'm afraid to answer the door when I'm home alone."

Sandra said she had begun to wonder if Eddie Navarre might have had something to do with Russ Douglas's murder.

"Why do you say that?"

"The stuff he told us. He said he'd been arrested for first-degree arson for burning down his medical supply business in the early nineties. I think he's still wanted for that in Florida. He's such a creepy man that I think the police here should be aware of him."

"Do you know where he's living?"

"The last time I talked to him, he said he was moving to Whidbey Island, and he was moving things from his storage unit in Renton."

Mike Birchfield had asked all the personnel assigned to the South Precinct to see if any of them had contacted an Eddie Navarre between December 26 and 31. A deputy working that weekend night shift said that he had been dispatched to answer a complaint about someone in a van who was trespassing on a homeowner's land.

"This guy—Navarre—was sleeping in his van. I gave him a verbal warning about trespassing and asked him to leave the property. He was cooperative."

With more information on the Chrysler van, Birchfield had sent out a request through WASIC (Washington State Information Center) and NCIC (National Crime Information Center) to be on the lookout for Eddie Navarre.

There were no recent hits. Birchfield had found that Navarre had a lengthy rap sheet that began in the 1970s and continued to 2000.

Neither he nor Plumberg could help but wonder if Eddie Navarre with his job selling franchises for juice bars might be the "headhunter" that Russel Douglas had mentioned during a holiday dinner with his extended family. Navarre was a persuasive con man. And Russ Douglas longed to have success and a larger paycheck. Even though he had just been upgraded to a new division at Tetra Tech, he might have been interested enough in Navarre's get-rich-quick franchises to meet with him.

If he was, that could have been the reason Russel had driven to a lonely location with which he was unfamiliar.

How he might have met Navarre was problematic. His family had heard of a headhunter, but they had never heard Navarre's name. Neither his Washington State friends nor the people he kept in touch with at the University of Phoenix were familiar with the name.

Plumberg drove to the mainland to retrace his and Birchfield's steps and seek out possible information they had not come across before. He took with him an enlarged photo of Douglas, along with two photos of Eddie Navarre that he had received from the Scottsdale, Arizona, Police Department. Navarre was still a strong "person of interest," and the detective hoped to find someone who could help him link the two men.

He went to the Fred Meyer store in Renton where store director Rick Nestegaard set up interviews with employees who might have waited on Russel. Would any of them recall seeing Eddie Navarre with him?

A clerk in the toy department quickly recognized Russ's photo. "He used to come in a lot to look at Hot Wheels cars."

"When was this?" Plumberg asked.

"Not recently."

"Could it have been six to eight months ago?"

"Yes. I remember he was very athletic looking, but I haven't seen him for a long time."

Shown Navarre's picture, she shook her head. "I've never seen this one."

A woman working in the health food section of Fred Meyer recalled someone who looked like the murder victim. He often bought nutrition supplements and lotions for his face and skin.

"When did you last see him?"

"Maybe about a month ago."

"He died last December," Plumberg said.

"It could have been that long ago. I'm not sure."

The clerk didn't recognize Eddie Navarre at all. Mark Plumberg went from store to store: Safeway, Starbucks, another Fred Meyer store, back to Gold's Gym, showing photographs of the victim and the suspect to employees. Many recalled Russel Douglas—but no one was familiar with Eddie Navarre.

It seemed that the Island County detective had

better news when he showed the photos to the manager at the Mission Ridge Apartments and she nodded vigorously. She thought Russ had often been with an older man, who was "creepy." When Plumberg asked about Navarre, she immediately recognized the name.

"He applied to get an apartment—but he had a criminal history and we didn't rent to him."

It seemed like a breakthrough after almost seven months! The apartment manager said she would check her records to find out more about Navarre.

And she did. There had been someone by that name who wanted to move in, and he did have a criminal record. But this applicant was African American, and Eddie Navarre was definitely Caucasian.

It was a huge disappointment for Plumberg.

He came back to the mainland day after day, showing the photographs at myriad stores, gas stations, banks, and restaurants from Renton to Tacoma. Surely someone must have seen Russel Douglas with Eddie Navarre.

But no one had.

Mark never found Eddie Navarre. The man he had tracked to Florida had the same name, but it turned out that *he* was the one with the long rap sheet. The "Eddie Navarre" who had stalked Sandra Malle on Whidbey only had one charge, and that was for selling a tear gas weapon in California in 1978. "He might not even have known that was against the law," Plumberg said.

As he spun his outrageous lies and behaved so eccentrically, Eddie Navarre came close to being charged with murder. Perhaps he realized that himself, and traveled far, far from Whidbey Island.

There were other leads that seemed—at least initially—to have merit. One man came forward, a part-time Whidbey Island resident who was an avowed homosexual. He recalled that he'd once met Russel Douglas in a bar and that they had had a "one-nighter."

"He said he'd never done that before, but that he was curious about it. I never saw him again."

When shown a lay-down of several photos which included Douglas's, the man could not absolutely identify him, having met so many strangers in bars in Washington and in Hawaii.

PART FIVE

Mark Plumberg

CHAPTER THIRTEEN

TWO DAYS AFTER JULY 4, 2004, Mark Plumberg returned from vacation. Commander Mike Beech called him into his office and informed him that he was now the lead detective on the Russel Douglas case. Mike Birchfield was leaving the Island County Sheriff's Office and joining another island city's department, and Mark would step in. (Tragically, Birchfield died in his early forties of pneumonia a few years after he left the department.)

Plumberg was both elated and challenged by his new assignment. This was a case that only grew more convoluted as months passed.

Mark Plumberg seems born to be a detective, although law enforcement was a career he had never aspired to in his early years. Tall, muscular, and highly intelligent, he started life in Kansas City, Missouri. Now close to fifty, he is a man of many interests and avocations, representative of a new generation of police officers who are anything but the doughnut-eating, hard-drinking, tough-talking cop caricature of decades ago. And that image in itself was a reputation given to them by macho writers and reporters. (In thirty-five years of writing true crime, I've never met a cop who ate doughnuts!)

Plumberg could well be a college professor teaching zoology and ichthyology. As an avid scuba diver and underwater photographer, he was the first to film the procreation of sand lance—a type of fish that burrows beneath the sand to spawn in tidal flats—a huge step forward for ichthyologists.

The Island County detective hikes in the Cascade Mountains, bikes for miles, enjoys the symphony, makes plum wine and beer, and also cooks holiday dinners for his two grown daughters.

Plumberg is a devoted father, and as his daughters grew up, he spent every vacation with Natasha and Heather—and only them. They wanted to go back to the places they'd visited when they were younger and their dad took them to Idaho, to Craters of the Moon and Glacier Park. He recently became a grandfather to a beautiful baby girl—Kennedy.

Long divorced, Mark lives in a home with easy access to Puget Sound, and sweeping views of mountains on all sides. He grows quinoa, barley, and kale in the backyard and raises chickens.

The youngest of eleven children and raised in the Midwest, Plumberg went to college on a football scholarship as a linebacker, but he didn't finish the four-year program. Instead, he joined the marines and stayed in the corps for eight years. He has lived in Hawaii, southern Spain, Asia, Corpus Christi, Texas, and too many areas of the world to note. He is fluent in Spanish. When he moved to Whidbey Island, he knew he was "home."

He pursued various careers for a time and became friends with local cops who suggested he consider being a reserve officer with the Island County Sheriff's Office.

Somewhat reluctantly, he gave it a try. Plumberg graduated from the Reserve Academy in 1996. His police friends urged him to take the civil service exam to become a regular deputy. He did, and graduated from the Basic Law Enforcement Academy in 1997 in the number-one spot. He joined the Island County Sheriff's Department and found that law enforcement was a perfect fit for him.

The Island County Sheriff's Department doesn't have that many detectives—only four—so each wears many hats. Mark Plumberg handles homicides, sex crimes, fraud, robbery, white-collar crimes, and arson. "Everything, really," he comments. "I *love* it—but it's draining *because* I love it so much."

As part of his arson training, he attended the Emmetsburg, Maryland, National Fire Academy.

"As I worked full-time," he recalls, "I quickly began to understand everything I learned in the academies."

One aspect of law enforcement troubles Plumberg, however. "I can't *protect* people. I try to tell people that. It's a rare occasion when I can actually prevent a crime. I have to deal with the aftermath."

It is the age-old dilemma for good cops. Solving crimes can be challenging and even exciting, but sadness and regret come inextricably bound together in a homicide case. They grieve for the victims' lives, even as they try to give them some kind of justice.

WITH EDDIE NAVARRE, PLUMBERG had a suspect who could be quite easily wedged into the empty spots of the jigsaw puzzle that Russel Douglas's murder had created. Not exactly fitting, but doable. But Plumberg wasn't satisfied with that. There were many other scenarios to explore, quite possibly suspects who had yet to be revealed. It was maddening that the motive for Russ Douglas's murder was still obscure.

If Russel had met Eddie in a bar—in Redmond where he worked, in Renton where he lived, in Lynnwood or Mukilteo or somewhere on Whidbey Island—he might have fallen for Navarre's crafty line of patter about a fortune to be made in juice franchises. He might even have been curious about a promise of gay sex. But it would have taken a series of coincidences for their paths to have crossed.

Even though Mark Plumberg continued to look for Navarre, he didn't allow himself to have tunnel vision. He had more people to interview or reinterview.

BRENNA DOUGLAS HAD STOPPED talking to the sheriff's investigators months before. Now, Brenna's attorney, Jessie Valentine, contacted Island County prosecuting attorney Greg Banks and asked for a meeting.

Shortly before three 3 P.M. on July 15, Plumberg, Banks, and Brenna met in Valentine's office. Susan Wilmoth, Valentine's legal assistant, was also present. Brenna and her lawyer provided her phone records for December 2003, and for January and February 2004. They also turned over her bank statement for December; they validated where she had made purchases on December 27. Jessie Valentine said she had no problem giving the investigators her client's appointment book at Just B's, showing a client list from December 22 to 27. They couldn't offer any more, citing Brenna's need to protect the privacy of her clients.

"Nobody needs to know who gets their hair dyed or what color."

This was to be a difficult interview for Greg Banks and Mark Plumberg; Jessie Valentine often made comments that precluded Brenna Douglas from answering questions spontaneously. At times she seemed to be guiding Brenna back to a particular question when she became distracted, and seemed to be almost coaching her.

Plumberg had to remind Brenna of what she

had said when she was first notified of Russ's death and in the days that followed.

"I was told that you stopped cooperating with our investigation some time ago."

"Oh no," she insisted. "I wanted to help. The only time I didn't want to talk to Detective Birchfield was when the insurance investigator came to my salon. He treated me horribly and told me they weren't going to pay my claim. That was when I called Jessie."

Both client and attorney said they had tried to make appointments with Birchfield without success.

Brenna had brought her appointment book with her to help her recall specific dates. Russ had come to visit on December 19 when his mother was there. "He stayed that night and on the twentieth," she said.

"He told me then about some guy who called and wanted to talk to him—the headhunter—but he wasn't sure he should talk to him because he had just gotten a promotion at Tetra Tech."

Once more, the recent widow stressed that Russ had very few friends—and that any he had came from "my circle."

"Who do you think might have killed Russ?" Plumberg asked.

"I have no idea!"

"What would have been his connection to Wahl Road?"

"I have no idea," Brenna said again.

Mark Plumberg told her frankly that he was still a little surprised about how quickly she had walked outside in her robe late at night when there were two strange men—himself and Mike Birchfield—in her driveway.

"I thought it was Russ coming home," she said. "My son woke me up and said there were lights in the driveway. I was angry—pissed—because I was thinking 'Great! He finally shows up after I've gone to sleep.' When I saw you, I didn't think you were any threat to me."

Brenna didn't think it odd that her girlfriends had called her so late at night.

"That's just what girlfriends do."

Jessie Valentine agreed with Brenna, adding that it *was* what women often did.

Still nonplussed at the way Brenna had responded to the news that her husband was dead on the night of December 27, Plumberg bore down harder.

"You only asked us in a kind of off-handed way why we were there. And we talked to you a long time and asked you some very pointed questions and you still didn't ask us what had happened. Even after Mike Birchfield told you that Russ was murdered, you didn't ask us why or where. Why was that?"

"I guess I was in shock. I assumed something bad had happened to him or you wouldn't have been there asking questions. I'm not a retard!"

Brenna seemed a bit indignant.

"I guess I just emotionally shut down. Russ couldn't swim very well," she said. "Actually, he swam like a rock. I guess I thought something had happened to him because he was going surfing the last time I saw him. I just didn't know what had happened that night."

Jessie Valentine chimed in once more, assuring Banks and Plumberg that *she* wouldn't have asked what happened in the same circumstances.

But Greg Banks and Mark Plumberg weren't there to find out how Jessie would have responded; it was Brenna's demeanor that made them curious.

At times, Brenna Douglas seemed to have been most aware of Russel's banking and email accounts and passwords, but often she seemed confused. She did not know anything about two payments made on the Tracker—one on December 24, 2003, and another on January 8, 2004—nine days after Russ died.

As for his email, she said she hadn't bothered to look to see who he was writing to—until he told her he had broken off his relationship with Fran Lester.

"Then I looked to see if he was telling me the truth."

Even though Brenna said she hadn't trusted her husband after he allegedly had an affair with a woman in Wisconsin three years earlier and she had put spyware on his computer, she appeared sad as she told the prosecutor and the detective that she and Russ had done "okay" as friends in their marriage.

Their Christmas reunion, if not perfect, was at least amicable while he was there. Some of their friends thought they might actually bind up the wounds of their marriage and give it another try.

Russ often stayed with the children, and was available to help Brenna with repairs and chores. He had helped her move a washer and a dryer.

"Did you have a key to his apartment in Renton?"

"I did, but I only went there once when he wasn't home. The kids and I were shopping on the mainland and we all had to go to the bathroom—so we went to his apartment."

"What was he wearing the last time you saw him?" Plumberg asked.

"Pretty average clothes—I think maybe blue jeans, a tank top, and a jacket. We were talking Christmas night and I asked him to wear 'normal' clothes when he was in my space—"

"And that is?"

"Whidbey Island, Everett."

Brenna said she had been embarrassed by some of Russ's weird outfits.

Asked to remember their discussions at Christmas about their relationship, Brenna said they had decided to take reconciliation slowly and see what happened. They had talked about building up trust and seeing how that went.

"How did Russ feel about that?"

"He was okay. We were having a great time, taking it slow."

"You told us before that you and Russ had sex on the morning of the twenty-sixth and you took a shower after?"

"Mmm-hmm."

Finally, they came to the end of a long session. Russel Douglas's widow still claimed he was unfaithful and sexually demanding, quick to anger, and unpopular. But she had also acknowledged that on the last day of his life, they were looking toward a future where they might retrieve their marriage and avoid divorce.

It was so hard to evaluate where she was coming from. If she had guilty knowledge about Russ's murder, why would she have initially been so vindictive about his flaws? Wouldn't she have played the grief-stricken widow to throw off suspicion?

Now, six months after his death, she still badmouthed Russ, but she seemed less virulent. Plumberg sensed even a tinge of regret as Brenna recalled the almost nine years the two had spent together.

Seizing an opportunity, he asked her if she would now consider taking a polygraph exam.

"I won't allow her to do that," Jessie Valentine said quickly.

"Do you agree with that, Brenna?" the detective asked.

"I have to do what my attorney tells me to," she answered.

CHAPTER FOURTEEN

WITH MIKE BIRCHFIELD GONE, Mark Plumberg tried to do the work of two investigators. They had been to Tetra Tech and talked to Russel Douglas's co-workers there, and found nothing at all that would suggest someone who might have wanted him dead.

A number of the female staff members were very attractive, and several of them said that Russ hadn't been an acquaintance but a "real friend." Still, when Mark Plumberg asked them if Russ had "come on" to them, they shook their heads.

"Absolutely not," one secretary said. "I'm married."

"That doesn't necessarily mean that Russel wouldn't have tried—"

"But he never did. His wife—Brenna—used to come to our office and she brought their children with her. We all knew that they sometimes had problems in their marriage, and that Russ was un-happy about that."

Plumberg moved back to another job on Russ's résumé. He took the ferry from Clinton to the city of Mukilteo to speak with the staff there. He found that many people who worked for the city had known Russ Douglas—from temporary employees to Mike Murphy, who was Mukilteo's chief of police.

Almost universally, Douglas had been liked.

"He loved his kids," a woman in the personnel office recalled. "He was a nice young man."

It was true, she said, that Russ often spoke of his depression and thoughts of suicide. He knew he had problems with his temper and told her he was seeing a therapist to get better.

Her opinion was echoed by a number of Mukilteo employees. In his last year or so working there, Russ had struggled with depression, sometimes locking himself in his office and even burning candles.

Many of the Mukilteo staff commented that they were hurt when they weren't notified of Russ's memorial service.

"We all would have gone," one secretary said.

A woman in the Mukilteo Planning Department said that about 90 percent of her contact with Douglas was via correspondence—phone or email.

"The last time I actually spoke to Russ was sometime in October last year," she said. "He was the happiest I'd seen him in a long time. He liked his new job and it seemed as though he might be getting back with Brenna. He told me that he had stayed with her and his kids on Whidbey Island two or three times. He also told me that he was dating someone else—but he wasn't living with *her*."

Mark Plumberg asked a question he had put to many people: "Did he ever talk about being homosexual or bisexual?"

"No! I never had any indication of that."

As he had with many of his Mukilteo coworkers, Russ had been open about his mood swings.

"He had very high highs and very low lows."

"Tell me about when he was feeling down."

"He'd just withdraw from everyone. When I heard he had died, I wouldn't have been surprised to find out it was suicide. He had a tough childhood and many problems—especially with his mother—when he was growing up."

"He told you that?"

"Yes."

Mukilteo Police Chief Michael Murphy said Russ would come in to talk with him at times.

"He was interested in police work, and he even said he was thinking of becoming a cop."

Murphy said that Douglas rode the ferry to work with a number of the other men in the office, but hadn't seemed particularly close friends with most of them. Sometimes the male employees went to a bar after work, a place they called "Cheers II," and he went with them.

After interviewing a dozen or more city hall staff in depth, and hearing them describe Russ

Douglas as "a nice guy who was really depressed," Plumberg felt again that if the killer had used an untraceable "drop gun," and left it at the scene on Wahl Road, Russ's manner of death would quite possibly have been determined to be suicide.

And the true manner of death would never have come out.

Another woman at city hall told the Island County detective that she had noticed how much Russ had changed almost a year before he was terminated from his Mukilteo position.

"He began to pump weights and change the way he dressed—and then he got an apartment by himself.

"He came by to see me sometime in the fall of 2003. I had just posted a new job opening and I was afraid he might be coming to apply for that position. I didn't want to rehire him, and I wanted to avoid any discussion about that with him."

"Why wouldn't you rehire him?"

"I was the one who wrote his performance evaluations and I really tried to cover for him at the end because he was in a very deep down place. His professional judgment was off, and he couldn't seem to perform, couldn't even start a task, work it efficiently, or follow it through. Sometimes he was angry and he swore and we had to ask him not to do that at the front counter."

But she, like everyone else, described Russel Douglas as a nice guy who was friendly and whom they all liked.

Mark Plumberg continued to canvass everyone who had known Russ at the Mukilteo City Hall. He spoke with a man named Ralph Randolph.*

"I saw you at the front counter and I said to myself, 'That's a cop,'" Randolph blurted. "I wondered why you hadn't talked to me."

Before their interview in the mayor's office began, Randolph explained that he had "a problem" with one eye, so if he seemed to be looking at Plumberg strangely, that was why.

He was quite agitated during the interview, and could barely sit still. He folded his hands in his lap, but he pressed them together with so much force that his thumbs turned white.

Randolph seldom looked at Plumberg, averting his face at a forty-five-degree angle. His skin often turned blotchy—red and white—and he kept pointing out that he knew that was happening because he could feel it.

He felt he had known Russ very well and said they had many conversations about everything from diet to music to mood changes. Plumberg studied Randolph's body language and wondered why this man was so antsy.

Finally, Randolph told Plumberg that he would probably find out about his being investigated by the FBI. They had "tracked him down" because he had once purchased a fairly rare replacement barrel for a gun he owned. He believed that had probably had something to do with the still-unsolved, much-publicized murder of a federal prosecutor in Seattle.

Oddly, Ralph Randolph said he had never seen that Russ Douglas was depressed. Every other employee in city hall had noted that moroseness—but not Randolph.

And then, within minutes, he reversed himself, saying that he had wondered if Russ had committed suicide when he learned he was dead.

"He was very smart, you know. If he wanted to, he could have killed himself and made it look like a murder so that insurance would pay off."

Almost as if he was talking to himself, and still facing away from Mark Plumberg, Randolph went through some outlandish scenarios of how that could have happened.

"Maybe Russ used springs to make the gun fly a long way, or some laser-activated device. Something that would propel the weapon into the water."

Plumberg hadn't mentioned anything about water at the crime scene, beyond saying that the road ended near beachfront homes.

He wondered just how springs and lasers could vanish from the Tracker.

Plumberg changed the subject. "Did Russel have insurance?"

"Oh—I don't know. We never talked about it."

More and more, Randolph veered away from answering questions directly, taking a long-winded, circuitous route before he addressed the subject. He said he and Russ Douglas liked the same kind of music, like Black Sabbath.

"He ever talk about alternate lifestyles or cults?"

"No!"

"You ever think he was gay or bisexual?"

"No."

Ralph Randolph acted spooked when the detective asked him where he lived. Again, he went into a winding story, this time about his divorce, some woman he'd met on the Internet who was "the love of my life," but he never actually gave Plumberg an address or his home phone number.

"Did Russel ever evince any problem with pornography?" Plumberg persisted.

"We joked about it sometimes because Russ put together the Mukilteo City Adult Entertainment Ordinance."

"You seem very nervous about something," Plumberg said.

"I *am* nervous."

"If you want to tell me something, I can put my pen away and stop taking notes—"

"No, I can't really think of anything to tell you."

Mark Plumberg's sense was that Randolph was simply a very agitated man most of the time, acutely self-conscious, and possibly had cop paranoia. The more Randolph explained his eye problem, his sinus problems, and his tendency to blush, the redder he got.

Maybe the FBI probe had frightened him; maybe he was just a nervous Nellie, but Plumberg would check him out.

He thought he knew a red herring when he saw one, and speculated that he had just spent a long time talking to one.

As it turned out, he was right. Randolph proved to have nothing at all to do with Russel Douglas's death.

PART SIX

Peggy Sue
Stackhouse

CHAPTER FIFTEEN

AS JULY MOVED TOWARD August, Mark Plumberg thought of the many times he'd thought he'd struck gold in his investigation—only to have it disintegrate into dust. He had no way of knowing that there *was* someone far away from Washington State who was wrestling with his conscience. Should he call the sheriff on Whidbey Island, Washington? Or would that be a devastating act of disloyalty to someone he considered his close—perhaps *closest*—friend?

Had Plumberg known, he would have been considerably cheered to know there was a witness detectives only dream of.

For the moment, he continued retracing the steps he and Mike Birchfield had taken early in the game. He moved along Admiralty Way and Wahl Road, talking with residents there. It wasn't rainy or snowing now, and the deciduous trees had leaves, while flowers bloomed in most yards. But

July 26 was a discouraging day. Plumberg wasn't finding any relevant information. He had talked to dozens and dozens of people who should have known something, some of them twice or more.

And then he received a call on his cell phone that took him in a whole different direction.

Island County Detective Sue Quandt told him that she had answered a phone call from a man who asked if the Island County Sheriff's Office had an unsolved homicide that had supposedly happened around Christmas 2003! She couldn't get the caller to give his name—or where he was calling from—but it certainly sounded as though this was something that should be followed up.

Quandt had confirmed to the caller that indeed there was an open case of a murder on the island—on December 26, 2003.

There was silence on the line and she wondered if the man had hung up.

"I have information," he finally said. "But I'm scared to talk about it."

Sue Quandt then transferred the call to the detectives' commander, Mike Beech.

The caller was frightened, but he sounded as if he was compelled to tell what he knew. Beech was able to establish some rapport with the man and felt he had gained his trust—or at least some of it. The informant said that the "shooter" was a friend of his.

"He told me about what he had learned in February," Beech said.

Mark Plumberg wasn't present during that first phone conversation, but he went to the Coupeville office as fast as he could get there.

"Have you found any connection with anyone who used to work at the Just B's salon and then she moved to Las Vegas with her boyfriend?" Beech asked.

"Yes!" Plumberg said. "I've contacted a woman who told me she was friends with both Brenna and Russel Douglas. She drives a limousine in Las Vegas. I don't know anything about her boyfriend, but I do know she used to work for Brenna in her salon."

"That meshes with what this guy—whoever he is—told me," Beech said. "Evidently, the boyfriend has—or had—a wife in Florida and they owned a business together. He said that the guy has a girlfriend who worked in Brenna's salon, and then the two of them moved to Las Vegas."

So far, Mark Plumberg and Mike Beech had validated everything the informant told them. But Plumberg had been through that scenario before. After so many detours, it almost seemed too easy. He kept waiting for this, too, to blow up in his face.

He wasn't ready yet to ask Brenna about her connection to Peggy Sue Thomas, but there was a woman Mike Birchfield had talked to who was a former hairdresser at Just B's. Jennifer McCormick now had her own salon in Freeland, and it happened to be in the same building as the sheriff's South Precinct substation.

He immediately contacted Jennifer McCormick and asked her if she knew Peggy Sue Thomas.

She did. She said that she and Peggy had worked at Brenna's salon at the same time. When Peggy moved away, she had referred her list of clients to Jennifer—a thoughtful gesture on her part that Jennifer appreciated.

"Do you know anything about Peggy's boyfriend?"

"She's had a lot of boyfriends, but I don't know the current guy's name," she answered. "But I heard that he had a wife in Florida and they had some kind of business together. He was supposed to be divorcing his wife—and he and Peggy moved to Las Vegas together. I heard the guy has a brother on Whidbey who owns a bed-and-breakfast. And I heard through the grapevine that Peggy's boyfriend just recently left her in Las Vegas."

Jennifer McCormick had always had a friendly relationship with Peggy when they both worked at Brenna Douglas's salon.

"The only thing that concerned me was one time—when I think she was kidding—she came into Just B's and she warned someone about something. Then she lifted her arms as if she was holding a gun and pointed and said, 'You'd better remember that or I'll come back and go 007 on you!'"

At this point, Mark Plumberg didn't know exactly what they had with the Florida caller, or where this new angle was going. He and Commander Mike Beech were very committed to keeping their tenuous contact with their nameless informant. They didn't want to alarm him and lose track of him.

Beech's relationship with the unknown caller held firm. The detective commander established certain times on particular days when the tipster could call him back. He hoped they could ask him more questions about how Peggy Sue and her as-yet-unknown boyfriend might be involved in Russel Douglas's murder.

The informant kept contact, calling them at the prearranged times. During each conversation, Beech and Plumberg learned a little more about what seemed to be an unbelievable hostile plot to kill Douglas.

But they still didn't have a possible motive.

Whoever the caller was, he was careful that he could not be traced, hanging up before they could isolate the phone from which he was calling.

But he had finally come to a point where he felt trusting enough to describe how Russel Douglas died.

"This person put the gun to Russ's head and shot him."

The detectives knew, of course, that Douglas had died of an almost-contact wound, and not from a "distance of one foot away" that local newspapers had reported.

"This led us to believe that the tipster wasn't

getting his information from media sources that anyone curious about the homicide could seek out," Plumberg recalls. "He knew that the murder gun was a .380 handgun, but he didn't know what make it was."

Commander Beech subtly attempted to find the source of the caller's information; he asked him where the murder had occurred.

"He didn't talk to me about that, but I want to say it was near an apartment complex."

This was wrong. Television and newspapers had written that the site was in the country, and even named Wahl Road, saying that the body was found in a private drive about twenty-five yards off the road itself.

It was becoming more clear that the anonymous man was not repeating something he'd found out in public media.

And then the mysterious caller said that the suspect's girlfriend was named "Peggy."

Mark Plumberg recalled talking with Peggy Sue Thomas in the one phone conversation he'd had with her. She certainly hadn't seemed nervous or concerned, and she'd readily acknowledged that she was a good friend of Brenna Douglas, and also considered Russ a close friend. It was difficult to believe that someone who might truly be a person of interest had been so relaxed, even charming when he talked to her.

"The victim's wife was probably involved, too—or knew what was going to happen," the informant continued: "By that, I don't mean to say that she was directly implicated at the scene."

He still hadn't given the Island County investigators the name of a suspect—but now they knew they were so close.

"The shooter told me that he and Peggy lured the victim to the place where he was shot. They told him that they had a Christmas present for the wife—"

Plumberg held his breath. This was almost the same story that Peggy Sue Thomas had told him—about going to Russ's apartment with that gift. And Brenna Douglas had mentioned that she didn't really question Russ about where he was going around 11 A.M. on December 26. She said he was going to pick up a tablecloth for her—as well as going surfing after that.

Peggy Sue Thomas and whomever her boyfriend might be had been only blips on Plumberg's intense investigation. It had been far easier to connect Eddie Navarre—a likely headhunter—to Russel, or someone the victim might have met at a swingers' club (if, indeed, he ever went to one). It also could have been a former coworker.

What possible motive could Brenna Douglas's friend and her lover have to plan a cold-blooded murder?

It didn't make sense. Not at all.

Chapter Sixteen

IT SEEMED TO MARK PLUMBERG that several principals in the murder probe were getting restless. Brenna Douglas called him in late July 2004 to ask if he would like to go with her when she emptied the storage unit where she was keeping Russ's possessions. He told her that he would. At the same time, he reminded her that she had promised to bring him her Nextel cell phone records.

"I'm having a hard time getting them because it's not in my name," she said.

She explained that she had taken over payments from a friend for a year, but she'd never changed the account name. Plumberg suggested she have the account owner phone Nextel; it would be simple for him to get the records.

She called him back later and asked if there was anything in the Tracker, which was locked in the evidence garage, that he could release. She wanted her kids' sleds, a power converter, and some paperwork from the glove box. There might be other items she hadn't thought of.

"I don't know," she said. "Just anything . . ."

AND THEN, AT LAST, the mysterious caller was ready to give up the name of the person he believed had shot Russel Douglas. He told Mike Beech that it was his friend James E. Huden, fifty-one, who had grown up and gone to school on Whidbey Island. "I think Jim Huden still has family on the island—a brother who was an air force colonel."

There weren't that many current or former residents of Whidbey Island who had brothers who were retired air force colonels.

Plumberg found that Huden's brother owned a bed-and-breakfast called Sea Shell Manor.* He had a good reputation and his business was doing well.

This was the first time that the investigators had heard the name Jim Huden. The informant said Jim was having a rough time financially; he was about to file bankruptcy.

"He and Peggy do nothing but party when he's in Las Vegas, and they're living on credit cards."

There was the name Peggy again. Asked to identify her, the caller said she was Jim's love interest and she lived in Las Vegas.

That, of course, struck a chord; this had to be the same Peggy the investigators had spoken to on the phone.

Mark Plumberg had obtained Brenna Douglas's

phone records. He found numerous calls between Brenna and the number he had for "Peggy." They had apparently talked a great deal in the month of December *before* the twenty-sixth. After Russel Douglas was murdered, there had been only eleven calls.

Things seemed to be coming together. At last, the secret informant was ready to tell Mike Beech who *he* was. He gave his name as William R. Hill, fifty-six, and said he lived in Port Charlotte, Florida.

"I didn't know if I was going to spill the beans or not," Hill said with some regret. "Jim's my best friend."

It had indeed been a difficult decision for Bill Hill to come to, but the thought of the man who had been murdered seven months before haunted him.

And initially he had been afraid of reprisal. In the end, he had called the Island County Sheriff's Office and told them what he knew.

A search of Hill's background showed him to be a solid citizen with no criminal history. He had lived at the same address in Florida for years. Bill Hill had been part of a musical group Jim Huden started called Buck Naked and the X-hibitionists. Jim was, he said, a very talented guitar player and they had played regular gigs in and around Punta Gorda, Florida.

Mark Plumberg felt they should move ahead rapidly, and his instincts were correct. On August

2, Bill Hill phoned Mike Beech once more and told him he had just had lunch with Jim Huden.

"He told me that we were having lunch so he could say good-bye to me. He said he'd heard that there was a new investigator on the case, and the sheriff's detectives were going to come looking for him, so he was packing up and heading for Vegas in the next few days. He said he needed to get together with Peggy so they could get their stories straight."

Mark Plumberg felt this gave credence to Bill Hill. He clearly wasn't the tipster who knew all about the sheriff's probe. *Mark* was the new investigator on the case. Someone on Whidbey Island or Las Vegas had their ears to the ground and had passed that information on to Jim Huden very rapidly.

How Jim had learned that the sheriff's detectives were close to contacting him was a mystery. They themselves had only heard his name recently, and Beech and Plumberg had kept that intelligence to themselves.

The two detectives agreed that they should fly at once to Florida so they could interview Jim Huden before he left for Las Vegas. While they were headed east, detectives Shawn Warwick and Ed Wallace flew south to the Las Vegas area to interview Peggy Sue Thomas, the woman with whom Huden had reportedly had an affair.

Mark Plumberg applied for search warrants through Island County's superior court. He was granted two—one for Huden's residence in Punta Gorda, Florida, and the other for Peggy Sue's home in Henderson, Nevada.

It seemed possible—*if* they could get to Punta Gorda before Jim Huden left—that they might open another pathway to solving Russel Douglas's homicide.

They didn't know then just how long their investigation would stretch into the future. Or how frustrating it would become. At this point, they didn't know all that much about the relationship that existed between Huden and Peggy Sue Thomas. Was it a casual affair or an intense bonding?

And it was vital that they learn about that.

CHAPTER SEVENTEEN

ALTHOUGH BOTH OF THEM lived far away from the serene island in Puget Sound in 2004, Jim Huden and Peggy Thomas had grown up on Whidbey Island. Their paths barely crossed over the years. During their school days, Jim was much too old for Peggy Sue.

Jim had been married twice—to his first wife, Patti, and then to his current wife, Jean. In 2004, Peggy Sue, who was a dozen years younger than Jim, had also been married twice. Jim and Peggy had initially seemed unlikely lovers. After all, she was living in Las Vegas and Jim was in Florida.

Jim's father died when he was young. He, his brother, and his mother eventually moved to Clinton on Whidbey Island and his mother remarried. His stepfather was reported to be a physically abusive man who often beat Jim's mother and sometimes got in some swats for him and his younger brother. Jim wasn't twelve yet and he wouldn't

have had the physical strength—or the courage—
to defend his mother. He reportedly felt humiliated
and ultimately frustrated.

Some sources opined that he never got to avenge
his mother. In his midteens, when he was finally
big enough to fight back and protect her, his stepfather suddenly died in bed of natural causes.

One school of thought said that Jim carried
that hatred for domestic abusers who hit women
and children throughout his life. Was this really
true? It created a background for Jim that might
one day offer a feasible reason for his actions as a
middle-aged man. But it also may well have been
apocryphal. His own brother insists that no abuse
happened in their boyhood home.

Jim Huden was a nice kid whose grades usually
didn't reflect his high intelligence. He got along
fine with his peers in grade school. Many of those
boys, who are now in their fifties, remember him
as a "typical kid."

When Jim was in the fifth grade, the local school
levy failed to pass and South Whidbey Elementary
School had no choice but to combine fifth and
sixth grades.

"We were both in that combined class," longtime friend Lloyd Jackson recalls. "I think I was
actually supposed to be a year ahead of him. After
that, they were able to raise school taxes and we
went back to single classes. My next clear memory
of him was in high school."

Asked if he'd ever gone to Jim's home, Jackson

shook his head. He didn't recall Jim ever talking about a "mean stepfather," although he himself had seen the man from time to time in their small town. If Jim had bruises that were apparent in gym class or the football locker room, those could be explained away. Most young athletes sustain bruises.

Lloyd Jackson recalled that Jim's stepfather "looked like the actor Dan Hedaya, who played Nick Tortelli—Carla's husband on *Cheers*." He was a dark and swarthy man whose eyebrows grew together over the bridge of his nose.

Naturally, Jim looked nothing like him. One of Jim's most outstanding features was his hair. It was dark blond and thick and shiny; he styled it like most of the teenage boys in the Langley High School class of 1971—parting it far off to one side with bangs and then plastered down with hair gel. The male students who had enough of a beard to do so affected sideburns.

Huden was still a fairly thin kid in high school when he, Dick Deposit, Ken Kramer, Tom Stackhouse, and Lloyd Jackson were among those who turned out for football for the Falcons at Langley High School.

"As I recall now," Jackson said, "Jim wasn't particularly gifted—but he was a 'gamer.'"

The athletic star of the class of 1971 was Ken Kramer, and Jim didn't come close to his skills when they played football, basketball, and ran track. Ken was the quarterback who carried the football across the goal line so many times, and Jim was a guard. But they were both first team.

And they were both popular. In 1970, Ken Kramer was class president for the first semester of their senior year and Jim Huden was president for the second semester in 1971.

Jim was generous and well liked, but he occasionally got into trouble at Langley High School because he was "a little bit wild." Although he made the honor roll in his junior year, he was also suspended in the eleventh grade for drinking.

In the school yearbook for 1971, Jim Huden was voted "the biggest cut-up."

Jackson and Jim drifted apart after Lloyd's high school graduation, although Jim remained close to some of his childhood friends, particularly Dick Deposit and Ron Young.

Many of Jim Huden's friends left Whidbey Island to go to college or join the service. One formerly close friend he lost touch with was Ken Kramer, who had been offered a number of athletic scholarships. True to his basic generosity, Jim never seemed to be jealous of Ken. The message he scribbled in Ken's yearbook demonstrated that, and in other ways may have been prophetic:

Ken—
  If you had enough pages, I could almost start to write about all the junk we've done. Football was best of all, though. If there is one thing it's taught us, it's to do

anything to win. You got the talent so re-
member that. Do the best in everything you
do, and best of luck to you.
                              James E. Huden

Lloyd Jackson didn't run into Jim again until about 1976 when Huden returned to Whidbey Island after serving in the air force.

"I was coming off the stupidest thing I'd ever done," Jackson said. "And getting a divorce. Anyway, we started hanging out together, sometimes where he was living, at Ron Young's house. Ron got married and added two kids, and I asked Jim if he wanted to move in with me. I had a house with a spare bedroom. I guess he stayed with me about a year. It was the start of a long, real friendship.

"It was good having him around. I was kind of depressed from my divorce and Jim helped me get over that."

After a while, Jim moved on to a place of his own. In 1980, Jim met his first wife, Patti Lewandowski. Patti worked for the telephone company as a lineman and she could scamper up the poles just as well as any man. Like the rest of Jim's friends, Lloyd liked Patti and was happy to see Jim settle down with a nice woman. Patti was "attractive—but no beauty."

The couple bought a house on the mainland in the north end of King County, and Jim was working for AT&T, too.

Jim Huden and a couple of his friends were

fascinated with computers and their possible future capabilities. In the mideighties, Jim and his coworkers quit the phone company and began to write a software program for Microsoft.

It was an extremely intense project. Patti Huden confided to Lloyd Jackson that Jim would often work himself to the point of exhaustion.

"He was so tired at times," she said, "that he would just start to cry."

But it was all worth it. Bill Gates's burgeoning Microsoft bought Jim's software program, and suddenly Jim and Patti were wealthy. None of their friends knew exactly how much the software netted them, but there were strong rumors that Jim's cut was forty thousand dollars a month over a very long time.

First, Jim and Patti bought a much bigger, more expensive house. They put it on the market a few years later and bought a large motor home with all the bells and whistles anyone could ask for. They embarked on a dream that many people have, but few can afford. They quit their jobs and took long, luxurious road trips back and forth across America.

When Jim and Patti came back to Whidbey Island between trips, they reunited with their friends for great get-togethers. It seemed that Jim Huden had everything a man might want—a good wife, a *lot* of money, and the freedom to enjoy a life of retirement when he wasn't yet forty.

Eventually—when they had seen every corner

of the country that they wanted—he and Patti sold the motor home and bought a lavish house on a golf course near Orlando, Florida. The idyllic weather was a far cry from the wind-whipped storms that often scoured Whidbey Island. The couple had seen most of the country and picked the spot that seemed to be the perfect place to live.

In early 1991, Jim called Lloyd Jackson and invited him to Florida for a visit. Lloyd accepted and he found Jim and Patti gracious hosts. They did everything they could to make his time with them memorable.

"They took me to Walt Disney's theme park at Epcot," Jackson recalled. "We went racing mini Indy race cars, golfing, and we watched Super Bowl XXV when the New York Giants played the Buffalo Bills."

Jim and Patti seemed happy together, but they had lived far too lavishly. They were running out of big money. Within a year, they took jobs as managers of the Chevy Chase golf course, just outside of Port Townsend, Washington. As one of the perks of the job, they lived in quarters above the pro shop. It was a definite step down from their plush lifestyle.

After a few years, the Hudens were able to move back to Florida. Jim's expertise with computers inspired them to start a new company. It went well at first; Jim was even voted businessman of the year in Punta Gorda. The couple returned to

Whidbey Island sporadically to hook up with their longtime friends.

Lloyd Jackson got a shocking phone call from Jim Huden in 1994. Jim told him that he was having an affair and that he and Patti were breaking up. He asked Jackson to fly to Florida, and drive Patti and their Chevy Blazer back to Washington State.

"I liked Patti—I was close to her," Jackson recalled. "But I was involved in a new relationship and had too much on my plate at the time to take a week off to bring Patti home. I felt bad because she apparently got the idea that I was taking Jim's side. I wasn't—I avoided taking either side. I didn't even know who Jim was having an affair with, really didn't care to know. It could have been his next wife—Jean—or it could have been someone else."

Jean, who was born in Orange, New Jersey, was a tall, slender, rather plain woman. When his divorce from Patti was final, Jim Huden married Jean. They remained in Florida for a number of years. Jim continued to visit Whidbey Island occasionally, always drawn back to where he grew up and the memories he shared with his old friends. Sometimes he brought Jean with him.

One of his old friends said that he liked Jean, she seemed "nice enough," but that they'd all felt much closer to Patti. It was difficult to picture their longtime friend with anyone but his first wife.

THE JIM WHO HAD become a "high roller" after his financial bonanza from the software program he sold to Microsoft had changed. As far as any of his friends knew, he hadn't cheated on Patti until near the end of the almost fifteen years they were married. By the time he married Jean, he was middle-aged, drank more—Crown Royal, in particular—and they were concerned that he might also be doing drugs. Jean Huden used drugs. Moreover, Jim had begun to notice women outside his second marriage, but he didn't elaborate on that side of his life with his island buddies.

Huden's high life couldn't last forever. Like all advances in the brave new world of technology, Jim's software program had run its course and was rapidly becoming obsolete.

Jim Huden was lean but muscular, and now he wore his hair pulled back in a ponytail. Not truly handsome, he was what most women would call "hot." Jim resembled actor Mickey Rourke (*before* Rourke's disastrous boxing injuries and bad plastic surgery). On the outside at least, Huden had become a "bad boy" type, a man who fascinated many women.

And, after all, he *was* Buck Naked, the leader of the band. Female fans crowded around the stages in clubs where the X-hibitionists played.

As in most relatively insulated communities, many of Whidbey Island's residents were connected in one way or another. Two of Jim Huden's oldest friends on the island were Sue and Neil Mahoney. Susan, a warmhearted woman the old gang called "Sweet Sue," and Neil had both lived through unhappy first marriages. As it happens with many slightly older couples, Sue and Neil were very much in love and grateful to have found each other. Their home was a gathering place for both the old high school group and their families.

Invariably, whenever Jim Huden returned to Washington, he would visit Sue and Neil Mahoney's home and he could expect to find old and new friends there.

Of the many people whom Jim Huden treasured, the Mahoneys were near the top. When the stress of his life grew too heavy, he knew he could always count on them.

CHAPTER EIGHTEEN

AS SHERIFF'S COMMANDER MIKE BEECH and Detective Mark Plumberg prepared to fly to Florida in August 2004, they realized that they could not have chosen a worse time. They would be literally flying directly into a storm of horrific magnitude. Hurricane Charley, the strongest hurricane to hit the United States in a dozen years, was gathering strength in the Caribbean Sea and heading directly toward Punta Gorda. At its peak, Charley was expected to have winds measuring over 150 miles an hour.

The weather warnings only made the Washington State investigators feel more urgency as they headed for Florida, hoping that they would get there in time to talk with Jim Huden. They didn't have the luxury of waiting for calmer skies; Huden could be long gone by then.

The plan was for Beech and Plumberg to go to Florida, and when they were finished there, Commander Beech would join Detectives Shawn Warwick and Ed Wallace and fly to Nevada to interview Peggy Sue Thomas again, if need be. Mark Plumberg would stay on Whidbey Island, organizing the case and seeking any further warrants they might need.

Nevada in late August/early September would be extremely hot. But that was nothing compared to an encroaching hurricane.

Beech and Plumberg arrived in Punta Gorda on August 3, beating the hurricane there. They did not, however, know if they could head back to Washington State before it hit.

They immediately called Bill Hill and told him they would be staying at the Best Western Hotel and asked if he would meet them there. He was still conflicted and they could hear it in his voice. At first, he declined to meet them, but he called them back a short time later and said he had changed his mind; he said he was actually at the Best Western—waiting for them in the parking lot in his van.

For the first time, Mike Beech and Mark Plumberg saw the man whom they had spoken to so many times on the phone.

After they checked in, Hill accompanied the detectives to their room. They sensed his angst at once; he clearly hated the thought that he was betraying his best friend, but he felt compelled to help them solve a murder.

Bill Hill confirmed everything he had told them in his series of phone conversations.

"Would you be willing to wear a wire while you talked to Huden?" Plumberg asked.

"No, no—I couldn't do that," Hill stammered immediately.

Nor would he provide them with a written statement about what Jim had told him. He remained ambivalent, torn between loyalty and duty.

"He's just too good a friend," Hill explained.

Hill felt that Jim was going to try to get Peggy Sue back, explaining that Huden was very much in love with her, even though he still lived with his wife, Jean.

"But I guess Peggy came to Florida last weekend, and she met with him and Jean," he said. "Jim isn't sure whether she will come back to him."

It was late and Beech and Plumberg had traveled all day. They agreed to meet with Bill Hill the next morning to continue their interview.

Hurricane Charley stayed on top of the news, and all around them, those Floridians who realized the danger to come were nailing plywood sheets over plate-glass windows, bringing in outdoor furniture and plants, and generally battening down their hatches. Still, Mike Beech and Mark Plumberg were so focused on talking with Jim Huden that they barely noticed.

At 3 P.M. on August 4, 2004, they met with Detective Tom Lewis of the Punta Gorda Police Department, who went with them to Jim and Jean Huden's home on Yucca Street.

There was a stillness in the air, an odd heaviness as Floridians waited for the storm to swoop in. Every once in a while, a ripple of wind caused the tropical vegetation to tremble and the jalousie

windows to rattle. Still, the TV weathermen were
assuring Punta Gordians that the storm was likely
days away from landfall in Florida.

As the Whidbey Island detectives neared the
front door of what was reputed to be Jim Huden's
home, Plumberg could see a man sitting on a sofa
and a woman standing nearby. He knocked on the
door and Jean Huden opened it.

"I identified myself, telling her in a loud enough
voice for the man inside to hear me that I was from
Whidbey Island, Washington. I asked if Jim Huden
was home and if I could speak to him. She let us in."

The man stood up and held out his hand to
Plumberg, saying: "I'm Jim Huden."

He didn't seem at all surprised to see the detectives
who had flown across America to speak with him.

Mike Beech interviewed Jean Huden in one of
the bedrooms, while Plumberg talked to Jim in the
living room.

"I assume you know why we're here," Plumberg said.

"No—not yet," Jim said.

Twice more, the detective told Jim Huden that
he and Beech were from Island County, Washington, but Huden still didn't seem startled or ask
why they had come to his door in Florida.

"We're here to investigate a crime that occurred
in Island County."

Huden's expression remained unreadable.

Read his rights under Miranda, Huden said
he understood and waived his rights verbally.

Jim Huden didn't ask *what* crime the investigators were asking about, but he didn't seem shocked when Mark Plumberg started asking him about the murder of Russel Douglas almost eight months earlier.

Only moments into the interview, Plumberg wanted to shake Jim Huden up. He told him that they were in Punta Gorda because they suspected *him* of taking part in the unsolved murder of Russel Douglas.

"You've been implicated in his death," Plumberg said bluntly. "I know that you're the man who pulled the trigger."

"I don't know why someone would say that," Huden said softly. "I've never even owned a gun."

As Plumberg questioned Jim Huden in Punta Gorda, Florida, in the summer of 2004, he made sure that Huden knew he could leave at any time. He was not under arrest.

Jim agreed readily that he and Peggy Sue Thomas had traveled from Las Vegas to Whidbey Island during the past Christmas holidays.

"I drove Peggy's Lexus up, and Peggy flew up with her two daughters."

Mark Plumberg reminded Huden once again that he was not under arrest, that he was free to go at any time. Huden nodded, but made no move to leave. The detective continued the interview by asking for more details about the trip Jim and Peggy had made just before Christmas 2003. Jim repeated that he had driven Peggy's car, and she and her daughters had boarded a plane.

"Can you describe Peggy Sue Thomas's car?" Plumberg asked.

"It's a dark green 1992 four-door Lexus sedan, and the license plate says FIRYRED. That's kind of Peggy's image."

"So when did you get up to the Seattle area?"

"A day later than I planned. But a day before Peggy was going to fly. I stayed that night at my friend Ron Young's house."

"Do you recall which day that was?"

"I'm not sure—I'd have to look at a calendar. I drove down to Sea-Tac to pick up Peggy and the girls the next day. We stayed together in a hotel north of Seattle in the Alderwood/Mill Creek area. Then Peggy and I drove to Whidbey alone the next day."

"What about her daughters?"

"I'm not sure how they got to their dad's— Kelvin's place—but I know they were with him."

Jim Huden said that he and Peggy Sue had stayed at his good friend Dick Deposit's home from the Friday before Christmas, December 19, to Monday or Tuesday of the next week, either December 22 or 23.

"Peggy was cutting hair at Just B's from that Friday until the next week, and then we left the island. We stayed at a hotel by the airport next."

Suddenly, Jim Huden interrupted the interview, saying, "Can I ask you a question?"

"Go ahead," Plumberg said.

"Is Peggy angry enough at me that she would implicate me in this crime?"

At this point, Mark Plumberg hadn't indicated that Peggy Sue Thomas was in any way connected to Russel Douglas's murder.

"Why would Peggy be angry with you?"

"I guess because I hurt her and wasn't truthful with her. Early this year, I led her to believe I was coming back to her but I never did. You know, I helped her move from Whidbey Island to Las Vegas in August 2003 and I stayed in Vegas with her until January of this year."

It was not easy for Plumberg to see where this was going or how the relationship troubles that Jim Huden and Peggy Sue were entangled in might possibly have *any* connection to the homicide probe.

He tried another tack.

"Have either Peggy or Brenna Douglas ever talked to you about Brenna's having financial difficulties?"

Jim shrugged. "I know Brenna was late with the rent for the house a few times. Peggy owns the place where Brenna and her kids live, and she really doesn't like being a landlord."

"Brenna have any reason to be mad at you?"

"Maybe she might be mad because I hurt Peggy."

Huden appeared to be fishing for what Peggy Sue and/or Brenna Douglas might have told investigators about him.

Plumberg didn't really answer him directly.

The sheriff's detective returned to more intense questioning about how Jim and Peggy Sue had spent their days on Whidbey Island around the

previous Christmas. That chill wintertime seemed
so far away now as the Washington detective sat
in the oppressive Florida heat.

"Did you two get together with Brenna Douglas
while you were there?"

"We meant to—and we tried, but it never
happened."

"How did you pay for the hotel by the airport
in Seattle?"

"We put it on Peggy's credit card."

Plumberg pulled out photos of Russ Douglas
and of his yellow Chevy Tracker.

Huden shook his head. "I don't recognize him
or the car."

"Did you by any chance interact with Russel
Douglas while you were in Washington?"

"On the night that Peggy and I left the island
to go to the airport hotel—that'd be Monday or
Tuesday before Christmas—I took a present for
Brenna over to Russel's apartment in Renton."

Although Plumberg's expression didn't change,
a bell went off in Mark Plumberg's head. Peggy Sue
Thomas had given him a different scenario having to do with a present for Brenna. She had told
him during one of their phone conversations that
she was the one who took a present for Brenna to
Russ's apartment. Why would the couple tell him
two different stories?

"Where was Peggy at that time—when you
took the present for Brenna to Russ?"

"She was back at the hotel. She saw a lot of clients that day, and she was pretty tired from being on her feet all day at the salon."

"Why didn't Peggy just give Brenna her present when they were both at Just B's that day?"

"Well, the two of them made a pact that they weren't going to give each other anything for Christmas—but Peggy wanted to buy a present for Brenna. She just had to make sure all the stores were closed for the day so Brenna couldn't run out and buy her something in return."

Huden said he hadn't talked to Russ himself before he took the present to him; Russ had given the directions to his apartment to Peggy to pass on to him.

(This was another small flaw in their scenario. Peggy later told the sheriff's detectives that Jim had spoken directly to Russ to get directions.)

"I parked directly in front of Russ's building—but out in the street because there weren't any parking spots left inside. I ran up the stairs and knocked on his door. When he opened it, I asked him if he was Brenna's husband, gave him the present, said it was for Brenna—and then I left."

"That would have been on December 23?"

"Yes."

"Had you ever met Russel before?"

"No."

"Did Peggy tell him that you would be bringing a present?"

"I don't know."

"Did he know who you were—that you were Peggy's boyfriend?"

"I suppose he did because Brenna and Peggy talked about everything."

That answer made it seem even stranger that Peggy claimed she only learned of Russ's murder belatedly—*days* after it happened. Why wouldn't she have been one of the first people Brenna Douglas called when she learned that Russ was dead? But Peggy had been emphatic that it was Doris Matz, her mother, who notified her. And this was well after she and Jim were back in Las Vegas.

"Did Peggy call Brenna when she heard?"

"No, I don't think so," Jim Huden said. "I told Peggy that it would just be another phone call with everyone calling Brenna and that she would understand and know Peggy didn't want to overwhelm her with more phone calls."

Mark Plumberg asked Jim if he would be willing to accompany them—voluntarily—to the Punta Gorda police station to provide a full statement on tape. The suspect agreed to that and immediately started putting on his shoes.

"You do know that you're not under arrest," Plumberg reminded him one more time, "and you don't have to go with us."

"I know," Huden said. "I'll go."

"Even though I told him many times that he wasn't under arrest," the Island County detective recalled, "it seemed to me that he *thought* he was in custody."

A Punta Gorda police officer drove Jim Huden to the precinct, and Mark Plumberg prepared to follow them.

Before Plumberg left the house, however, he spoke with Jean Huden, telling her that Jim was willing to go with them.

"Has Jim ever owned a gun?" he asked casually.

"No! Jim hates guns. Is Jim under arrest?"

"No, ma'am, he's not. He's voluntarily going to give us a statement."

Jean didn't ask why Jim might be in trouble or why he would be arrested. Commander Mike Beech and Detective Mark Plumberg had never before encountered a homicide probe where the people they interviewed asked fewer questions or who reacted with such little emotion. Particularly Jim Huden. Was it because Jim and Jean were in shock?

Or perhaps their demeanor was so flat because they already knew the answers.

AS THEY WAITED FOR audiotapes and a video camera to be set up in an air-conditioned interview room at the Punta Gorda police headquarters, Plumberg and Huden made small talk. The suspect was hard to read. He didn't seem particularly nervous; his mien was more one of calm acceptance.

When the tapes started to roll, the detective read Jim his Miranda rights once again.

Jim began to answer questions, and he confirmed several major points on the record, knowing that one day his voice, image, and statements might indeed be used against him in a court of law.

Plumberg jotted down the salient points, filling about ten pages of his yellow legal pad, and he watched Jim's reactions to certain questions:

1. During the Christmas holidays in 2003, Jim Huden had driven Peggy Sue Thomas's Lexus from Las Vegas to Seattle. At the same time, Peggy flew from Vegas to Sea-Tac Airport.

2. Jim and Peggy stayed at Dick Deposit's home on Whidbey Island from Friday, December 19, until Monday or Tuesday, December 22 or 23.

3. Jim said he went alone to Russel Douglas's apartment in Renton to drop off a present for Brenna—either on that Monday or on Tuesday.

4. There were apparently several phone calls between Peggy and Russel arranging the present delivery on the day Jim said he took it to Russel.

5. Jim drove Peggy's Lexus to Russel's apartment.

6. Peggy did not accompany Jim, but stayed at the hotel because she was "tired" after cutting hair all day.

7. Jim's relationship with Brenna Douglas was because she was Peggy's friend. "They have a telephone re-

lationship," he said. "And I'm kinda just a guy in the room."

8. Peggy's mother called them in Las Vegas days after the murder to tell them that Russel was dead.

9. Jim Huden and Peggy Thomas were both in deep debt on their credit cards—just as Bill Hill had told detectives earlier.

10. Huden confirmed that Bill Hill was a friend of his and that they had lunch on the Monday before the current interview. "I told him I needed to get back to Peggy in Vegas."

Who delivered the Christmas gift for Brenna from Peggy—and if indeed there *was* a gift—might not seem important. But it was. One or both of the two suspects was either failing to recall the details—or lying.

Mike Beech told Jim Huden that his own best friend, Bill Hill, had called the Island County Sheriff's Department and told Beech himself that Jim had confessed to him.

Huden wilted when he heard that. Until now, he had not asked directly just why he was being questioned. Surely he knew from the direction of the questioning, but he seemed reluctant to say anything specifically, even after Mark Plumberg accused him of being the shooter.

Within a very short time, Jim asked for an attorney. Plumberg assumed he would want to be taken home where he could contact a lawyer, but he remained in the police station, dialing a number of law offices. He had no luck. It was after business hours, too late at night to reach anything but answering machines.

"We even tried to *help* him find a lawyer," Plumberg said.

When Jim Huden couldn't locate an attorney to come to the police station, he asked Plumberg, "What happens next?"

"That's up to you."

Huden mulled it over for a while, and then he asked if he could have a ride home.

A Punta Gorda police officer provided that transportation.

THERE WAS NO QUESTION that the Island County detectives felt they had the person who had either shot Russel Douglas or conspired with someone else to do so—but they couldn't prove it.

They had no gun. They had a single, battered bullet from Russ Douglas's brain. They had no solid physical evidence or credible eyewitnesses. And, most puzzling of all, they had no motive. Apparently Huden and Douglas hadn't even known each other!

It was true that Jim Huden and Peggy Thomas had run through their money and were approaching their credit card limits, but killing Russ hardly seemed a feasible way to get money. He didn't have much money—certainly not enough to kill for.

All homicides have *some* motivation, however obscure, but this case was as baffling as anything they had run into before.

Hurricane Charley was getting closer, but neither Mike Beech nor Mark Plumberg was anxious to leave Punta Gorda. They wanted to canvass Jim Huden's neighbors and friends to see if they could learn anything more about him, something that might help them get an arrest warrant.

The Hudens' next-door neighbors on Yucca Street weren't able to provide much information, nothing beyond finding them "nice people." They *had* noticed that Jim was not living with Jean for several months in 2003.

"I think he left right before Memorial Day last year," the wife said. "And then he was back in January or February."

The detectives contacted a man named Roy Boehm, said to be a friend of Jim's.

"I know him, and I occasionally went flying with him—but we aren't close," Boehm said. "I think I know Jean, his wife, better."

Mutual friends said that Jim admired Boehm and wanted to emulate his bravery and toughness in some way.

"You ever go shooting with him?" Plumberg asked.

"No! I don't know if he even owns a gun. I know he left Jean for a while and went back to Washington to visit his brother and a friend who lives there."

Asked about any other friends Huden might have, Boehm mentioned a local called "The Mayor." He wasn't really the mayor, but people called him that.

"Jim liked to play golf—I think he used to work on a golf course. That's about all I know about him."

The two Island County detectives next located the musicians who had played in Jim's band, Buck Naked and the X-hibitionists.

"We've started a new band we call Buck Naked II, and we play in a place called Tallulah's in Sarasota," one member told them.

The man gave them the names of three other band members, including Bill Hill, but his answers were terse and he didn't seem to want to discuss Huden. He did tell them, however, that Jim had told someone he might be leaving the area soon, and they wouldn't see him again.

Bill Hill couldn't fathom why the Jim he knew would have killed anyone. On August 8, 2004, hearing that the Washington State detectives had talked to Jim and that they had drawn quite a bit of information from him, Hill provided Mike Beech and Mark Plumberg with a taped statement of what he had told them earlier on the phone.

While Hill was doing that, another of the Buck Naked performers dropped in to his house.

The drummer said that he'd known Jim since 1994 or '95, but they hadn't been very close since Jim came back from Las Vegas.

"Lots of people are angry with him," the drummer said. "About a week ago last Sunday, he announced he was leaving town and our band again!"

"Does Jim have a gun?"

He shook his head. "I don't know about any firearm and I've been to his house many, many times."

It was beginning to look as if Jim Huden had already left town. When Beech and Plumberg knocked on Jean and Jim's door, no one answered. A neighbor said he had seen Jean come home in her Corvette, but she left again in Jim's red car.

Jean's brother, who had no particular love for Jim, said that he hadn't seen Jim but that Jean had said she was getting out of town for the weekend, going to the beach to lie in the sun. She didn't say *which* beach she planned to visit.

"She said she had asked Jim to move out."

Jean had known about the other woman in Las Vegas for some time, but she had hinted that there was "another problem."

"I asked her if it was a legal problem, but she didn't answer," her brother said. "Jean doesn't tell about other people's business or personal problems."

Jean told her brother only that the other problem was why the Washington State detectives were in Florida at the moment.

Many people knew that Jean was leaving for a few days during the prior week, but no one recalled having seen Jim for a week to ten days. Jean had returned to their house and continued her usual routine and neighbors expected Jim to drive up at any moment.

Almost everyone the investigators talked to said that Jim had been "a different man" or "not himself" since he'd come back from Las Vegas months before. He had seemed depressed and distracted. Some even thought he might be ill.

Jean's brother didn't know what to make of it all. When he spoke to Jean on the phone, he sensed that Jim might be listening in, but she swore he wasn't with her.

She told her brother that she had hidden her gun so Jim couldn't find it; he was so depressed. They all knew about Jean's gun, but no one was sure Jim had a gun of his own. They doubted it.

"Jean told me that Jim needed to see a shrink and that he was having problems," one female acquaintance recalled.

One thing was clear: Jim Huden wasn't in Punta Gorda. Surely someone would have seen him, but it appeared that he had left Punta Gorda shortly after he gave a statement to Mark Plumberg and Mike Beech.

Most people who knew him believed he had flown to Las Vegas, and the two detectives weren't that worried about finding him as they headed west just in time to escape the hurricane. He had been quite cooperative with them.

But Jim Huden was not nearly as predictable as everyone thought. At least at the moment. He wasn't in Las Vegas, although he was in touch with Jean. They had plans to meet in a hotel miles away from Punta Gorda after the investigation simmered down a bit.

Whether Jean Huden had somehow aided her husband in his vanishing act was hard to tell. According to their close friends, they had been having marital problems, and she was considering divorce. Since Jean obviously knew about his obsession with Peggy Sue Thomas, it wasn't surprising that their marriage might be in big trouble.

Jim had left Jean once before. This time, he hadn't been home in Florida with her for more than four or five months, and now he was gone again.

Jim had told Bill Hill that he was going to try to get Peggy Sue back. Jean Huden would have to be a saint to want to help him evade the Island County investigators, especially after Peggy Sue had come to Florida and Jean had seen her husband and his lover together. Even so, if she still loved him, Jean might have delivered his red sports car to him.

Mark Plumberg's search into Peggy Sue's background was unearthing tangled and complicated secrets.

Were it not for the vicissitudes of fate, karma, and even sheer coincidence, Peggy Sue Stackhouse Thomas might never have been born.

And, some said, that would have been a good thing . . .

CHAPTER NINETEEN

ON AUGUST 18, 2004, the Island County Sheriff's Office authorized a press release, hoping that might encourage someone to come forward with information. They officially named Jim Huden and Peggy Sue Thomas as "persons of interest" who might be connected to the unsolved murder of Russel Douglas.

The story was carried by print, radio, and television media that night.

It paid off, and it led to the most important piece of physical evidence the Island County investigators retrieved since the night Russel Douglas died.

At a quarter to one the next day, Commander Mike Beech received a call from Investigator Boeglin of the Doña Anna County Sheriff's Office in New Mexico.

"We just had a weapon turned in," Boeglin said. "A citizen named Keith Ogden brought in a .380

caliber Bersa pistol. He thinks it might have been used in the homicide up your way—victim might have been a guy named Russel Douglas."

It seemed almost too easy. If this was the death gun, the murder probe might be coming to a successful conclusion. It had been a frustrating eight months for the investigators.

But if they thought they were home free, they were mistaken.

Commander Mike Beech and Ed Wallace were on a plane for Las Cruces, New Mexico, early the next morning. They took custody of the possible murder weapon from the Doña Anna County sheriff. Keith Ogden had turned in a two-tone Bersa Thunder, .380 caliber—serial number 573168. Its manufacturer and the caliber could well be a match; the Bersa was one possible gun pinpointed by ballistics experts.

How it ended up in Las Cruces, New Mexico, was a mystery.

Mike Beech and Ed Wallace phoned Keith and arranged to meet him and his wife, Donna, at their home in Radium Springs, New Mexico.

They learned that Ogden's connection to Jim Huden was through Keith's cousin, Preston Collier.* Ogden was a retired police officer from Multnomah County, Oregon. He and Donna had known Huden when they were living in Las Vegas.

"My cousin called us after he read information in a press release," Ogden said. "He told us that there was a search on for a Bersa that was missing after a homicide up in Washington."

It took less than twenty-four hours before Keith Ogden went to his local sheriff and handed over the gun. "Keith hated to do it—we both liked Jim," Donna said. "But we both agreed that we had to go to the police with that gun."

The Ogdens weren't positive about when they met Jim Huden, but believed it was sometime in mid-2003.

"Let's see," Ogden said. "We met Jim about three weeks before the Johnny Rivers concert at a casino in Henderson, Nevada."

(Mike Beech contacted the concert promotions manager for casino artists, and was able to pin down the date of the Rivers concert as August 29, 2003.)

"Several months after that," Ogden continued, "might have been six months, maybe less—Huden called me and asked if I had any guns to sell because he was looking to buy one."

Keith Ogden didn't have any guns for sale, but Jim Huden had shown up at his house in Las Vegas a few days later with a .380 Bersa pistol he'd purchased.

"I taught him how to clean it and operate it."

The two men had then taken it to the Ogdens' backyard near Las Vegas where Keith and Donna test-fired it into the dirt there.

"We fired it into a pillow to cut down on the noise."

"Do you recall just where that was in your yard at your last place?" Beech asked.

"I do," Donna Ogden said. "You walk out the back patio door. There's a pool facing you. Then you would turn left onto the grassy area, past two clumps of ornamental grass plants set in gray gravel. Just about two feet beyond that was where we were firing into the ground."

Asked to isolate the time this happened, Keith and Donna Ogden thought it had been more like four months rather than six after Huden was first looking for a gun in August.

They were positive the test-firing had occurred *before* Jim and his girlfriend, Peggy, had left to go to Washington State in December.

After the couple came back from their Christmas trip, Keith said that Jim had contacted him again. Now that he thought about it, Jim said he was worried about having a gun in their house because of Peggy's young daughters.

"He asked me if I would take care of the gun for him, and I agreed," Keith said. "We were over at Jim and Peggy's house for lunch, and I remember that Peggy's mom called that day to tell her that someone on Whidbey Island had died or was killed. Come to think of it, it was right *after* that that Jim called me and asked me to keep the gun for him."

As far as Keith knew, the test bullet rounds that were fired were still in the ground at their former home.

"We moved to New Mexico on July 6, 2004," Ogden said.

"Did you do any landscaping in the backyard before you moved?" Detective Ed Wallace asked.

"No, sir. But, if anyone dug a shovel in there, they might not even touch the rounds. They penetrated several inches down."

The gun that Jim Huden had left with Keith Ogden might be worth its weight in gold. If it was the *right* Bersa Thunder. Mike Beech treated it tenderly as he hand-carried it back to Whidbey Island for ballistics tests.

Mark Plumberg delivered the .380 Bersa pistol to the Washington State Police lab. There it was swabbed for DNA testing. That didn't yield a match, but within a day, he received a fax from criminalist Evan Thompson.

The gun that Keith Ogden had turned in microscopically matched the extractor and ejector marks on the shell casing recovered from Russ Douglas's yellow Tracker. Moreover, the lands and grooves striations on the single bullet recovered from the victim's brain also matched the Bersa's barrel!

This, at last, was a vital piece of physical evidence. The link between Jim Huden and the death weapon had been made.

It should have been enough to arrest Huden, *if* they could find him.

Jim was proving to be extremely elusive.

CHAPTER TWENTY

ON *AUGUST 31, 2004,* Commander Mike Beech and detectives Shawn Warwick and Ed Wallace from Island County arrived in Henderson, Nevada. Accompanied by Detective Daniel Leath of the Henderson Police Department, they served a search warrant on Peggy Sue Thomas.

Beech, Wallace, and Warwick talked to Peggy Sue for two days. They saw that she was a very tall, striking woman with long, reddish-tinted hair. She would certainly stand out in any crowd.

Peggy Sue explained that she was working for a limousine service in Las Vegas. Her day planner and appointment book verified that. She kept very precise records on her clientele. She saved business cards, and jotted down her regulars' favorite snacks and drinks. She also put in the hourly base rate for the limousine and noted tips. One group might leave her a five-hundred-dollar tip, while others left ten dollars. Of course, when she drove a celebrity, she mentioned that, too.

Peggy Sue's attorney—Gerald Werksman of Los Angeles—was present when the Washington State detectives interviewed his client.

She was accommodating and didn't seem upset when they removed the hard drive from her computer, five sealed and labeled bags of possible physical evidence, and a laptop computer in a gray case. The items were shipped securely back to the sheriff's office on Whidbey Island.

Peggy's business cards featured a photo of her draped over a luxury limousine, wearing a clinging black dress that was open almost to the waist.

Apparently, Peggy's fortune had risen since Jim left for Florida; some of her tips were a thousand dollars or more! Hers was a transportation business that attracted high rollers—many of them men, but she also had glowing thank-you notes from couples who had visited the Vegas Strip.

Her Henderson, Nevada, home was upscale, the golden stucco of the southwest with lavish landscaping of palm trees, cacti, and paloverde trees.

Peggy Sue had good recall of the Christmas season now eight months in the past. She had flown to Seattle, she said, with one of her daughters.

"Jim drove my Lexus up before I got there, and he picked us up at Sea-Tac Airport."

Werksman wanted Jean Huden's phone number, but Peggy said it would be better if she had Jean call him.

When Jean called Peggy's attorney a short time later, she verified that she'd heard Jim say that he had shot Russ Douglas. It happened while he was going out for cigarettes.

Werksman disagreed. "I don't think he did it."

But Jean Huden insisted. "He keeps saying he did it."

Werksman told Jean that this was a very important statement, and she had to be certain. Werksman, too, was concerned that Jim might commit suicide.

"I told her that she ought to call Plumberg. And then I told her that it was very decent of her—knowing the strain she'd been under—to talk to me."

Werksman said he had Peggy write down a statement about what, to the best of her memory, was closest to what had actually happened during her Christmas visit to Whidbey Island.

Peggy was prepared to sign the one-page statement. Warwick and Beech exchanged glances; how could Peggy sum up everything that occurred on the prior December 26 in just one page?

Asked once again about who had delivered the present for Brenna to Russ, Peggy said that *both* she and Jim had gone to his Renton apartment.

That, of course, presented a continuing problem with their separate versions of the errand, but the investigators didn't correct her.

Peggy's appointment book showed that her last hair appointment was on December 23, 2003, at

Just B's—the day the couple both said they left Whidbey Island and moved to a motel near Sea-Tac Airport.

Peggy told Shawn Warwick that she realized she still had the key to Dick Deposit's house on Soundview Drive in Langley where they'd been staying for four days.

"We drove back to Whidbey on the twenty-sixth," she said. "Jim left me at Dick's house for thirty, maybe forty-five minutes and drove off in my Lexus to get some smokes."

This was a very important date, the day that Russel Douglas was murdered, and the investigative team from Island County was eager to hear about Peggy's memories of that day after Christmas.

Dick Deposit's guest house was about five miles from Wahl Road, where Russ Douglas was shot, but neither detective betrayed any particular interest when they heard this. They listened intently, however, as she recalled the day after Christmas.

She said he had returned in that time period, bringing some Swisher Sweets cigars with him. These cigars were an item that few stores carried. Peggy said she still had the receipt for them. However, she hadn't saved receipts for gas, ferry tickets, or other purchases she and Jim made on December 26.

Peggy recalled that while Jim was gone, she noticed the sheets from their bed had been washed—but she'd forgotten to put them into the dryer. She rectified that, turning on the dryer and then making the bed.

When he came back about noon, she said they had left the island again, taking the Keystone ferry to visit a friend, Bill Marlow. After that, they had driven to Vancouver, Washington, to see one of Peggy's sisters.

Heading north again, Peggy Sue said she and Jim stayed at the Marriott Hotel near Sea-Tac Airport.

She had left out one stop on their quick trip down I-5, almost to Portland. Initially, Peggy didn't mention stopping at the Red Lion in Longview at about 6:30 in the evening of December 26.

Their friend Rick Early verified to Detective Sue Quandt that Peggy Sue and Jim had stopped to share a holiday dinner there, but they had only eaten appetizers and drank coffee, and left before others in the party ordered dinner.

In this second interview with Shawn Warwick, Peggy went into more detail about catching the Keystone ferry on the day after Christmas. She said they had missed the noon ferry, and taken the 12:45 to Port Townsend to visit Bill Marlow. But the Washington State Ferry System said there *was* no 12:45 ferry; the next ferry would have been at 1:30 P.M.

Detective Quandt reported to Mark Plumberg that she had contacted Bill Marlow in Port Townsend.

"He said Peggy and Jim didn't come to see him

at all during the Christmas holidays. Jim was supposed to meet Marlow and other musicians for a band practice on the twenty-third, but he never showed up. Jim called him instead and said that he and Peggy were in Seattle."

It appeared that Jim and Peggy had attempted to fill the day of Russ Douglas's murder full of occasions where they had been with people who would validate them. But some of them simply didn't mesh.

Peggy's recall of the vital day placed them around noon at Dick Deposit's—returning a key, buying Swisher Sweets, drying sheets, and then on the Keystone ferry to see Bill Marlow, next heading south on 101 either to Vancouver (which now seemed doubtful), before going to Kelso-Longview, Washington, to join friends for dinner.

And then the pair had set out for Las Vegas.

As Detective Shawn Warwick interviewed Peggy Sue again before he and Ed Wallace left Nevada, Peggy wanted to correct something she had said earlier. She said she had been mistaken when she said that Jim had been gone from Dick Deposit's house for half an hour to forty-five minutes. Thinking back, she thought he'd been away only about fifteen minutes.

Any homemaker knows that would not have been enough time to dry a load of sheets and pillowcases.

Odd.

Whenever the interview with Peggy began to

veer into areas where Gerald Werksman appeared to feel uneasy, he changed the subject. He went into great detail about the baseball games he'd placed bets on since he had arrived in Las Vegas, or asked the detectives about how they liked the hotel where they were staying.

It was an obvious ploy to take some of the heat off of Peggy Sue's answers.

THE DETECTIVES HAD HEARD about that Christmas trip many times.

They listened patiently, detecting slight changes. And then they showed Peggy a photograph of the death gun found in Radium Springs, New Mexico, only two weeks earlier.

Peggy Sue denied ever having seen it before, but the stunned look on her face spoke for itself. After this first day of interviewing and finding more items listed on the search warrant, the detectives called it a day. They wanted to give Peggy Thomas time to mull over the fact that the Bersa had been found and perhaps wonder which of her documents and files had been taken into evidence.

She had also appeared shaken when her prize car was impounded.

After they left, Peggy immediately called Jean Huden. She said she was shocked when the detectives showed her a picture of a gun.

"I was thrown for a loop," she said. "My car was impounded. I have to find Jim and see what in the hell is going on."

Peggy Sue told detectives the next day that the only possible phone contact with Jim Huden would be at the house he shared with his wife, Jean, in Punta Gorda.

"I called Jean and told her what had happened—and asked if she knew anything about it. She put Jim on the phone. That was a first, 'cause I never talked to him."

"Yesterday," Shawn Warwick cut in, "you kept mentioning that you had been talking to Jean—but you didn't mention talking to Jim."

"I *hadn't* talked to him when you were here yesterday," she explained. "I didn't think he'd been home since Detective Plumberg was down there. But Jean was with him yesterday so I got to talk to him. He got on the phone and asked how I was doing. I said, 'How do you think I'm doing? My car's been taken—what's going on?' And he just said, 'I'm sorry, I love you. I never meant for you to be involved in this—but *I did it*. I did it when I went for cigarettes.'

"I said, 'It can't be!' And he said, 'Just know I love you, and you're never gonna see me or hear from me again.' That was it. He hung up."

Peggy Sue said that she was hysterical, shocked at what Jim confessed to her—so she had called Gerald Werksman, her attorney, who advised her to call the Island County Sheriff's investigators.

Gerald Werksman validated what his client said, and that he had urged her to call the sheriff's office.

"This was the first time she ever called with tears [in her voice]. And I was naturally most interested in not only did he say he did it—*when* did he say he did it? She told me when he went out for smokes."

Mike Beech finally asked Peggy an obvious question: "The first thing that struck me last night—and again this morning—is nowhere in here do you go, 'Why? Why did you kill him? Why did you do this?' That's a pretty normal human response, I would think."

"If you would have seen my demeanor yesterday, I couldn't even hardly function," Peggy explained.

"Before your phone call with Jim yesterday—or after?"

"No, when I got the phone call."

"You mean when you *made* the phone call," Shawn Warwick corrected.

"Yeah, I mean when I got to talk to him [Jim]. I mean, I called up very frank and ended up with the phone being hung up on me, and I'm left in hysterics."

"Well, what do you think—about why he might have done it—killed Douglas?" Warwick pressed.

"I don't know anyone who would do that," Peggy said.

Peggy's attorney reminded her that she had told him about Jim's growing up in an abusive household. And that Bill Hill had told Werksman that Jim believed Russ was abusing Brenna.

Peggy Sue denied that she had ever told Werksman anything like that.

It seemed that they were mapping out a scenario right there in front of the detectives—one that would totally absolve Peggy and point fingers at Jim as the shooter.

Gerald Werksman's explanation for the "why" of Douglas's inexplicable murder grew more convoluted.

"Now we start speculating," he said. "And this whole thing is speculation."

"Mmm-hmm," Mike Beech mumbled, not giving away his own opinion.

"But I came away from where—either I read or what you said, as now you've switched, at first, you—" Werksman fumbled. "I was told that the motivation for this was insurance. I don't know where I heard that, but now I'm sayin' to myself, now, because motivation seems to, you know, be an obvious question, maybe in his own sick way, Jim was avenging the abuse he—that he may have heard from Brenna that she was getting or her kids were getting from Russ.

"Okay. And from what I've heard about Huden, he's wacky enough to—to somehow, in his own mind, thought he was a . . . an avenging source or something, that as, as far-fetched as that may seem."

"Well, everything in the past two years has been far-fetched," Peggy cut in.

"Well, regardless of his motive, would he and

Brenna—would Jim and Brenna have had a chance to have a discussion?" Shawn Warwick asked.

"I don't think so," Peggy said.

"Do you know that Brenna is driving a new SUV?" Warwick asked.

"No."

Peggy Sue said that Brenna's plan to buy her house hadn't materialized. She had told Werksman that it was against Brenna's financial interest for Russ "not to be around."

"Yeah," Werksman added. "When Russ was alive, there was the hope that she, Brenna, would buy the house."

The interview wound around and around like a spinning top, the lines at the top disappearing into the vortex, but they came out changed. Peggy Thomas insisted that she and Jim *had* taken the Keystone ferry to Bill Marlow's house on December 26—after they left Dick Deposit's house.

"He and his wife were the only ones there," she said. "They must have forgotten."

One thing was clear to the three detectives. For a woman who had allegedly been passionate about Jim Huden, Peggy Sue Thomas had no compunction about throwing him to the wolves, trying to find reasons he was "wacky" and impetuous and capable of murder.

AS HE WENT OVER all the reports that came across his desk, Mark Plumberg was accounting for every time, every minute that Peggy and Jim had been on

Whidbey Island during the 2003 Christmas season. He was also ferreting out seemingly insignificant slips, different versions of the same situation, and peculiar comments. It was akin to stringing a line full of tiny Christmas lights. Every once in a while, something didn't match. That tended to make the entire rope of "lights" go black.

Taken separately, those jarring mismatches didn't matter all that much. As a whole, Plumberg believed that someone had to be lying.

This was most assuredly not a slam-dunk case. The circumstantial evidence was mushrooming, but it wasn't enough to arrest anyone on murder charges.

The homicide case on the shooting death of Russel Douglas remained open.

PART SEVEN

The Stackhouse Family: 1963–2002

Chapter Twenty-one

JIM HUDEN WAS MISSING, and could possibly be dead—a suicide. That was what his wife, Jean, said she was afraid of. Back on Whidbey Island, Mark Plumberg moved along a winding path toward what he hoped would be the truth. He had met all of the principals who might have even a sliver of knowledge about Russ Douglas's murder.

All except Peggy Sue Thomas. He had spoken with her on the phone and found her easygoing and accessible—unlike Brenna Douglas, whose emotions were so erratic that they were almost impossible to chart.

Plumberg had heard talk on the island that Peggy Sue's very large family, fathered by Jimmie Stackhouse, had suffered many tragedies in the past. Indeed, there was an almost "Kennedyesque" sense about them, a black cloud of violence, misfortune, and sudden death that seemed to stalk them.

If Peggy Sue Thomas *did* have any complicity or

guilty knowledge that would help close the Russel Douglas homicide case, Plumberg needed to find out as much as he could about her.

A vicious, sadistic murder that occurred two states away and forty years earlier had made Peggy's father, Jimmie, a widower with six children to raise.

The tragedies that Jimmie Stackhouse and his family endured had nothing whatsoever to do with Peggy Sue. She was born on September 2, 1965— two years and three months after Mary Ellen Stackhouse, Jimmie's first wife, was murdered at the age of thirty-two.

Jimmie Stackhouse would surely have remained with his original family—his wife and six children—and he wouldn't have been a single man when he met the woman who would bear his seventh child.

That baby, of course, was Peggy Sue Stackhouse.

Almost every family, traced back generations, reveals startling and disturbing events, some best left unexamined. If ever there was a family damned to tragedy and pain, it was Jimmie Stackhouse's. I share that family surname, although I haven't found any direct connections—for which I am thankful. Again and again, those on the family tree underwent unbelievable losses. Jimmie Stackhouse suffered so many.

IN THE EARLY SUMMER of 1963, despite the many blows in Jimmie Stackhouse's early life, he had some happier times. Jimmie spent his adult life serving in the navy as a chief petty officer, service he was proud of. By the time he was thirty-one, his life was complete with everything a man might wish for. A perfect family. A career he loved.

Jimmie met the girl he would marry on Whidbey Island. Mary Ellen Hower came from a very wealthy extended family back in Findley, Ohio. The Howers started the Quaker Oats company, and lived in a mansion that they eventually donated to the city of Akron. Now known as the Hower House, locals and tourists alike flock to view its historic luxury.

Mary Ellen's branch of the Hower family wasn't particularly wealthy, however, and she went to high school in Coupeville, Washington, rather than an exclusive finishing school for girls.

Jimmie Stackhouse met her there, and felt lucky to have won such a beautiful bride. As Jimmie was stationed from one base to another—in Hawaii and California—Mary Ellen gave birth to six children in eight years. Both she and Jimmie welcomed them, and they were very happy.

And then, a horrifying crime in San Jose, California, stopped Jimmie Stackhouse's world, changing his family's future in untold ways.

Stackhouse was stationed at the Naval Air Station at Moffett Field in Mountain View, California, thirty-five miles south of San Francisco, a short distance northwest of San Jose, and only a mile from San Francisco Bay.

Moffett Field has a long and rich history going back to 1931, with huge wooden hangars that once housed dirigibles (blimps like the ill-fated *Hindenburg,* which crashed and burned in Lakehurst, New Jersey, in 1937). Later Moffett provided space for fighter jets. The naval facility was decommissioned in 1994, and both NASA and private corporations now occupy the fifteen hundred acres there.

For Stackhouse, his wife, Mary Ellen, and their three boys and three girls, Moffett was a good duty station. The temperature was moderate, there were flowers everywhere, and even the fog that hovers so often over San Francisco is held back by the coastal range of mountains before it hits San Jose. At the time, Moffett was rumored to have the best commissary in America, and navy families abounded so that Mary Ellen and their children had no difficulty finding friends.

Jimmie bought a split-level house for his brood on Ruskin Drive in the Berryessa neighborhood in San Jose. There were plenty of bedrooms and a green sweep of grass where the Stackhouse children could play.

They were a handsome family. Jimmie was a big, rugged man with wavy, red-blond hair that he combed into an imposing pompadour. Thirty-year-old Mary Ellen was a tall, slender brunette who was attractive enough to be a model. Tommy, eight, was the oldest and resembled his mother, while Mike, seven, Lana, five, Brenda, four,

Rhonda, three, and Robby, eighteen months, all looked like Jimmie.

Jimmie had thirteen years in the navy and he loved it. A flight mechanic, he planned to stay in the service until he retired. Mary Ellen had her hands full with six children under eight, but she occasionally worked as a cocktail waitress at the navy base and also helped out with wedding receptions there. To add a little more to the family's income, she sold Avon products.

She was fiercely protective of her children, particularly when Jimmie was gone for training or active duty.

In early June 1963, Jimmie was far away from home. He was attending navy classes at Stewart Air Force Base near Nashville, Tennessee. Mary Ellen missed him, of course, but she wasn't lonely—not with six active children running through their new house.

Although she had close neighbors, friends she knew well, Mary Ellen was always careful about locking her doors and windows at night. Once she got the children in bed, she allowed herself some "alone" time to watch television and relax.

On Tuesday, June 4, Jimmie called her, something that was unusual for him, and she was happy to hear his voice. But she had Robby in his high chair and was feeding him supper. He demanded her attention; either he or his bowl of food were in danger of falling out of the chair, so she couldn't talk long. She and Jimmie agreed they would try again soon to have a calm conversation.

Later, with the house finally quiet, Mary Ellen poured a cup of coffee and dished up some ice cream for herself, carrying them to the living room so she could watch one of her favorite shows.

At 10:30 P.M., the sun had finally set. It was a warm night, and she still had the windows open. Uncharacteristically, she put off locking the outside doors, even the one that opened into the lower level of their house. But she was involved in watching television.

None of the children or nearby neighbors heard anything unusual during the night . . .

But things were far from normal in the Stackhouse household. No one woke the children up on the morning of June 5 to tell them it was time to get ready for school.

Lana, who at five was the oldest girl, was the last to see her mother alive and the first to find her that morning. As she stumbled sleepily down the hall, Lana found Mary Ellen lying on the floor, blocking the top of the stairway to the midlevel of the house.

"I had fallen out of my bed about ten P.M.," Lana told a California parole board a very long time later. "I believed for years that if I had only stayed awake, my mother would still be alive.

"I knelt near her and tried to get her to wake up. It wasn't real. I thought that my mommy was just sleeping. I knew she would wake up."

Lana saw Mary Ellen's "tattered throat wounds," and her blue eyes staring blankly at nothing, eyes that would haunt Lana forever after.

Her brothers Tom and Mike were only seven and eight, and their bedroom was in the basement level of the house. When Lana screamed for them, they rushed up the stairs. They found their mother there, lying on the floor outside the room where Rhonda, Brenda, and Lana slept. But she didn't answer when they tried to talk to her, and there was some kind of red liquid underneath her. It was a sight no children should ever have to see.

Tom and Mike realized that she would never answer them again.

They also knew instinctively that it was up to them to get their three sisters and baby brother out of the house.

Rhonda Stackhouse was just three years old. She would never be free of certain flashes of memory, crazy, jagged bursts of light and color as if she was watching a screen in a nightmare.

Rhonda can still picture the pajamas her brothers were wearing: "They had a pattern of cartoon figures on them," she recalls. "My brothers carried us over my mother's body, and I could see that one of her eyes was bulging out of its socket. That image has stayed with me."

Using strength they shouldn't have had, Tom and Mike somehow managed to lift Brenda, Rhonda, and Robby over their mother's body and lead them out the front door where they hurried to their neighbor Madeline Cassen's house. She and Mary Ellen were good friends, and they hoped she would know what to do.

Rhonda recalls that Madeline's hair was very blond and "puffy." She took the youngest girls by the hands and Lana walked ahead as they walked back to the Stackhouses' front door.

"She opened the front door," Rhonda says, "and she looked up the stairs at the landing. I remember her letting go of my hand, and I looked up at her face and she was screaming and screaming. I can still see her bright red lipstick and her blond bouffant hair as I stood there looking up at her."

Within minutes, the quiet morning air was pierced again, this time by wailing sirens as one squad car after another drew close.

Their lives changed on that Wednesday morning in the first week of June. It was a school day, very close to summer vacation, and all the children had been looking forward to that.

"I didn't know what had happened," Rhonda recalls. "Our whole world just evaporated that night. No one told us anything. Men with cameras took pictures of us, but nobody talked about what was wrong with our mother. When I look at the pictures of us that appeared in the *San Jose Mercury News* that day, Robby's crying and the rest of us just look confused. I could see blood staining Brenda's shoes.

"Brenda—who's a year older than myself—simply stopped talking for six months; she didn't utter a word. All of us knew something terrible had happened, but we didn't know what. I don't think we even believed our mom was dead at that point. My dad came home from Tennessee, but he didn't explain anything, either. I do know we never went back to that house—not until we were mothers ourselves."

For thirty-two years, what Mary Ellen had suffered, and the way she died, was never mentioned in Jimmie Stackhouse's home.

"And we never asked our father," Rhonda says. "Because we knew it would make him feel bad. He never volunteered anything. He may have believed he was doing the right thing. A long time later, I found out that he sold our house for a dollar—and a handshake. He asked for an immediate transfer to another base, and the navy granted it. We moved to the Whidbey Island Naval Air Station in Washington State. I sort of remember that we had some of the furniture from our old house, but I'm not sure if that's just my imagination."

Brenda would never remember her mother at all, even though as an adult she consulted therapists to help her open up that padlocked part of her brain.

Mary Ellen died three weeks before Rhonda's third birthday, and she would retain only fractured memories, blurred scenes of being with her mother. She can recall sitting in a high chair near a big window and watching Tom, Mike, and Lana walk down the sidewalk to catch the school bus, and she remembers sitting on the landing of the stairs, while Brenda, who was sixteen months older, was trying to tie her shoes.

"I could picture waking up and my mom was carrying me to her bedroom—and having a warm washcloth put over my eyes because I couldn't open them. I must have had an eye infection. There were small things like sitting on the kitchen counter, with my mom holding me and reaching to get something out of the cupboard."

When Jimmie Stackhouse hopped off the plane, he had immediately gathered his children around him.

"My dad never went back into our house," Rhonda said. "I think my Aunt Ellen flew down from Whidbey Island to be with us. And I believe we lived with her and Uncle Cat—who was a tugboat captain when we first moved up there, and Dad was building us a house."

When someone praised Jimmie for keeping his family together, he was puzzled. Why was that so brave?

"Of course I took care of my children," he said. "I would never walk away from my family. I had six small children. My main concern was to get them out of the house, out of San Jose—where reporters were hounding us—and get them settled. I didn't discuss it with the children. I didn't know they wanted to."

He was still young, a man who had truly loved his beautiful wife, now suddenly widowed. His adult life was well nigh perfect until sometime between 10 and 11 P.M. on that warm June night. Jimmie Stackhouse was doing the best he could, believing that if his children didn't know all the horrifying details about their mother's death, they would adjust soon enough.

Jimmie had learned to be stoic. His mother had died from childbirth complications when he was only nine days old, and he was raised by an angry and abusive grandmother. At seventeen, he left her South Carolina house and never went back.

"No one explained a thing to us," Rhonda said. "It took years to forgive my dad for the hell us kids went through and his part in brushing it all away without really investigating if his children were okay. It was right there in front of him that we were not, but I don't fault him. He coped the way he knew how."

They didn't have therapy; therapy wasn't the automatic answer to post-traumatic stress disorder (in 1963, the term itself was yet to be coined).

Lana felt overwhelming guilt, Rhonda needed to know the truth, and Brenda had been struck dumb. Robby was too young to even remember his mother, and the big boys were doing their best to be brave.

When they fled their house on the morning of June 5, Tom, eight, had insisted on taking his toy pistol, saying, "I'm going to get the person who hurt Mommy."

CHAPTER TWENTY-TWO

MARY ELLEN'S MURDER MADE the kind of headlines newspaper editors in the sixties cherished. Words like "sex fiend," "bloody enigma," and "telltale clues" were common in describing homicides.

The hunt didn't last long. Mary Ellen had recently confided to a close friend that she was afraid of prowlers who might be watching her. She had received several obscene phone calls from a man who seemed to be disguising his voice.

"He's threatening to kill me," she said fearfully.

For some reason, she did not report the calls to the police, but she had her phone number changed to an unlisted number, telling herself that it was just a prank caller and if he didn't have her number, he couldn't call.

Although tracing phone calls to their source is much easier today than it was fifty years ago, there were ways police and phone companies of the sixties could have put a pen register on her phone and kept a record of the numbers her threatening caller had used. Unless he was calling from a pay phone, or hung up too quickly, or used other methods to hide his identity.

Would it have saved Mary Ellen Stackhouse's life? Quite possibly—but one can never be sure. The caller might have been her killer or someone else entirely. Many pretty women whose husbands are often away on military duty receive weird phone calls.

If it was the murderer who had made the calls, investigators had no feasible way to sift through the thousands of military personnel around Moffett Field.

Fortunately, several tips that came into the police offices named a possible suspect even before the sun set on the day her body was discovered.

Neighbors on Ruskin Drive and adjoining streets told homicide detectives that Mary Ellen had had some issues with a teenage neighbor boy who lived with his parents in a house located directly behind the Stackhouses' home. More accurately, he lived in the garage outside *his* family home. The rumor was that Gilbert Thompson, sixteen, wasn't allowed to sleep in the house because he was "strange sexually" and his parents didn't want him sleeping so close to his female relatives because he was molesting them.

Thompson had a German shepherd that was allowed to run free, and the dog had dug up the

Stackhouses' front lawn and garden that Mary Ellen tended so carefully. She had scolded Gilbert, saying he should keep his dog fenced in. He had been very angry. Indeed, just before Jimmie left for the Tennessee training facility, he had given their own bulldog to a farm home because it too was destroying their freshly planted grass.

If only the Stackhouses' dog had still been in the basement, Mary Ellen would have had some warning.

Shortly thereafter, Gilbert's dog disappeared and he was convinced that Mary Ellen had called the dogcatcher to take his pet away. Whether she had done that is moot; she would never be able to say. There were other neighbors who were concerned about the dog and also might have reported it to animal control.

In the days before Mary Ellen's murder, witnesses told the investigators that Thompson had blamed her and shouted at her "in unpleasant terms" about his dog's disappearance.

No one said "person of interest" in 1963; police just came right out and said "suspect," and early on Gilbert Thompson was definitely a prime suspect in Mary Ellen's homicide.

Ironically, Gilbert's parents—who had lived in the neighborhood for only six months and had six children of their own—had been among the first to offer to care for Mary Ellen's children until Jimmie Stackhouse's flight from Tennessee landed.

Within hours after they had responded to the

Russ Douglas worked hard to be physically fit. Besides building his muscles at a gym, he scuba dived and hiked difficult trails in Washington State mountains and foothills. But being in good shape could not save him when someone with a gun stalked him.

Gail O'Neal

Russel Douglas photographed when he was in the army. He had so many dreams, so many goals, but very few of them worked out—even though he was highly intelligent.

Gail O'Neal

Russel Douglas at his wedding to Brenna. They were a toxic combination, two people who never should have dated—much less married.

Gail O'Neal

Brenna Douglas prepares to share wedding vows with Russel. They already had a son.

Gail O'Neal

Russ Douglas with his son, Jack. Russ loved his two children—Jack and Hannah—but he and Brenna fought constantly. She tried to distance him from his family. Even so, they both seemed to want to keep their marriage together. After Russ moved out, he was on call to help around the house they rented and see his children. He came home for Christmas 2003, and it looked as though they might be able to reconcile after all.

Gail O'Neal

Russ's yellow Tracker where it was found on December 26, 2003. It sat in the driveway of an isolated cabin on Whidbey Island for more than twenty-four hours before horrified neighbors called 911. The first deputies to arrive were shocked at what they found inside.

Police file photo

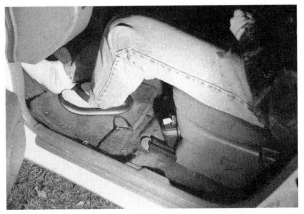

Russ Douglas was found slumped behind the wheel of his new yellow Tracker. It seemed clear that he had no warning as someone armed with a gun approached. Or was his instant death a suicide? What was he doing in this lonely place?

Police file photo

This gun wasn't found at the scene, ruling out suicide. Criminalists thought the death weapon was a Bersa handgun. Investigators found a single slug and a bullet casing—but they needed the gun they came from to make a case. Still, any killer with good sense would have thrown it into the deep water around Whidbey Island so it could never be traced back to him—or her.

Police file photo

Russ Douglas was highly educated, but sometimes he made the wrong choices.

Gail O'Neal

Washington investigators looked for expended bullets in the backyard of this Nevada home where someone had test-fired a handgun. They found casings that they hoped would match those fired from the death gun.

Police file photo

At one time, Brenna and Russ sold sex toys at home parties. These were found in Russ's apartment. Later, they had a more successful business—a beauty salon called Just B's.

Police file photo

This gated estate was right next door to the cottage where Russel Douglas was found murdered. A "person of interest" had once lived there, but the Island County investigators didn't know that when their homicide probe began.

Ann Rule

Patrol officers in Freeland, Washington, guarded the crime scene where Russel Douglas perished on the dark, rainy night of December 26, 2003. Detectives would need daylight to thoroughly search the woods around Douglas's yellow Tracker.

Police file photo

The driveway where Russel Douglas was shot. The morning after his body was discovered, Island County investigators found tire tracks that they hoped to link to a killer's vehicle.

Police file photo

Prosecuting Attorney Greg Banks and his paralegal assistant, Michelle Graff, worked together on what seemed to be an unsolvable—or, perhaps, unprovable—homicide case on Whidbey Island, Washington.

Leslie Rule

Island County Sheriff's Detective Mark Plumberg was assigned to lead the investigation into Russel Douglas's murder in mid-2004 and worked for nearly a decade on a case that appeared to have no motive, and no physical evidence. He never gave up and found a sad kind of justice for the victim.

Ann Rule

Jim Huden, the man his long-time friends knew. He was voted Businessman of the Year in Punta Gorda, Florida. Huden was student body president of his high school on Whidbey Island. He was also an athlete there, and later a computer genius who sold the software he developed to Bill Gates's Microsoft for a very high price.

Jim Huden had dealt with a number of discouraging issues in his life. He'd gone from rags to riches and back again, but he kept trying. The one influence he couldn't deal with was a beautiful woman with whom he was passionately in love.

Peggy Sue Thomas was very young when she married for the second time, but she seemed content helping Kelvin with his personal trainer profession and taking care of her baby girls.

Peggy Sue met Kelvin when they were both in the navy. They had two beautiful little girls together, and Kelvin always had Peggy's back—even long after their divorce when they were both with other people.

Peggy Sue always had a tendency to gain and lose weight. She was very heavy just before her second daughter was born when she, her half sister Brenda, and Kelvin attended a county fair. Brenda loved Peggy, but she was afraid of her, too.

Peggy Sue Thomas was a chameleon. She could easily go from plain and plump to a woman the media called "Drop-Dead Gorgeous." It was an eerie nickname, all things considered.

Vickie Boyer

Brenda Gard, Peggy Sue's half sister, was emotionally fragile, and family tragedies seemed to hit her harder than her siblings—especially when there were so many secrets. Even so, she was prepared to testify against someone close to her.

Rhonda Vogl

Even in her midteens, Peggy Sue Stackhouse fancied herself a seductive glamour girl.

At almost six feet tall, Peggy Sue was a natural at basketball. She was also well coordinated and was chosen to play on an all-male team. She continued to play, coach, and work out at her old high school with girls much younger than she was.

Rhonda Vogl

Wedding photo of "Sweet Sue" Mahoney and Neil Mahoney. After the Mahoneys suffered a terrible loss, Peggy Sue Thomas and Jim Huden met at a funeral wake and began a hot affair, one that would lead one day to more tragedy.

She was tall and statuesque, and Peggy Sue Thomas shone as she competed in the Ms. Washington pageant. She won and went on to another pageant in Las Vegas.

When she was in her thirties, Peggy Sue Thomas became a beauty pageant winner, a femme fatal, and embraced her "fiery red" period. She even had it on her license plate.

Police file photo

Peggy Sue was skilled in many areas— aircraft mechanic, beautician, basketball star, beauty queen, and entrepreneur.

After divorcing Kelvin Thomas, Peggy Sue moved to Las Vegas and was a very successful limousine driver. She kept files on what shows her clients liked, what they drank, the restaurants they preferred. She was beautiful, and most of her client list asked for her as their chauffeur.

Her sisters said that Peggy married Tony Harris, a preacher, just to make her father angry. Whether it was because Tony was black and Jimmie flew the Rebel flag, or for some other reason, no one knew. At any rate, the marriage didn't last long.

Jim Huden and Peggy Sue Thomas. Both had loved before, but their affair was so passionate that they seemed meant to be together . . . at first.

When Brenda Gard realized that her younger half sister was trying to totally control her life, she moved out of Peggy's Las Vegas home and headed back to Whidbey Island. Although it looks as if the sisters are drinking milk, they are really White Russians. Peggy drank a lot, but she could hold her liquor most of the time.

Brenda Gard

Mary Ellen Stackhouse, Jim's first wife, bore him six children. They were a very happy navy couple living in California in 1963 when a silent stalker broke into their home. Jim was far across the country attending training sessions.

Jimmie Stackhouse when he married his first wife, Mary Ellen. He built them a split-level house in San Jose, near Moffett Field, where he was stationed. Looking back, one has to wonder how many lives were impacted when Mary Ellen died.

Mary Ellen took her children to see the Easter Bunny. *Left to right:* Tom, Mike, Brenda, and Lana in about 1960. The pictures of their early lives were hidden from the children and their questions about where their mother was went unanswered. Jimmie thought it was best.

Rhonda Vogl

The Stackhouse children were all adorable, and their mother sewed their clothes and costumes for holidays. *From left to right, back row:* Tom, Rhonda, Mary Ellen, Jim, and Brenda. *Kneeling in front:* Lana and Michael. Robby hadn't been born yet.

Rhonda Vogl

After the heartbreak he suffered in San Jose, Jimmie Stackhouse asked for a change of duty to Whidbey Island, Washington. He hired Doris Alton as a housekeeper and married her a year later. They had a single child together—Peggy Sue Stackhouse—who had red hair like her father. He doted on her. His first six children often felt left out.

Rhonda Vogl

Doris Stackhouse was the complete homemaker. She could sew like a professional, bake, and kept a perfect house—with the help of two of her daughters and three stepdaughters. Peggy Sue was much younger. All of her siblings loved her, but they resented the special treats she got.

Rob was Mary Ellen and Jimmie's youngest child. He grew to be six feet, five inches tall. He died when he tried to take a gun away from a drunken partygoer, protecting the crowd that the gunman was aiming at.

Rhonda Vogl

Jimmie Stackhouse had six children with Mary Ellen, and one with Doris. Rob was deceased when this was taken. *Left to right, back row:* Jimmie, Mike, Tom. *Front, left to right:* Lana, Brenda, and Rhonda. Their family fell apart after their mother was killed, and their father remarried twice.

Rhonda Vogl

Doris and Jimmie pose with their combined family. *Back row left:* Amy, Tom, Jimmie, Lana, unknown. *Front row left:* Doris, Sue, Brenda, and Rhonda. Anyone looking in from the outside would have thought that Doris and Jimmie had a perfect family. That wasn't exactly true.

Rhonda Vogl

Rhonda Vogl researched the story of her mother's murder in California in 1963. She and her sisters, Lana and Brenda, finally learned the truth in 1995, and they located her grave. It had been thirty-two years since her death. Rhonda carried a wreath all the way from Idaho, and Brenda kneels next to Mary Ellen's tombstone.

Rhonda Vogl

Brenna Douglas, who never remarried after she was widowed, and the children she had with Russ: Jack and Hannah.

Gail O'Neal

Although the case stretched from December 27, 2003 to February 15, 2013, Island County Prosecutor Greg Banks and homicide Detective Mark Plumberg never forgot the man who was lured to his death in the lonely woods.

Police file photo

Vickie Boyer and Peggy Sue Stackhouse were from the two largest families on Whidbey Island. Vickie was grateful for Peggy's support when she came out of an abusive marriage, and felt she had a friend for life. They both moved to the Southwest; Vickie was always there for Peggy—but one day she lost faith in the woman she had admired so much.

Vickie Boyer

Peggy seemed thrilled when she told Vickie about a new man she'd met in Las Vegas—a limousine client. She thought he might have money—a lot of money—and she asked Vickie to do some background research on Mark Allen. He was wealthy, and it wasn't long before he and Peggy Sue were engaged. Their ceremony was Western themed all the way.

Vickie Boyer

Peggy Sue and her daughter Taylor pose for her friend Vickie's camera just before her third wedding.

Vickie Boyer

Happy at last! Peggy Sue was beautiful as she posed just before her wedding to Mark Allen in Roswell, New Mexico, in the summer of 2008.

Vickie Boyer

Vickie Boyer, now working for Mark Allen, pins a boutonniere on the father of the bride—Jimmie Stackhouse. Both he and his ex-wife, Doris, were pleased to see their daughter marrying so well. Russ Douglas had been dead almost five years, and Peggy had long since broken up with Jim Huden.

Vickie Boyer

Jimmie Stackhouse proudly leads his daughter down the aisle where she will say her wedding vows for the third and hopefully last time. In his seventies, Jim had aged markedly with each disaster in his life.

Vickie Boyer

Peggy Sue's wedding to multimillionaire Mark Allen was perfect, with wildflowers, gladioli, and sparkling lights, thanks to Vickie Boyer, who handled all the details for the cowboy ceremony, just as she had for Peggy for years.

Vickie Boyer

Mark Allen leans forward to kiss his bride after they were pronounced wed. It seemed that Peggy Sue finally had everything she had wished and planned for.

Vickie Boyer

Allen was fascinated by the tall, beautiful redhead from almost the first time they met. He may have had some doubts, however. In this photo, Peggy Sue looks triumphant, but Mark has a "My God, what have I done?" look on his face.

Vickie Boyer

Peggy Sue Stackhouse Harris Thomas Allen posed with her original, somewhat fractured family. Daughter Taylor; father Jimmie; Peggy; mother Doris Matz; half sister "Sweet Sue" Mahoney; niece; and older daughter, Mariah.

Vickie Boyer

The new bride poses with (*rear*) Vickie Boyer, Taylor Thomas, "Sweet Sue" Mahoney, Mariah Thomas, along with flower girls.

Vickie Boyer

Rhonda and Mitch Vogl visit their older sailor son on his ship, with their younger son (*between them*). Rhonda was baffled when she got an invitation to her half sister Peggy Sue's wedding. "We hadn't been in touch for a long time, and I had no idea who Mark Allen was. None of her half sisters did! We didn't go to her wedding."

Rhonda Vogl

Peggy Sue, *left*, was very tall with long legs. She dances here at a reception. Vickie Boyer is on the far right, and another guest is in the middle.

Vickie Boyer

Peggy Sue could always twist her father around her little finger.

Vickie Boyer

Jimmie Stackhouse today—in his log home in Idaho.
After a life full of tragedy and loss, he looks tranquil.
But looks can be deceptive and the Stackhouse family
has not seen the end of strife.

Although Jimmie Stackhouse's marital record was
spotty, he was always free with advice for his children
and their spouses. At first, Mark didn't complain.

Vickie Boyer

Peggy Sue Thomas confers with her attorney in an early court appearance.

Gail O'Neal, the victim's mother, gives her survivors' statement and begs Peggy Sue Thomas to tell what really happened when her son was shot to death on December 26, 2003. For everyone involved, the big question was: What was the motivation to kill Russel Douglas? Peggy Sue did not respond.

Leslie Rule

Peggy Sue walking into the courtroom at her sentencing. She passed Detective Mark Plumberg (*center*) without looking at him. She had never expected this to happen to her.

Leslie Rule

Peggy Sue listens as Russ Douglas's family begs her to give a motive for his violent death, but she said nothing.

Leslie Rule

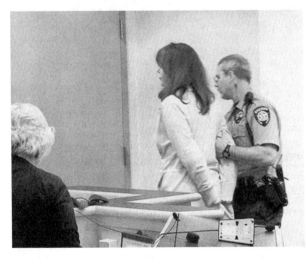

No longer free, Peggy Sue is led out of Judge Alan Hancock's courtroom in handcuffs.

Leslie Rule

On February 15, 2013, Peggy Sue Thomas talks to her attorney, Craig Platt, just before she is sentenced to prison for an extraordinarily short time in a murder case. Just behind her to the left is her daughter Mariah, and her ex-husband Kelvin Thomas.

Leslie Rule

Peggy Sue Thomas stands between her attorneys as Judge Alan Hancock pronounces her sentence for criminal assistance after the murder of Russel Douglas.

Leslie Rule

Superior Court Judge Alan Hancock was stern as he sentenced Peggy Sue Thomas, saying he regretted the Washington State statute that limited him to a shockingly short sentence. He urged her to tell the victim's family the truth.

Leslie Rule

Left to right: Island County Prosecuting Attorney Greg Banks, author Ann Rule, and Island County Sheriff's Office Detective Mark Plumberg, minutes after Peggy Sue Thomas was sentenced to prison in Judge Alan Hancock's courtroom.

Leslie Rule

Author Ann Rule, *left*, with Mark Plumberg at his home on Whidbey Island. Plumberg spent almost a decade tracking Russel Douglas's killer(s).

Peggy Sue Thomas in early 2013. She doesn't know yet what her future holds for her. Like *The Picture of Dorian Gray*, none of her devious plots show on her pretty face.

scene of Mary Ellen's murder that Tuesday, detectives went to the Thompson home. But there was no one there except for Gilbert's mother. She said her husband was a roofer, and Gilbert was, too, although he was employed by another company. They were both at work.

Mrs. Thompson was as upset and grieving as all the other neighbors the investigators had talked to. She offered again to take the Stackhouse children into her home until relatives arrived to care for them.

On Wednesday evening, Captain William McKenzie and Detective Sergeant John Mattern went back to the Thompsons' and asked to speak to Gilbert. By 9 P.M., it seemed clear to them that the sixteen-year-old had some guilty knowledge or involvement in the Stackhouse case. He and his father agreed quite willingly to go to headquarters to talk further, and if it was indicated, for the teenager to take a polygraph exam.

When the detectives spoke to Gilbert's father privately, they learned that the elder man had dealt with his son's oddly perverse sexual obsessions for a very long time. Eight years before—in 1955—the family had lived in Bakersfield. At the time his son was only eight, but Gilbert had been caught forcing a girl to strip as he pointed a knife at her.

Four years later, there was an incident in Missouri where the then twelve-year-old Gilbert was arrested for attacking a woman on the street, again with a knife. He was also accused of stealing from a teacher that year. Later, in Monterey, California, he was arrested for choking one woman and wrestling another to the ground.

"He used a knife in both of those attacks," his father finished grimly.

School authorities in Bakersfield had handled the first incident when he was eight. He seemed far too young to be dealt with by the police. There was no record of the events that had allegedly happened in Missouri four years later, and the San Jose detectives suspected that his juvenile record—if he even had one—had been shredded in Missouri.

Between some of the attacks against women, Gilbert Thompson had lied about his age and enlisted in the army. He wasn't very big, only about five feet, six inches tall and 140 pounds, and somehow he managed to convince recruiters that he was eighteen.

When he reoffended, the army quickly gave him an honorable discharge for "fraudulent enlistment," and turned him over to juvenile authorities in California.

There were more cases where he had been a suspect, but Gilbert Thompson had apparently avoided being in trouble with the law in San Jose County. If he was, he wasn't caught.

Or he was passed on to other agencies.

The salient factor, as far as Captain McKenzie and Sergeant Mattern were concerned, was that Gilbert Thompson had *never* submitted to any psychiatric counseling, or been placed in an institution.

And that was appalling.

If his attack on a fellow elementary school student when he was eight had happened in Santa Clara County—the county where he killed Mary Ellen Stackhouse—he would have been automatically referred to the Santa Clara County Juvenile Probation Department. There, he would have been seen by a psychiatrist and been given a battery of psychological tests.

In almost any case involving bizarre sexual acting out, a child like Gilbert would surely have been remanded for treatment to the children's section of Napa State Hospital.

Most sociopathic boys act out by the time they are five, usually by torturing animals or setting fires. Whether Gilbert would have been treatable at the age of eight, no one can say. It might well have been too late. But at least someone would have noticed a burgeoning social predator.

His parents had felt that he "was just going through a stage" in his early attacks. Moreover, they couldn't begin to afford the twenty-five dollars an hour that was the going rate for psychiatric treatment in the fifties and sixties.

With Mary Ellen Stackhouse's shocking murder, there were cries from the public, who blamed authorities, his parents, and the buck passing of different law-enforcement agencies for failing to treat Gilbert.

(Fifty years later, nothing much has changed. Blame for violent atrocities is still at the top of the

news, with much finger-pointing and little defini-
tive action.)

WHEN BILL MCKENZIE AND John Mattern joined
Gilbert Thompson himself for an interview, they
were surprised at how nondangerous he appeared.
He wasn't all that big, and looked smaller as he
slumped in a chair in the interview room. Gilbert
wasn't a bad-looking kid—he had wavy brown
hair, a sprinkling of freckles, and slight acne.

When he opened his mouth, however, Gilbert began to describe the fantasies that filled his
world. He said he'd had some homosexual encounters, but that he also thought a lot lately of
what it would be like to have forcible sex with
several women in his neighborhood. One of them
was Mary Ellen Stackhouse.

The teenager said he'd gone to bed in the garage
behind the family home. From there, a path led
through tall weeds about seventy-five feet to the
Stackhouse property. He wasn't able to fall asleep,
and he got up around 10:30, dressed, and crept
over to his potential victim's backyard.

When he tested the back door on the ground
level, he found it wasn't locked. He walked in,
moving silently past the two older boys—Tom and
Mike—who were sound asleep. Gilbert hadn't
brought any weapon with him, but he saw a hammer on a workbench on his way to the stairs that
led up to the living room.

He grabbed it.

As he reached the top of the stairs, he could see Mary Ellen sitting in an armchair, watching television, but she had her back to him and wasn't aware he was behind her—not at first.

And then there was some slight sound as he turned into the living room itself, maybe a creaking floor or even his own harsh breathing. Mary Ellen turned around, startled to see him inside her house.

"What are you doing here?" she shouted. "Get out!"

But he didn't leave. Thompson estimated that he then struck her on the head with the hammer at least seven times.

In his mind, there was no turning back. One of the women he'd assaulted in Monterey had identified him, gotten him into so much trouble that he was kicked out of the army. He didn't want any more trouble, so he went to the kitchen and found a steak knife.

"I cut her throat," he confessed to the detectives.

Then he carried out the rest of the obsession that had made him leave his bed and creep into the Stackhouse home. He ripped Mary Ellen's slacks off and raped her.

"I was very careful not to get any blood on my clothes," Gilbert added. "When I was done, I went to the bathroom on that floor and washed my hands. Then I went home and went back to bed."

Although he didn't mention exactly what his victim had done, the fact that Mary Ellen's body had been found at the top of the stairs leading to her daughters' bedrooms suggested that she had been fighting to save them, a mother lioness protecting her young, even as she died.

ON JUNE 7, 1963, Mary Ellen Stackhouse's funeral was held in the Darling-Fischer Garden Chapel with two Baptist ministers from churches she had attended performing the services. None of her children were there when Mary Ellen was buried in the Golden Gate National Cemetery.

That same day, Gilbert Thompson, his parents, probation officials, a court clerk, and a sole reporter attended a hearing regarding what jurisdiction would handle the teenager's trial. He was currently being held in Santa Clara County's Juvenile Hall. A further hearing was set for June 17 to determine if Thompson would be turned over to juvenile authorities or if he would face murder charges in superior court.

With his long history of sexual assaults, the latter seemed the best option. Gilbert Thompson's juvenile probation officer, P. R. Silva, described an early interview with him, a time when Silva had expected the teenager to show emotion or cry.

"Gilbert expressed regret over what he had done, particularly at leaving six children motherless, but he showed no physical signs of remorse."

The defendant hadn't cried or trembled. He neither blushed nor turned pale as he spoke of his vicious attack on Mary Ellen Stackhouse.

Gilbert first wanted to plead insanity, but then he decided to go for a trial.

Gilbert Thompson was charged as an adult in superior court, pleaded guilty, and was sentenced to life in prison. Because of his age, he would spend two years in a boys' reformatory before he was transferred to the California Men's Colony in San Luis Obispo.

He would be permitted to ask for a parole hearing every five years.

"This is one of my saddest days ever on the bench," the judge said. Gilbert Thompson didn't appear to share the judge's feelings. Instead, he motioned to the bailiff and asked, "Can you let me know the winner of the World Series game?"

He was only seventeen, but his sexual deviancy was deeply entrenched.

CHAPTER TWENTY-THREE

WHEN JIMMIE AND HIS six children arrived at Whidbey Island for his change of duty, he built a house for his family. Their Aunt Ellen opened her home to them until Jimmie had finished the new house. The navy gave him as much leave as it could, but eventually Jimmie had to go back to duty.

He hired a local woman, the divorced mother of two small daughters—Amy, who was four, and Sue, nine—to be a live-in housekeeper and take care of his children. Her name was Doris Alton née Anderson, and she was eight months older than Jimmie.

Physically, Doris was nothing like Mary Ellen. She was not a beauty as Jimmie's first wife had been, but rather a petite, average-looking woman. She wore her blondish-brown hair cut short and rolled up just below her ears and eschewed makeup.

But Doris pleased Jimmie with her ability at organization and homemaking. That was the most important thing to him as he tried to re-create at least the semblance of a normal household where he and his six children could move past the tragedy they lived through at Moffett Field.

Doris had just been divorced from her daughters' (Amy and Sue Alton) father, and she needed someone to help her raise them. Alton had signed away all of his legal rights to the girls.

Jimmie wasn't an outwardly affectionate man; he showed his love for his family by trying to provide everything physical that they needed.

Beyond his expertise in the navy, he was a man who could do virtually anything: carpentry, make furniture, and he was "smart as a whip" according to his children. He was a plumber, mechanic, and he had a photographic memory. Even so, he never could spell or sing.

He had built the fine house on Edgecliff Drive in Langley: seven bedrooms and three bathrooms. All by himself, he sanded, stained, and hung twenty-four mahogany doors.

When Jimmie poured cement for a window well, he let his children place their hands carefully in the wet cement, and then etched their initials beside the small handprints.

They are still there a half century later.

The Stackhouse children came to love Whidbey Island. Along with Sue and Amy, they rode their trikes and bikes all over the south end of the island, rushed down a well-worn trail to the beach every day where they scraped mussels off the pilings or caught minnows with fishing lines tied to their fingers—selling them to fishermen for bait. They swam like fishes themselves, bobbing in the waves. Langley was a small town then, where kids could count on free handouts from merchants: a cold hot dog from the Langley Meat Market or some treat from the grocer.

If there was anywhere the Stackhouse children could begin to feel safe and heal, Langley would have been the place.

Between Jimmie and Doris, they had eight children, all of them born between 1954 and 1961. Jimmie Stackhouse's new semifamily seemed to be the answer to how he could take care of his motherless children.

Jimmie was often out at night, going to bars and dating women. Doris told Rhonda how they decided to get married, but only after Rhonda was a grown woman.

"I waited up for him one night," Doris recalled. "When he finally got home, I told him, 'There's nothing out there that you can't get right here.'"

Within a year of Mary Ellen's murder, Jimmie married Doris. Their wedding picture is of the couple with all of their children clustered around them. It might have worked in a movie of that era starring Julie Andrews and Jimmy Stewart or Doris Day and Henry Fonda. All the elements for a fictional happy ending were there, but this was real life, and no matter how serene the Stackhouse family might have seemed to neighbors and Jimmie's navy buddies, it wasn't.

Like Mary Ellen before her, Doris kept a spotless house and was a great cook and seamstress. She was admired by those who lived in Langley for her self-sacrificing efforts to raise six motherless children along with her own two daughters. Still, the facade Doris Anderson Alton Stackhouse showed the world was only that—a facade.

No one can see through the outside walls of someone else's house, and Jimmie's children by Mary Ellen felt that they were always treated like second-class citizens to Doris's daughters.

"Doris put on airs," Rhonda recalls. "As if she was a loving, devoted mother—but she wasn't. There were many times when we realized that we didn't really matter to her.

"One time, we all missed the school bus. Our brothers and Lana, Brenda, and I started walking in the rain. Then we saw Doris's car, with Sue and Amy in it, but Doris drove right by us."

And soon, Doris was pregnant with Jimmie's child. She would be the only baby they had together. Peggy Sue Stackhouse was born on September 2, 1965.

She was an adorable baby with burnished auburn hair, much doted on by her father and her half siblings.

"I finally got my redhead," Jimmie crowed. He had always had flaming red hair, and he was covered with freckles from head-to-toe. But Peggy Sue was his first child to inherit those genes.

"Of course we loved her when she was little,"

Rhonda recalls. "But she was spoiled—and head-strong as she grew up."

With Peggy Sue's birth, Jimmie's older children moved another step down the ladder. "We were third best now."

Doris continued to impress people in Langley with her devotion to *all* her children. For reasons Mary Ellen's children never understood, she had their birth certificates changed, removing their natural mother's name, and replacing it with her own.

She was, in her stepchildren's opinion, "an angel on the street and a devil at home." Butter wouldn't melt in her mouth as she presented herself to the Langley community as a long-suffering stepmother who was doing her best to raise six children who weren't even hers. Some people saw her as heroic; others were suspicious of her saintly persona.

"She fulfilled our basic needs," Rhonda remembers. "We got all our shots, and went to the dentist regularly—but she didn't even try to meet our emotional needs."

Doris was such an exceptional seamstress that she won a contest and received a top-of-the-line sewing machine, a model used by professionals. She was an artist when it came to sewing.

She insisted that Jimmie's girls take sewing lessons—which they hated—but were later grateful for.

She also taught them how to maintain a perfect house. Lana, Brenda, and Rhonda were required to clean house on Tuesdays after school and all day Saturday. Doris wanted to be sure that all Jimmie's girls learned how to bake, although they barely knew the rudiments of cooking, and she didn't care if they couldn't cook plain food.

Jimmie's three oldest daughters had to clean house so thoroughly that even a hard-boiled army sergeant would approve. They had to scrub the bathroom tiles with a toothbrush until they were clean enough to suit their stepmother.

If Lana, Brenda, and Rhonda sometimes "forgot" to come home and clean on Tuesdays after school, there was hell to pay, just as there was when Doris disapproved of their decorum.

"One time," Rhonda remembers, "I fought back and sassed my half sister, Sue. Doris beat me with the vacuum cleaner cord. She also used a paddle with holes in it when she spanked us. I always wet my pants even before she started to hit me because I was so scared!"

Although they weren't exactly "Cinderellas," the older girls did not have a truly happy childhood. Her sisters remembered Mary Ellen, but Brenda still completely blocked the memory of the night in June when their mother was murdered. Mute for a long time, Brenda had finally begun to speak after many months on Whidbey Island.

But she didn't talk about her dead mother. And none of the children really knew what had happened to Mary Ellen. They recalled the blood and being wakened early by Tom and Mike, being lifted over a woman who didn't look like their mother, and the older ones recalled men with cameras and strobe lights.

As they grew older, they knew that Mary Ellen had been murdered, but they didn't dare ask about it for fear it would upset Jimmie.

Christmas was a time when Jimmie's children felt more left out than ever. "Sue, Amy, and Peggy Sue got *tons* of presents, and our stepmother never seemed to notice how unequal it all was—or maybe she did," Rhonda says. "I don't know what she was thinking."

Jimmie and Mary Ellen's six children got "one big gift" for all of them, a present from one of Jimmie's aunts.

Even then, Doris would give the present to Sue to "monitor" to be sure her stepchildren weren't too hard on whatever it was.

Jimmie's children got along fairly well with Doris's two daughters; Sue, sometimes called "Sweet Sue" with affection, was a nice girl. So was Amy, although she was shy and tended to fade into the background.

For a blended family, they may have fared better than many such relationships. Of them all, Peggy Sue was the one who was most indulged— the baby of the family.

Peggy was a chubby child, and Doris watched her closely, fearful that her beautiful baby girl might truly become fat. Peggy was allergic to eggs and chocolate, and she had to be on a special diet. Instead of milk, she drank Strawberry Quik. Peggy had sugar-free candy because she was allergic to chocolate. This wasn't really Peggy Sue's fault; she couldn't help having allergies—but Doris coddled her excessively.

"If I hurt myself," Rhonda said, "I didn't go to anyone for help—I just found a Band-Aid. It was the same for all of us. We knew she wasn't our *real* mother."

But Doris watched over Peggy Sue all the time.

"Once, Rob was spinning Peggy on his feet," Rhonda remembered. "They were laughing and having fun until she got launched into the air and broke her arm. My stepmother was livid."

Doris bragged about Sue and Amy when they earned good grades, but whenever Jimmie's kids got a D or an F, she told him, "That's *your* child—not mine."

Jimmie noticed that her own children got preferential treatment, and although he was seldom angry, he complained to Doris: "You draw a line down this family!"

Doris was a good manager of her household money and in handing out chores. Jimmie appreciated the comfortable home she kept. She liked the new house that Jimmie had built, but she had her eye on another house next to the one her new husband had provided. It was also on Edgecliff Drive. It was smaller, just an old—but quaint—farmhouse, and it wasn't big enough to hold their large family. Doris wanted Jimmie to buy it for her and their children. But it was something that Jimmie simply would not give her.

A long time in the future, Doris would have that farmhouse, although she wouldn't live in it with Jimmie Stackhouse.

Even though Tom, Mike, Lana, Brenda, Rhonda, and Robby were fond of Sue, Amy, and Peggy Sue, Jimmie's first children were all afraid of losing each other. They had already lost so much, as amorphous as their memories were, and dreaded some unknown danger that might attack one of them.

It doesn't take a trained psychiatrist to spot the reasons behind their anxiety. As the years passed, none of the children born to Mary Ellen Stackhouse ever found out exactly what had happened to her. She was there one night when they went to bed, and she was lost to them in the morning. Some of her six children remembered seeing her bloodied form on the floor, while others blocked that image or were too young to understand. A dark horror sometimes consumed them—especially Brenda. She still cried out in her sleep in terror.

She always would.

Wakened, she could not remember what her nightmare was about.

One morning when Brenda was ten, Rhonda nine, and Robby was six or seven, they waited for the school bus in the pouring rain. Suddenly, Robby broke away from his sisters and ran to get at the front of the line of students waiting to board. But he slipped on the loose gravel and puddles, and fell. The bus driver didn't see him, and drove the massive bus right over him.

The other youngsters shouted to her to "Get off of him!" totally confusing her so that she put the bus in reverse and backed over him.

"We thought he was dead," Rhonda says. "We had seen him pulling with his arms to try to get out from under the bus, and at first he was screaming. We got pushed onto the bus and Doris told us we had to go to school. No one would tell us how he was. The school called an immediate special assembly on bus safety, and we thought that meant for sure that Robby was dead.

"*Finally,* they got around to telling Brenda and me that Robby was alive, but he was in the hospital. He was hurt quite badly; his ankle was crushed and his shoulder was dislocated. He came home in a wheelchair with his injuries in casts. It took him several weeks to recover."

And, once again, the truth had been withheld from the Stackhouse children, which made them feel that they were standing on unstable ground.

Peggy Sue had a more solid childhood; she lived with her natural mother and father, all of her half siblings loved her, and she got virtually anything she asked for.

She had no awful memories to repress. Like Sue and Amy, Peggy Sue slept in the room next to Doris. If she had a bad dream, she could run to her mother and be comforted in seconds. Doris would always favor her youngest daughter.

Lana, Brenda, and Rhonda slept far away in another part of the house. When they had bad dreams or believed that someone—or something—was trying to get into their rooms, Doris pooh-poohed their anxiety, saying "Don't be silly."

Doris gave Rhonda a two-by-four and told her to shove it up under the doorknob. "And nothing can get you."

That didn't help. Many nights, they lay awake, frightened of what might be hiding in the dark.

Doris and Jimmie's marriage lost much of its luster as the years passed. The older children were in middle school and then high school. They were, of course, several grades ahead of Peggy Sue.

All of Jimmie's children were natural athletes, and even the girls excelled at basketball and baseball. Tom played football and basketball with his teammate Jim Huden. At that time, Jim was sixteen and Peggy Sue was only seven and their paths didn't cross.

Peggy Sue would be a basketball star when she reached high school, not just because she was six feet tall but because she was strong and graceful. She was the only girl in an Everett basketball league, and they were glad to have her.

"Peggy Sue was *good*!" Rhonda said.

Besides sports, Lana, Brenda, and Rhonda also developed an interest in the opposite sex. They were all pretty and popular, as were Doris's girls, Sue and Amy. It was probably ordained that little Peggy Sue would grow up fast and be eager to date.

Sometimes her rebelliousness was funny and sometimes it was troubling.

In her teens, Peggy Sue entered a Jell-O wrestling contest where she and her opponents wore bathing suits and jumped into a huge vat of orange Jell-O!

"We went to see that and it was hilarious," Rhonda recalls.

When she was fourteen or fifteen, Peggy often hitchhiked out of town—whether it was to go to a party or to run away, and she hitched a ride with the Wonder Bread man! She got home safely, and the Stackhouse girls—Peggy included—laughed about it for years.

Rhonda remembers that Peggy once asked her to lie and give her an alibi. She had a date with a much older boy. She needed a reason to stay out late, and wanted Rhonda to say she was staying overnight with her. But Rhonda shook her head. She was not going to lie for her baby sister.

A few years after that, Jimmie and Doris Stackhouse were obviously becoming estranged. She was gone a lot, leaving his older girls to run the house, but she eventually came home.

Jimmie retired from the service as a Master Chief when he was thirty-nine and relocated to his former home state of Idaho in 1973. He bought a home in Bonner's Ferry. That house burned to the ground, and Jimmie set about building a very large log cabin–style home. His son Tom helped him. It was almost as if Jimmie hoped that a strong house, built with his own hands, could keep his family safe.

Doris didn't like it there and there were other arguments. She wanted to be close to her family on the coast—her mother, brother, and sister. Shortly thereafter, she moved back to Bellingham and the couple split up. They filed for a legal separation and then divorced. Doris and Peggy Sue moved to Bellingham, Washington.

In 1984, both Jimmie and Doris remarried— Doris to a wealthy older man named Paul Matz, and Jimmie to his third wife, Terry Little. The log house Jimmie and Tom built burned down, too. Undeterred, Jimmie built another log house, larger than the last.

And Paul Matz bought the farmhouse on Edgecliff Drive on Whidbey Island that Doris had always wanted.

Doris and Jimmie's divorce was hardest on the most sensitive members of the family, Amy and Brenda. Amy was so upset about it that she lost control of her mother's car on the way to high school one morning and wrecked it. Fortunately, she survived with slight injuries.

Shortly after high school graduation, Amy married Mr. DeBoer and soon gave birth to six children, one after the other.

Although Doris had taught Jimmie's girls to bake, they really couldn't cook—but Lana, Brenda, and Rhonda learned fast.

Before he settled down with Terry, Jimmie was

single for a time. He was still a ruggedly handsome man, much sought after by single women. It was he who taught his girls how to cook the basic things they needed to know. They were, of course, already adept at baking.

"We did the shopping, too," Rhonda recalls. "My dad would give us money to buy groceries and he didn't seem to mind when we bought other things we needed from the market—mascara, shampoo, makeup.

"I remember cooking my first Thanksgiving dinner when I was sixteen. It turned out fine, except no one told me to take the bag of giblets out of the turkey before I roasted it."

When Jimmie Stackhouse married Terry Little in December 1984, his tally of children expanded once again. He was now stepfather to Jason, twelve, Tiffany, ten, and Josh, nine. That made an even dozen children that Jimmie had supported during his adult years.

He cared about them all, but Jimmie and his offspring had suffered through another tragic homicide almost two years before he married Terry. Rob Stackhouse, twenty-one, the last baby that Mary Ellen gave birth to, had joined the navy right out of high school. He was a big man—six feet, five inches and about 250 pounds. Rob was handsome, blond, and easygoing, as big men often are; Rob had nothing to prove and was a gentle giant.

On January 21, 1983, shortly after he was mustered out of the service, Rob attended a house party in Alaska. Despite his misgivings, Rob agreed to an arm-wrestling contest with another of the male guests who had clearly had too much to drink. Of course, Rob won easily and the loser was enraged. He pulled out a gun and began to fire wildly at the house, over the heads of partygoers.

Afraid the man might actually hit someone, Rob lifted him up by his armpits, took away his gun, and placed it on a car hood. He struck the drunk in the chest to get his full attention, and said, "You're gonna kill somebody!"

Humiliated and angered further, the shooter pulled another gun out of his belt.

Rob had no idea it was there. In a split second, the shooter pulled the trigger on his second gun and fatally wounded Rob Stackhouse.

Once again, murder had struck the Stackhouse family. Rob's life had barely begun, he had never married, and he was one of the kindest members of their family. His death hit them all hard.

Rob and Peggy Sue were close in age, only a little over three years apart. When Rob was killed, she was seventeen and living in Bellingham with Doris, her parents long since divorced.

Tragically, Jimmie and his third wife, Terry, lost her son—Josh—when he, too, was twenty-one. Jimmie had raised Josh since he was in fifth or sixth grade and loved him as he did his biological sons. Josh was killed in a fiery car crash in Salt Lake City in 1995.

Jimmie's red hair turned stark white as he tried

to deal with losing so many people he cared about to violence.

And the world moved on.

AMY HAD MARRIED IN 1978, Rhonda in 1980, Lana in 1981, Brenda, Mike, and Sue in 1987, and Tom in 1989. Several of Jimmie's children would go on to happier second marriages, although Amy Alton DeBoer's marriage lasted. Lana Galbraith never remarried after she divorced Steve Galbraith. Peggy Sue married Tony Harris, a preacher in a somewhat different religion than her Baptist roots, but it didn't last long. Tony was black and, jokingly, Peggy told her half sisters that she married Tony just to get her father's goat. They believed her. She had always said she was going to marry a black man just to "bug" her father. Jimmie Stackhouse had always hung both an American and a Rebel flag on his property.

It was getting more difficult to keep the family together, although all the Stackhouse daughters worked hard at it. Rob was gone, of course, and Tom and Mike married and drifted far away— Tom to California and Mike to Connecticut and then Virginia. For a time, Tom seemed to disconnect from his father and siblings. After he helped Jimmie build his first log house in Idaho, many years passed between Tom's visits home to the Northwest. He would reconnect one day when his family was in chaos. Mike tried to call Jimmie once a week.

Most of the girls—now women—stayed close,

and family photo albums filled up with pictures of them and their husbands and many children.

Peggy Sue followed in her father's footsteps; she joined the navy in 1988. She had always done well at whatever she chose to do. Once more, she played basketball in the navy, and also became a highly skilled aircraft mechanic before she was honorably discharged in 1992.

Peggy Sue had met and married Kelvin Thomas in 1991 while she was still in the navy. Kelvin, too, was African American, but he wasn't anything like Tony. Compared to Peggy's first husband, Kelvin was a nice, normal guy, who was well respected on Whidbey Island. He and Peggy talked of having a family, and tried to find a way to have more than a paycheck-to-paycheck financial situation. They hoped to have a lot of money one day, and they tried various avenues to get there.

While Kelvin got a job as a cook in a Denny's restaurant, they once joined a class-action suit to sue Denny's for racial discrimination, and Kelvin probably got a modest settlement. The couple were living in Jacksonville, Florida, but they applied for jobs at B.F. Goodrich in Washington, and they were both hired. They moved home to Whidbey Island just after Mariah was born.

Kelvin Thomas's business as a personal trainer was going well. They were both athletically inclined. Peggy still worked out at Langley High School, exercising and both playing and coaching basketball with girls much younger than she was.

Many of her glory days as a teenager had revolved around her skill at that sport.

Peggy was no longer fragile; she had grown to be a very large woman, standing over six feet tall in her bare feet, but she was perfectly proportioned as long as she watched her weight carefully. She was Amazonian—and extremely attractive to most men who met her.

Peggy and Kelvin had one daughter—and then a second—and they proved to be good parents to Mariah and Taylor, both of whom had red-blondish curly hair, adorable faces, and high intelligence.

Peggy Sue told her half sisters that a photo of Mariah reading a book, her chin propped on her hands, was chosen by Oprah Winfrey herself as the model for a statue she had commissioned to encourage children to read.

They didn't know if that was true or not.

But that was Peggy; she was a chameleon—both in her life and her looks. In some photographs, she had a slender figure and a sculptured, perfect face. In others, particularly her pregnancy pictures, her features appeared bloated and her midsection big enough to carry triplets.

Peggy did put on a lot of weight during her pregnancies, expanding so much that she didn't look at all like the "fiery red" woman who would emerge later as glamour personified. Peggy Sue had fought weight her whole life, but when she was slim she was gorgeous.

"Drop-Dead Gorgeous," as the news media would nickname her.

One day, Island County prosecuting attorney Greg Banks would comment that she was a woman who was capable of continually "reinventing herself."

That was certainly true.

But no one could ever say that Peggy Sue wasn't loved, however she looked or whoever she was. She sometimes complained, however, that her father didn't show her enough affection. Her half sister Rhonda told her to quit worrying about it, saying, "Dad is just Dad." Kelvin loved her, although she suspected that he sometimes strayed. Jimmie continued to dote on his "precious baby girl," and in his eyes, Peggy Sue could do no wrong, but he wasn't demonstrative. She was still tightly bonded to her mother, who had always treated her like a princess.

Wherever Peggy was, Doris Alton Stackhouse Matz was there, too. They were almost a matched set, a duo that drew "Do not cross" borders around their world.

Jimmie's first three daughters still resented the way Doris shut them out just as she had when they were children.

"The straw that broke my back," Rhonda says, "was how Doris favored Peggy's two girls over all of our kids. One time, I was over at Peggy's with Brenda's son, Kyle Gard, and Doris came over to get Mariah and Taylor, Peggy's daughters. She was going to take them to the beach, and she said, 'Come on, girls—we're going to the beach!'

"She didn't ask Kyle and he was just heartbroken. He stood in the driveway, holding his arms out and crying as they drove away. That was when I knew for sure that *we* would always be third place in Doris's world."

Nevertheless, all the half sisters remained in what looked like a solid family unit with birthday parties, baby showers, weddings, and other get-togethers. They filled countless scrapbooks with photographs, newspaper clippings, and mementos. When she was in town, Peggy Sue was almost always in those celebrations. Usually, her half sister Sue was the driving force to keep their wildly blended family close. Sue undertook the task of writing a kind of family tree with all their births, marriages, and deaths noted.

In their case, it *was* difficult to follow the action without a "scorecard."

Peggy Sue and Kelvin didn't become rich overnight, but they were doing quite well.

Peggy excelled in her job in Everett with B.F. Goodrich, and soon became the first woman ever promoted to lead mechanic with the company. She liked her job, but she quit, saying that she wanted to spend more time with her daughters.

She also went to beauty school, and earned her beautician's license in Idaho. She worked at a number of Langley salons: Atelier, Studio A, and opened her own salon—Baker Street Hair Theater. During tourist season, there were any number of wealthy women who sought out island beauty salons.

Peggy Sue sometimes helped Kelvin with the clients in his personal trainer business. In time, they made enough to buy a house in Langley, the house that Peggy would one day rent to Brenna Douglas.

ON JUNE 20, 1987, Doris's oldest daughter, "Sweet Sue," was married for the second time. Her first, very young marriage hadn't worked out. But this was a joyful wedding and reception. Her half sisters were happy to attend. Sue and Neil Mahoney were a true love match. Sue was in her early thirties and it was a wonderful happy occasion. They had found the loves of their lives. Sue brought a son into their marriage and they soon had a daughter together.

Neil, forty-four, grew up in West Seattle. When he graduated from high school in 1971, he worked and studied until he became a journeyman wireman, and belonged to the International Brotherhood of Electrical Workers union, and also taught electrical apprentices. He loved sports of all kinds and was an avid bicycle enthusiast. He also played the trombone and guitar.

That was probably how he connected to Jim Huden, playing in some of the bands Jim put together. As it is with many small communities, there were many connections among Whidbey Island residents.

Doris's oldest daughter was the "Sweet Sue" whom Jim Huden often visited on his trips home from Florida, but he wasn't able to attend Sue and Neil's wedding.

Jim might also have known of Peggy Sue before. Still, she was so much younger than he that they were like two sailboats tacking away from one another.

And, of course, when Peggy married Kelvin four years after the Mahoneys' wedding, Jim was far away in Florida, wed to his second wife, Jean.

If they had never met, it might have—probably would have—been better for everyone.

Sue and Neil Mahoney were to have only five years together. Two weeks after their fifth wedding anniversary, Neil wasn't at his job with an electric company, but he agreed to do a favor for his boss. He rode his bike to pick up his employer's van, and then delivered it to a garage for a regular maintenance check. Neil retrieved his bike from the van and headed for home in Edmonds.

A car struck him, leaving him in critical condition with multiple injuries. Sue had to make a decision that no loving wife should ever have to make. Neil was in a coma and showed no brain activity. She finally agreed to have him taken off the breathing machine and he died. He was only forty-nine.

Jim Huden was anguished when he got the news and he headed for Neil's memorial service and wake as quickly as he could. On June 8, 2002, after gathering a band from among some of their old friends, Jim played and sang at both the Edgewood Baptist Church service and the Irish wake afterward.

Peggy Sue was there, of course. Sue, the widow, was her half sister. Everyone had loved Neil Mahoney and the enormity of his tragic death drew so many friends and relatives that the memorial service and wake were crowded wall-to-wall.

Although they had always moved on the periphery of each other's lives, Jim Huden and Peggy Sue Thomas were so far apart in age in their younger years. He was a man when she was still a child. Now they were drawn to one another on this sad day in June. The spark lit then, even in the midst of mourning, was impossible not to notice. They were both married to other people, but that didn't seem to matter.

The air between them fairly crackled with electricity and mutual attraction.

Even so, both of them stayed married to other people for a time, but they were together every chance they got.

When Peggy found out that her husband, Kelvin, was also having an affair, she was shocked. He was dating a woman older than she was! That stung. It may have been the first time a man ever walked away from her. For all intents and purposes, their marriage was over and they divorced.

It was a friendly divorce and both of them continued to put their daughters, Taylor and Mariah, first, sharing custody and parenting decisions.

No matter that Peggy and Kelvin went their separate ways with new partners, Kelvin always had Peggy Sue's back.

CHAPTER TWENTY-FOUR

PEGGY SUE STILL SMARTED over the fact that Kelvin had chosen another woman over her. She needed to validate her own attractiveness. And she needed a female "wing woman" to help her achieve something big that would restore her confidence.

For a while in 2002, Peggy Sue and Cindy Francisco were best buddies. They always attended shows at the China City comedy night. It didn't take long for the crowd to notice them. Peggy Sue often heckled the comic onstage. They sat in front and got up frequently and left to order drinks, making themselves the center of attention.

Finally, one comedian decided to put a stop to all the interruptions during his routine. While the two women were out of the room, he asked the crowd to laugh at them when they came back.

"You don't need a reason," he directed. "But I need a break; just laugh out loud when they come back in."

The crowd obeyed, and Peggy Sue and Cindy couldn't figure out what was so funny. The third time this happened they didn't enjoy all the attention and their prancing in and out slowed down.

The restaurant was very popular in Freeland, and the building that housed it was large and impressive. It attracted many locals. It still does.

Cathy Hatt and her husband, Dean, lived next door to Dick Deposit's second house, and they watched over it when Deposit was away on one of his frequent trips. They handed out the key if Deposit told them whom to expect.

The Hatts were also frequent diners at China City and Dean often sang along on Karaoke Night. They watched as Peggy Sue flirted with men sitting at the bar.

"I saw her move in on one of my friend's boyfriends one night," Cathy recalls. "My friend was in the ladies' room and Peggy was all over her boyfriend when she came back. I actually thought there was going to be a fight." When Cathy's friend objected to Peggy Sue's physical advances to *her* fiancé, Peggy Sue stood up and turned around slowly, showing off her figure, and then she said, "Why would he want you when he could have this?"

Peggy Sue ran her hands seductively over her body and posed, and it took Cathy and several of their friends to stop a catfight. Peggy didn't care; she just laughed.

Cathy Hatt recalls one early summer evening.

"We were at a fiftieth birthday party for Ron Young—down on the beach—and Jim Huden was there. There were tents put up so no one would have to drive home drunk afterward. Peggy arrived later. Most of us thought she had her eye on Dick Deposit, but one of my friends said, 'No, she's with someone else. I can't tell you who it is.'"

Cathy didn't have to ask who it was. An hour or so later, she saw Peggy Sue crawling out of Jim Huden's tent, carrying a half-empty bottle of Royal Crown. "It was only about eight or nine in the evening, but she was very drunk."

Cathy is petite, and standing next to six-foot-tall Peggy, she looked even smaller.

"Peggy never seemed to remember me," Cathy said. "Dean and I were sharing a night out with Dick Deposit at China City, and I found myself standing next to Peggy Sue.

"She looked down at me, and she had a really condescending tone in her voice when she said, 'Do I know you?'

"I told her who I was, and she wasn't impressed. A week or so later, she was standing next to me again, and again, she asked me, 'Do I know you?' I just gave up—and said, 'No, you don't.'"

When Peggy Sue figured out that Cathy and Dean Hatt were friends of Jim Huden, she was nicer to them.

After Peggy and Jim moved to Las Vegas, one day she went to pick him up at the airport.

"She had rented a Mercedes Benz and was

wearing a tight, one-piece, black leather outfit," Cathy said. "She told me, 'All I'm wearing to the airport is a can of whipped cream.'"

Cathy remembered Jim and Peggy driving up to Dick Deposit's house on or about December 19, 2003. Rather, she saw Peggy.

"She told me that Jim was really, really sick that night. I never did actually see him on that Christmas trip. After they left," Cathy said, "Dick Deposit called me to ask if they had left his house key with Dean or me. And I really don't think they did."

Peggy could turn on the charm and seduce anyone she aimed for—both men and women. She wasn't interested in women sexually—not at all—and she had few women friends. But she usually had a *best* friend. One or another "best friend forever" came and went in her life.

There were two very large families in Langley—the Stackhouses and the Boyers. Vickie Boyer's mother bore eighteen children—outnumbering even Jimmie's brood.

Vickie was one of the younger children and she was sickly. No one in her family expected her to live long. When Clifford Peerenboom proposed to her, she was only fourteen. Her mother knew she was too young—but then she felt Vickie probably wouldn't live beyond nineteen or twenty and deserved to have some kind of a life. Vickie married Clifford and she didn't die; instead she suffered through a long and controlling marriage. As the nineties began, she had finally gathered the courage to divorce her husband. When Peggy Thomas befriended her, it made Vickie feel happier and more secure. She dropped her married name at once and went back to her maiden name. She and Peggy Sue were both coming out of the end of their marriages, and it seemed that they had so much in common.

Peggy, who stood a head taller than Vickie, was the confident one, and Vickie was more dependent after so many years in her emotionally abusive marriage.

Despite warnings from one of her sisters, Vickie and Peggy became close friends within a short time.

When Peggy made up her mind to enter the Ms. Washington contest, Vickie helped in any way she could; she raised money, distributed signs, and got Peggy as much publicity and media interest as she could.

Vickie was almost as thrilled as Peggy Sue was when she won the beauty pageant. They had done it together, and their friendship was solid as a rock. At least it seemed so to Vickie Boyer.

Peggy Sue Thomas's photograph appeared on television and in any number of newspapers. She wore a figure-clinging gown and the sparkling rhinestone crown on her head seemed made for her. She was in her glory.

The next step was a pageant in Las Vegas. Peggy entered the 2000 Ms. U.S. Continental Pageant. During the question-and-answer part of the pageant, Peggy Sue seemed self-assured as she described herself as a "trailblazer" who followed her own path.

"Women have to know it's okay to do things out of the norm," she told the judges. "They should set an example for their children. [That is] the greatest ethical challenge facing women today with all the violence, sex, and drugs in the media."

Peggy looked beautiful in her pale purple formal and four-inch pumps, and she won the evening gown competition.

But she didn't take first place in the pageant held in Las Vegas.

Peggy was anxious to get off Whidbey Island. She was skilled at many things, but she sought genuine affluence, not something that a beautician or a mechanic could earn. Peggy longed to be rich. It was nice to have her "Ms. Washington" title, but that would run out in a year.

She had persuaded a tall, handsome male friend who had a solid position at Microsoft to loan her seventy-five thousand dollars. Peggy needed "seed money"—money for her next transformation. The glitter in Las Vegas seemed like real gold and actual diamonds and she set her sights on moving there as soon as possible.

VICKIE BOYER MOVED TO Texas in 2002 to do some training for the company she worked for— the CVS pharmacy chain. Shortly thereafter, Peggy

Sue and Jim Huden were in the Southwest, too. By the summer of 2003, the couple were living in a high-priced rental house.

Peggy's two daughters, who were now twelve and ten, were living with them, but spending time with Kelvin Thomas during vacations and holidays.

Vickie still considered Peggy Sue to be her best friend, and she came to Las Vegas to visit Peggy and Jim in September 2003. While there she met another Whidbey Island expatriate.

Scott Mickelsen appealed to her, and she saw him often during the visit. She seriously considered moving to the gambling city.

When she came back in November, Vickie spent more time with Scott and she made plans to move to Las Vegas as soon as she could. Peggy said that Vickie was welcome to stay with her. Her house was big enough for a number of guests and her half sister, Brenda Gard, lived with her for a while, too.

Peggy and Jim, who seemed to be doing very well, were actually living on credit cards and the money Peggy had borrowed. Their economic situation grew tighter every month. To their disappointment, Las Vegas streets were not paved with gold after all.

Vickie Boyer moved into their large rental home on Christmas Day 2003. A few days later, Peggy Sue and Jim returned from their trip to Whidbey Island. They seemed exhausted from the drive, and didn't say much about their Christmas trip to Washington State.

Jim Huden didn't stay in Las Vegas very long. He told the two women that he was going back to Florida.

"They had run out of money, and Jim said he was going to go to Punta Gorda, but when he came back, he would have a lot of money with him," Vickie said. "I figured he was going to liquidate his business or something."

Jim and Jean Huden had run a successful business in the computer industry, but it had long since fallen fallow due to Jim's disinterest.

Peggy had to find some way to make money, too, because she and Jim were dangerously close to maxing out their credit cards. Soon, with neither of them working, they wouldn't even be able to pay the rent.

As the months passed, it became obvious that Jim Huden probably wasn't coming back at all and that he'd gone back to his wife, Jean. His once-thriving computer support company had perished from neglect, and he had no business left to liquidate.

Before Huden fell in love with Peggy Sue, he was voted "Businessman of the Year" in Punta Gorda. But now his life had crumbled into ashes.

He was a man filled with anxiety. He told his Florida friends that he longed to go back to Las Vegas and Peggy Sue—but he didn't leave Punta Gorda.

He and Peggy Sue had been "passionately" in love, according to most of their friends. Their mutual attraction was so intense that it had seemed they would give up whatever they had just to be together. Peggy had divorced Kelvin, and Jim seemed ready to split from Jean.

What could have happened to keep Jim from flying back to Las Vegas? He had told Bill Hill that he intended to fly back to the gambling city.

Why had Peggy let their relationship end so bleakly? Was she afraid contact with Jim might entangle her in a murder plot?

Jim was afraid of something, but none of his buddies in Florida knew what it was. Jim and Jean Huden did a lot of drugs, but an arrest for possession of illegal substances wasn't *that* intimidating, especially in the crowd of musicians that Jim ran with.

Something, however, was haunting Jim Huden. His band members—the X-hibitionists—were growing annoyed with him because he missed so many gigs and practices.

CHAPTER TWENTY-FIVE

PEGGY HAD TOLD DETECTIVES that she and Jim stayed at Dick Deposit's home during the 2003 Christmas holidays. All of his friends knew that Deposit, a certified public accountant, was meticulous and paid great attention to the smallest details. If anyone would remember the most minute aspect of his friends' visit, it would be Deposit. Now, on August 13, 2004, Plumberg went to Deposit's apartment to interview him. Dick Deposit said he'd known Jim Huden since they were in fourth grade together. Peggy Thomas's half sister, Sue Mahoney, was a dear friend of his. Deposit was aware that Jim had left his wife, Jean, months before, and moved to Las Vegas so he could be with Peggy.

The accountant didn't live in his house on Soundview Drive, but he often spent weekends there, usually with guests. And he allowed his friends to stay there. He left a key to the house with Dean and Cathy Hatt, and asked those who stayed in his guest room to return the key to the Hatts when they left.

"The only person who goes to my house alone, though, is my girlfriend," Deposit said. "Sometimes she goes there with her friends."

Deposit had heard the accusations and rumors about Peggy Sue Thomas and Russel Douglas's puzzling murder. Almost everyone connected to either Peggy or Jim had.

"Did Peggy deny those allegations?" Plumberg asked.

"My feeling was that she thought it was a total fabrication," the accountant answered.

Deposit said he hadn't seen Jim since the previous December, but he had seen Peggy a few weeks before at Sue Mahoney's birthday party.

"I think I saw both Peggy and Jim during the week of Christmas—probably that Sunday, the twenty-first," he said. "Jim, Peggy, Sue Mahoney, and her daughter were all at my Soundview house for dinner."

Asked if he'd gone to his house any other time that week, Dick Deposit thought he had probably dropped in on Christmas Eve.

"Do you have a room there that you've set aside for the guest room?"

Deposit nodded.

"Did you check the house to see if everything was okay?"

"I probably looked around. I usually do."

"Did you have to make the bed in the guest room?"

"I don't recall that—no. But I think I would have noticed if the bed wasn't made."

That was on December 24—a day after Peggy Sue Thomas and Jim Huden left the island. And yet, when they said they'd come back to leave the key on the twenty-sixth, Peggy Sue had been emphatic about having to dry the sheets and make the bed in the guest room.

It was another *small* disparity, but the string of events had more and more gaps with question marks.

PLUMBERG DECIDED TO CLOCK the time and distance between the Marriott Hotel near Sea-Tac Airport to Douglas's apartment in Renton. Although they had yet to find any present that either Jim or Peggy—or both—had given Russ, each had indicated that they had traveled from the hotel to the Mission Ridge Apartments. Peggy Sue's version was that Jim had left the Marriott headed for Russ's apartment, but had called within ten minutes saying he couldn't find it.

That was strange. The location was easy to find, particularly for someone who had lived in the Seattle area for years.

When Mark Plumberg did test drives in normal traffic conditions, he found one route was 9.3 miles and took twenty-one minutes. The alternate route was 5.6 miles and required twelve minutes' travel time.

Next, he drove from Dick Deposit's Soundview

Drive home to the crime scene on Wahl Road. The distance was only 5.1 miles. Peggy had recalled that Jim left to get "smokes," while she dried the guest room sheets and made the bed. In her first statement, she said Jim was gone for a half hour to forty-five minutes. Later, she corrected herself and told Plumberg that Huden had been gone only fifteen minutes.

With a search warrant, Plumberg obtained Jim Huden's December credit card bill. All the places he had used it correlated with his and Peggy's travels on December 26. They were in Washington all day, traveling up and down I-5. By the twenty-seventh, a credit card slip showed that they bought gas at a Chevron station in Fresno, California. This would have been on their way back to Las Vegas.

Jim Huden was no longer living with his wife, Jean, in Punta Gorda. When he left the first time in September, it wasn't for good; he had simply taken a weekend trip, and soon neighbors saw his red car back in the Hudens' driveway.

But he was definitely gone a month or so later. No one in Florida recalled seeing him for weeks. Nor had he been seen in the Las Vegas area.

Jean Huden claimed to have no knowledge of where he was, although she evinced concern that he might have been depressed enough to commit suicide.

If he was alive, she was one of the most likely people who might have heard from him. Detectives wondered if it was possible that Peggy Sue had, too.

Gerald Werksman, Peggy's attorney, was present on August 30, 2004, when Shawn Warwick, Ed Wallace, Sue Quandt, and Mike Beech went to Henderson, Nevada, for yet another interview with Peggy.

Peggy told them she was sure that Russ Douglas and Jim had never met each other until December 23, 2003, when they took the gift to him for Brenna.

Warwick asked Peggy about the gun that they had shown her photos of the day before. "I did not know about the gun," she said.

He asked Peggy if she saw the gun go from Jim's hands to "another person" who then gave the gun to the New Mexico sheriff.

"I did not. I did not see a gun," she said firmly. "I may have seen a pouch with a gun in it in February of this year."

ON SEPTEMBER 15, 2004, Brenna Douglas came into the Island County Sheriff's office in Langley carrying a huge wicker basket trimmed with ribbons, and filled with an assortment of fancy soaps, oils, and brushes. She explained that this was the gift she had received from Peggy Thomas. She said she thought she got it on Christmas Day from Peggy Sue herself, but she wasn't sure.

During September 2004, Mark Plumberg was able to get a temporary felony warrant and a

BOLO (be on the lookout) alert as Jim Huden had seemingly vanished.

And then the holiday season was once again approaching. On December 13, Mark Plumberg filed a follow-up report, saying, "I believe there is probable cause for the arrest of James E. Huden (b. 8/26/53) for the First Degree Murder—RCW 9A.32.030—of Russel A. Douglas (b. 9/09/71)."

Soon it would be the first anniversary of Russ Douglas's murder. Christmas lights in the small towns on Whidbey Island seemed to mock Plumberg, reminding him that his "persons of interest" were still walking free, and that one of them had disappeared completely.

CHAPTER TWENTY-SIX

ALWAYS RESOURCEFUL, PEGGY SUE Thomas had landed on her feet just as she found herself really broke in Las Vegas.

Vickie Boyer's boyfriend, Scott Mickelsen, recommended Peggy Sue to a company that operated an upscale limousine service. And she proved to be a natural. She drove wealthy clients and celebrities, and after one ride, most of her customers asked for her the next time they were in town. It didn't hurt that her business cards were very seductive. Wearing a blouse cut down to her waist, Peggy Sue posed for her cards, draping herself over one of the limos.

Before long she had a file full of prospective clients. They weren't just men. Several couples always asked for her when they came to Las Vegas.

It wasn't particularly unusual for Peggy to get a thousand-dollar tip. She kept track of the restaurants, hotels, and extras that her repeat clients enjoyed. She provided expensive liquor, snacks, and other sought-after items in the limo she drove.

Vickie Boyer looked after Peggy Sue's daughters, since Peggy was often working until six in the morning. Taylor and Mariah were used to their mother's involvement in other matters, but they also knew she loved them devotedly.

Her half sister Brenda had watched her nieces when she lived with Peggy in Las Vegas, and after she left, Peggy hired a series of women to watch over her daughters. Unfortunately, none of the sitters and housekeepers lasted more than a month before they quit.

Vickie was shocked when she saw what was probably Peggy's biggest tip or perhaps a gambling win: eighty-five hundred dollars in one-hundred dollar bills was stacked neatly on Peggy's dresser.

Whatever else she might be engaged in, Peggy adored her two daughters and they felt the same about her. "She has always loved her girls," Vickie recalled. "And so does Kelvin. The girls are pretty, smart, and well behaved, for the most part. But when Brenda lived with her and she did something that Peggy had forbidden, they tattled on her."

Both Rhonda Vogl, Peggy's half sister, and Vickie Boyer recalled that Brenda was "afraid" of Peggy. Peggy was probably more domineering with Brenda than she was with anyone. It got to the point where Brenda had to wait to make her morning coffee until Peggy said she could. She lasted about six months before she fled Nevada and returned to Whidbey Island.

Peggy Sue Thomas was a complicated mix of both good and bad traits. Once she got on her feet financially, she could be very generous to someone who might be down on his or her luck.

Vickie Boyer was sorry, though, to hear Peggy brag about how kind and giving she was. She seemed incapable of doing good deeds without taking credit for it.

At one point, Peggy read about a girl who couldn't afford a dress for her high school prom, and she arranged for her to have a four-hundred-dollar formal and a limo to arrive in. It *was* a very kind gesture.

"It sort of spoiled the picture of her being so benevolent to people," Vickie said wryly. "If she had just given someone something and kept it to herself, it would have been better. But she had to toot her own horn all the time. She told a lot of people about the poor girl who needed a dress and how she had stepped forward."

When Vickie Boyer was setting up a new house, Peggy Sue gave her a lot of her own used furniture. Again, it was a helpful gift and Vickie was grateful.

"But," Vickie said, "when anyone complimented me on how nice my house looked, Peggy just had to say, 'I gave her that,' or, 'That used to be mine.' She didn't want anyone else to give me things; she *had* to be the gracious giver, and she had to take credit for it.

"It was part of her need to be controlling, I guess. She had to be Lady Bountiful and she *had* to brag about it."

It was a minor irritant to Vickie; she continued to consider Peggy her best friend, and tried to ignore small disappointments in her attitude.

Sometimes, however, Vickie wondered if she was in another situation where she was being controlled by a strong personality.

Vickie and Peggy Sue had talked for a long time about quitting smoking. But the time was never right for Peggy. Finally, Vickie stopped smoking on her own. Peggy didn't notice until she suggested that they go outside for a cigarette.

"I don't smoke anymore," Vickie said. "I quit."

And she had done it herself, without Peggy's permission, without telling her.

"Peggy was so mad at me," Vickie recalled. "That was a control issue. She accused me of betraying her by quitting cigarettes without her. I guess I was getting stronger and I wasn't so submissive any longer."

After Vickie married Scott, Peggy seemed to resent their happy ending. She was single at the time with no real prospects in view.

The three of them often went to restaurants or clubs together. And Peggy pouted.

"I know you're just going to talk to Scott and ignore me," she told Vickie. "And you'll be dancing with him and I'll sit here all alone."

Vickie tried to include Peggy in her life. For all

her "fiery red" beauty, Peggy Sue *was* technically alone. Jim was gone and had been for a long time.

By 2007, Peggy Sue Thomas was making a good living driving limousines in Las Vegas. She was close to her father and mother and her half sister Sue Mahoney—but didn't spend much time with her half siblings from Jimmie Stackhouse's first marriage.

Her best friend, Vickie, married Scott Mickelsen on July 28 that year and moved to Roswell, New Mexico, with him.

Peggy Sue would be forty-two in September, still extremely attractive, and she kept her eye out for a man who might meet her criteria. Although Vickie was in the midst of packing up and moving, the two women were still close.

One night, Peggy picked up a man with a scruffy beard who wore a cowboy hat, an expensive suit, and shiny boots. She found him quite handsome, although she had been in Las Vegas long enough not to fall for a man just because he was good-looking.

They chatted as they drove past the millions of Las Vegas lights, and she thought he was fascinating. He told her he was a horse owner/trainer and rancher from New Mexico, and that his name was Mark Allen. He said he had a ranch in Roswell called the Double Eagle.

Later, Peggy was enthusiastic when she told Vickie Boyer about her passenger. She didn't know much about horses or ranches, but she thought

Mark Allen might have money. Big money. What he'd said had a kind of authenticity that she rarely encountered.

And the man named Mark Allen had promised to ask for her the next time he came to Las Vegas.

Vickie knew if Peggy ended up wanting this rancher, she could have him. She had yet to see any man who hadn't fallen for her best friend's guile. She was a virtual magnet for males from twenty to eighty.

Peggy Sue asked Vickie to get on the Internet and search for any information she might find about Mark Allen. Although she didn't really want to do that, Vickie complied and found out a lot that interested Peggy.

Mark was from a family with money and his father, William Allen, had made a fortune as an executive in the oil fields of Alaska. In 2008, Senator Ted Stevens, a well-thought-of legend in that state, was tried for corruption involving favors from Allen, who had allegedly paid for renovations on one of Stevens's homes.

In the ensuing trial, Bill Allen testified for the prosecution, and the beloved senator was found guilty of seven counts of lying, a disaster for his political career. Days later, he lost his reelection bid to retain his senate office. One faction accused his prosecutors of knowingly letting one of *their* witnesses—Bill Allen—lie in his testimony. The fallout led to a major political scandal.

Through it all, Bill Allen was most concerned

about dragging his son, Mark, into the Stevens scandal—and Mark never was.

Ted Stevens, whose career had been legendary only to be sullied by corruption charges, had his conviction thrown out in 2009 by a federal judge. It was too late. His political career was in ashes, and he was nearing seventy.

Ex-Senator Stevens died tragically in Alaska in a float plane crash a year later in October 2010 as he and a group of friends headed for a fishing trip. Secretary of the Navy Sean O'Keefe and his nineteen-year-old son barely survived, as did the thirteen-year-old son of another plane-crash victim.

MARK ALLEN HIMSELF DID indeed have money, more money than even Peggy Sue might have imagined. He did have a ranch, and he did own horses. He even owned some that might make a national name for themselves one day soon.

Mark looked like a good ole cowboy, but he certainly wasn't a show-off. Still, Peggy suspected he might actually *be* very wealthy. At fifty-two, he was more than a decade older than Peggy Sue. He wore well-polished boots, and either black or white ten-gallon hats, and he affected a grizzled look with a few days' stubble of whiskers.

He had a John Wayne persona and Peggy rapidly began to see him as a good candidate for the next jump in her life. Perhaps because he had never seen Peggy angry or unpleasant and because she was stunning, Mark Allen was soon "smitten" with her. She was in her "fiery red" stage, at the peak of her beauty.

At first, when Mark came to Las Vegas, he asked if Peggy was available. Soon, he insisted on having her be his limo driver.

"She caught my eye," Allen said later. "She drove me and some friends a few times, and after that, I started calling the company and asking for Peggy. I paid a lot of bills for her before we even got married—credit cards and stuff like that. But, hell, I liked her. Then she started telling me how to take care of horses!"

Even though it was obvious to him that Peggy knew very little about horses, Mark Allen took Peggy to visit his ranch. He didn't need a horse expert; he needed *her*. Although the farmhouse there was just a three-bedroom, two-bath older ranch home all on one floor, the stables, other facilities for his horses, and the sprawling acres that surrounded it all were obviously extremely valuable.

It was true that Peggy didn't know very much about horses, but she recognized Mark's stables were inhabited by fine equine specimens, and his trainers were top notch. Mark was particularly enthusiastic about a small chestnut gelding with a swirl of white on his forehead—Mine That Bird. He told Peggy Sue that he hoped to buy him. To look at him, Mine That Bird wasn't particularly prepossessing, but Mark's trainer, Chip Woolley, predicted great things for the horse, and encouraged Mark to buy the gelding.

Mark's new relationship didn't look nearly

as promising to Woolley. "Hell, she didn't know which end of a horse to put the bridle on!"

At the moment, however, Mark Allen was obsessed with Peggy. He asked her to marry him, and within a few months of their meeting, they invited those close to them to their wedding and lavish reception.

Mark's parents were there, along with Peggy's mother, Doris, her father, Jimmie, her stepmother, Terry, her daughters Mariah and Taylor, her half sister Sue Mahoney, and of course, Vickie Boyer, along with a few dozen other friends and relatives. None of her six half siblings from Jimmie's marriage to Mary Ellen attended. They were invited but had never heard of Mark Allen and they had virtually no forewarning of the wedding.

The couple married under a pergola in a white, red, and gold–themed ceremony. Peggy Sue wore a snow-white halter dress, a diamond pendant, a crown of Austrian crystals, and carried eighteen pure white and yellow-red roses. Mark dressed in a black leather tuxedo and a black ten-gallon hat.

As Jimmie Stackhouse walked his daughter down the rose-petal-sprinkled aisle, Peggy Sue's future seemed as golden as the decor.

The reception that followed featured a large cake with a cowboy-hatted bride lassoing a groom on its top. There was even a frosted stack of hay next to them.

Mark and Peggy's favorite alcoholic drink was Patrón tequila, an expensive liquor made from the blue agave plant. It cost around sixty dollars a bottle, but money was no object that night.

Or any other night. The couple always kept lots of Patrón on hand.

The guests celebrated into the wee hours, and Peggy had never looked happier.

And yet, there were soon harbingers of trouble ahead.

For most of their eight-year friendship, Vickie Boyer believed Peggy when she said she didn't do drugs—until the day that she surprised Peggy snorting cocaine. She knew that Peggy was a heavy drinker; she couldn't hide that, and after she married Mark, that continued unabated. Vickie was shocked to learn at last that Peggy Sue was heavily into illegal substances.

Mark Allen hired Vickie to be his assistant. Her salary wasn't all that much—forty-five thousand dollars a year—but he was more than generous to her and her husband, Scott. Allen bought Vickie a truck, and gave her thirty-five thousand dollars to put down on a house she wanted to buy.

Mark was openhanded with many people he knew, including his bride. He had his house remodeled, adding two bedrooms for Peggy's girls, two new bathrooms, and a fully outfitted kitchen. In the backyard, he constructed a swimming pool with a slide, and a barbecue.

One feature of the farmhouse had been less than ideal when Peggy Sue and her daughters moved in. The master bedroom was adjacent to the ranch office, and the only doors in between were swinging, tavern-style doors. There was no real door to shut, much less lock, and the trainers and cowhands came and went often.

Not surprisingly, they had little privacy. Mark added a new bedroom for them at the other end of the house, with a lockable outside door.

"She had her mother move in," Mark recalled. "They were a package deal. Peggy Sue said she wanted all 'her people' to take over from my employees. That wasn't gonna happen." Outside of that, Mark gave Peggy everything she asked for. He bought her mother, Doris Matz, a cozy fifth-wheeler to park at the ranch, as well as a new car.

They had joint bank accounts without any limits on Peggy Sue's withdrawals.

Because Mark's driver's license was temporarily suspended, Peggy suggested that any vehicle, boat or other expensive equipment should be registered in her name. It would make things so much easier. He agreed.

Mark was generous to her parents. He sent Jimmie and Terry on lavish vacation trips, bought them presents, and always welcomed them into his home.

"Mark bought a posh houseboat and named it the 'Peggy Sue,'" Vickie Boyer recalled. The *Peggy Sue* was plenty large enough for them or guests to live aboard, just like a real house. When a chunk of Mark's oil money came in, they paid $253,000 for a pontoon boat for day outings on the water. Mark also bought numerous vehicles for them.

All of their acquisitions continued to be in Peggy's name only.

Vickie Boyer's job with Mark forced her uncomfortably into the private lives of her new boss and Peggy Sue. With her office being in their home, she couldn't help but overhear their arguments, and she was far too close to many of Peggy's financial machinations. Vickie liked working at the Double Eagle Ranch, but being at Peggy's beck and call every day allowed her to see small fissures in the perfect image she had initially seen in her best friend.

Peggy Sue had been Vickie's rock, the one person she believed she could count on. Being an unwilling ear-witness to Mark and Peggy's arguments could be dismaying. Vickie knew that Peggy was interested in money, but she had also thought that she sincerely loved Mark Allen when she married him.

A few months into the marriage, Vickie wasn't so sure about that.

Jim Huden had been gone for more than three years and Peggy rarely spoke of him or seemed to care what had happened to him. According to Vickie, beyond Mark, there weren't any men in Peggy's life.

Life on a ranch in Roswell, New Mexico, wasn't nearly as exciting as driving a limousine in Las Vegas, and although Peggy had pretended to be interested in horses, she really wasn't. Mark spent so much time out in the stables and ring with his head trainer, Chip Woolley. She resented that. And she didn't care for most of the people who worked for Mark on the ranch.

Mark had bought the gelding without much promise from a breeder in Canada, the small horse that was born with splayed legs. Somehow, despite his physical handicaps, Mine That Bird had won four out of six races at the Woodbine Racetrack in Toronto. In 2008, "Bird" was voted the Canadian Champion two-year-old Male Horse.

Running in the 2008 Breeder's Cup Juvenile race, Mine That Bird came in dead last. But Mark believed in him, and the small horse had heart. He won two more races, and he qualified for the Kentucky Derby!

His odds weren't good: fifty to one. Peggy couldn't see what all the fuss was about.

She hated the way most of the ranch hands ignored her, answering only to Mark. If Peggy made remarks or did something to ruffle their feathers and Mark called her on it, she blamed Vickie. She said it was Vickie's fault, that Vickie was the one who had complained about them.

"Oh, don't be mad at her," Peggy would say. "Vickie didn't really mean that."

Mark continued to be bighearted with Vickie Boyer. When one of her brothers died, Mark gave Vickie five hundred dollars to buy a plane ticket home for his funeral. When her aunt died in Wisconsin, Mark asked Peggy to give Vickie a thousand dollars. She did, but Peggy wasn't happy about that.

Mark was easygoing and trusted people.

"To him," Vickie said, "a handshake was a contract. He was a good businessman but he believed most people were as good as their word."

Once Mark and Peggy had their new bedroom with its outside door, Vickie was relieved that she could no longer hear most of their quarrels. But Peggy often complained to her about Mark. That puzzled her best friend.

"She had everything she'd always wanted: money, a good man who loved her, fabulous vacations, a husband who was kind and generous to her daughters and parents, *anything* she wanted. But she still complained."

Peggy Sue had always been soft-spoken, using her subtle wiles to seduce men. Still, sometime in early 2008, Vickie became concerned for her.

"Peggy started yelling and screaming. That scared me because she had never done that before."

When she and Mark disagreed, he wouldn't fight back. As she screamed at him, Mark simply stepped back, waiting for Peggy to calm down. She had become a different person from the woman he married. He was seeing a side of her he'd never encountered before.

Before Christmas 2007, Mark had asked Vickie to buy two airplane tickets and make reservations at a posh resort in one of the Grand Cayman Islands in the western Caribbean Sea. It would be the ideal place where he and Peggy Sue could relax and enjoy each other, and hopefully sand down some of the rough spots in their fledgling marriage.

It sounded as though they were working their problems out, but just before they were to leave, Mark and Peggy Sue had a serious fight.

In view of that, Mark said he wouldn't go to the Grand Caymans. Peggy Sue would have to find someone else who might like to share that exotic—but now ruined—vacation with her.

"But no one wanted to go with her," Vickie recalled. "In the end, with Mark's permission, I said I'd go."

It was not a pleasant trip. All the expensive restaurant visits and Patrón tequila had made Peggy Sue's slender Vegas body a thing of the past. Most days, she didn't want to go to the pool or the beach where someone might see her. When she did go, she wore "old lady" bathing suits that covered her from her shoulders to her knees.

"We mostly stayed in the room," Vickie said. "For four or five days, with all that wonderful scenery in the Caymans and so much we could have done, Peggy wouldn't go out, and it wasn't fun for me to go out alone."

Peggy ate and drank her way through what should have been days in the sun. Vickie was vastly relieved when they finally boarded a plane for New Mexico.

More and more now, Peggy Sue was stockpiling money and *things* she wanted to keep. She showed Vickie a storage unit where she had secreted a small sports car, jewelry, and a rare John Wayne gun. She wanted Vickie to hide the pontoon boat in another storage unit. Vickie refused. Peggy had convinced Mark that they should store the pontoon craft and he agreed as long as it was close by. In actuality, Jimmie Stackhouse soon hooked onto it and towed it behind his truck to his place in Idaho.

Peggy was certainly acting like a woman who was anxious to be single again. But she didn't want to be single and poor again.

Peggy dipped deeply into the bank account she shared with Mark. She took $354,000 from that account and deposited it into a Wells Fargo account that was solely in *her* name.

Vickie didn't know about that at first, but she found out and was relieved when Mark managed to reverse that huge transaction.

She realized that Peggy was stealing smaller amounts from Mark, too. Mark had given her ten thousand dollars to pay the pool man. She never did. Instead, Peggy put the money into her own account.

When Vickie asked her why she was putting things in the storage unit, and diverting funds into her own bank, Peggy Sue just smiled and said inscrutably, "Because you never know . . ."

What did she mean by that?

Vickie Boyer was concerned that Peggy Sue was going to dump Mark as soon as she had enough stockpiled in her storage units and bank accounts. That would probably hurt him a lot because he seemed to have tried everything to make his bride happy.

Peggy Sue asked Vickie to spy on Mark, pore over his accounts and investments so she would know exactly what his assets were.

"I couldn't do that," Vickie said. "For the first time ever, I lied to Peggy and told her I couldn't find any information on Mark."

There was no telling how much Peggy might receive in a bitter divorce. Still, Vickie wasn't worried that Peggy would *physically* hurt Mark. He could take care of himself.

That changed one night when Peggy Sue and Vickie were sitting in a local bar, talking to a regular there, a man named Ollie. Peggy had had a great deal to drink and she was upset about yet another disagreement with Mark.

After listening to her complain, Ollie—who was none too sober himself—offered, "I could take him out for you."

"I have his gun," Peggy said slowly. "A John Wayne hand gun . . ."

Ollie saw the humor in that. "Wouldn't that be ironic," he said, "to shoot a guy with his own gun?"

"But *this* time I'll know to throw it in the water," Peggy commented.

Vickie, who wasn't drinking because she was the designated driver, heard that and suddenly everything came clear. She had never believed that Peggy was connected to the murder of Russel Douglas. Peggy Sue might need to be the belle of the ball wherever she went, and she could be mean sometimes, but Vickie had always put up with it because that was just Peggy Sue.

Afraid for Mark, Vickie took the gun away from Peggy.

"But I thought about it and thought about it. When she said that about throwing a gun in the water, I knew in my heart that she was really *evil*."

Vickie feared for Mark Allen's life, even more so when Peggy said to her, "If he dies, I'll get everything. I'll be the one telling the ranch hands what to do."

Vickie called Allen and told him about the conversation in the bar. "And I have your gun; I got Peggy to give it to me," she said. "And I told him about the things Peggy had said in the bar. Mark agreed to pick it up or have her bring it to him, but he himself was beginning to worry about how far his bride might go.

"In the end," Vickie recalls, "he arranged to have a friend of his meet me in the parking lot at Wal-Mart and I gave *him* Mark's gun."

Fortunately, Mark remained in good shape. If indeed Peggy Sue had any plans to eliminate him and inherit his considerable wealth, she probably found herself blocked before she got very far with her nefarious plots. Ollie from the bar was a drunk, and he couldn't be counted on to keep his mouth shut. As isolated as she was in Roswell, Peggy Sue didn't have anyone else in her life who might accommodate her.

By mid-2008, things were no better in Peggy and Mark's life. It became clear that their marriage was headed for oblivion. Peggy Sue called her longtime friend when she was very intoxicated and said she was afraid she was going to commit suicide. She still had a rifle in her possession.

"Someone has to take this gun away from me, Vickie. I don't know what I might do."

Things around the Double Eagle grew increasingly tense. Vickie was planning to resign her job with Mark and remove herself from the continuing battle. But before she could do that, she heard screams coming from the master bedroom. It was Peggy Sue calling to her.

"Vickie! Vickie!" she hollered. "Dial 911 right away!"

Vickie did.

When Peggy came running out toward Vickie, her blouse was ripped. Peggy cried that Mark had physically attacked her.

The Allens had been married for not quite eleven months. For all intents and purposes, it was over in the summer of 2008. When Peggy Sue's domestic violence complaint against Mark went for settlement a week later in a New Mexico court, she assumed that he would be banned from the Double Eagle.

The judge shocked her when she said that it was Peggy Sue who had to move out. She wouldn't even be allowed to get her belongings.

The judge relented when Peggy pleaded and said that Vickie would go with her to oversee that she did not take anything beyond her own possessions.

She had already taken far more than her share of Mark's assets. In July 2008, Peggy Sue had her burgeoning bank account, the houseboat, the pontoon boat, several cars, jewelry, and probably valuables that no one knew about. Even so, it rankled her to think of the truck and the thirty-five thousand dollars that Mark had given to Vickie. She told her former best friend that the truck wasn't really hers, and that the thirty-five thousand dollars for a mortgage down payment was meant to be a loan—not a gift.

Vickie went to Mark Allen and asked him if this was true. He shook his head, and immediately signed an affidavit that said the mortgage money was a gift. Then he said, "The truck is yours. It always will be. It always was."

While Peggy Sue was banned from the Double Eagle Ranch, her mother, Doris, stayed on, comfortable in her fifth wheeler. Mark had always been good to Doris, and she was in no hurry to leave his generosity and protection. She urged Peggy to rethink what she was about to lose by going ahead with the divorce.

Annoyed, Peggy told her firmly: "This is not your divorce! This is *mine*!"

Few women would hug a divorce to her breasts and brag about it, refusing to share that "honor." But, for Peggy Sue Stackhouse Harris Thomas Allen, the upcoming divorce was like a trophy she had won after carefully making her plans succeed.

She moved into her houseboat, the seagoing

luxury pad. One of the first things she did was re-name it. No longer the *Peggy Sue*, its new name was *Off the Hook*.

Vickie Boyer and Peggy Sue exchanged some vituperative emails, however. Peggy was still angry about the truck and the thirty-five thousand dollars Mark had given to Vickie. Peggy considered them hers—and not Vickie's. Vickie was upset because Peggy had rented a house to one of her daughters without consulting her and because she had finally had to accept that her caring friend had feet of clay. Peggy was badmouthing Vickie to anyone who would listen. She allegedly claimed that her longtime best friend was "a money-grubbing, bad bitch" who was only her friend to get at her money.

For most of the eight years they were best friends, Peggy really didn't have that much money to speak of and Vickie had always stood by her.

In one email, Vickie wrote, "You never look at the whole circle, Peggy. I gave you plenty, did plenty, backed you up a hundred percent all the time and never did one thing to dishonor you. And you call me names, throw out words like people are nothing to you when all I was doing was covering your ass. You were so damn drunk you don't even know what you said to strangers, let alone your friend. I brushed it off, but no more! Don't fucking tell me about using people, Peggy. Don't tell me how it was all me using you. You know better. You know I did everything you asked."

Vickie recalled Peggy's conversation with Ollie

in the bar. "By the way, while you were disgustingly talking about taking Mark out, you said, *'This time I will know to throw the gun in the water.'*"

Peggy responded scathingly. "You are such a fucking liar, Vickie . . . Ollie *jokingly* asked if I wanted him to take Mark out and I said, 'No way!' I explained to him what I'd been through with Jim, and I didn't want to hurt Mark. I wanted all of this shit to be over. You know damn well I never said anything about throwing anything in the water because I didn't have anything to do with that shit Jim did . . ."

Peggy's email was an example of how she had always before managed to convince Vickie that she was right. She insisted that Vickie knew "in her heart" that she had always been innocent, and that she had maintained that to everyone and never, ever said she was guilty.

But Peggy Sue had been intoxicated when she blurted out her regret about not getting rid of the gun—the gun that Jim Huden had used to shoot Russ Douglas. And Vickie was drinking ginger ale. She had no doubts at all about what Peggy had blurted out in the bar. That was why she had talked Peggy out of the gun and seen that it was returned to Mark Allen.

Peggy accused Vickie of keeping any potential friends away from her because Vickie was jealous.

"So, Vickie, throw out your low blow and try and threaten me with me saying something that I didn't. That hurts more than anything, and you might as well just put a knife through my heart."

Peggy told Vickie to keep the $35,000 and the truck Mark had given her, but she predicted that Vickie would never have integrity. Ironically, she emailed that she had finally discovered how wicked Vickie was.

"I guess I am the fortunate one to have finally seen it."

Peggy Sue sarcastically wished that Vickie would be happy, and ended with a flourish of guilt, saying that she would never have any contact with Vickie—and blaming her once-faithful friend for hurting her (Peggy) more than anyone ever had.

"Remember what you told me. You only get in this life what you give. I hope you get yours . . ."

Peggy Sue had accused Vickie of subtly threatening her about the Ollie conversation, and now there was little question that Peggy was threatening, too. She sounded very angry—and frightened—that she would be connected to Jim Huden in the murder of Russel Douglas.

The two longtime friends never met again. Mark Plumberg included the exchange of emails in his constantly expanding case file.

Even after Peggy was banned from Mark Allen's property, her mother, Doris, remained living in her cozy motor home at the Double Eagle Ranch. Always a superb baker, she took Mark cupcakes and cookies. She was, of course, a constant reminder of his unpleasant months with his red-haired bride, and Mark finally managed to get Doris to leave.

CHAPTER TWENTY-SEVEN

PEGGY SUE HERSELF LAY low on her houseboat. She was terribly angry with Vickie, and felt betrayed. Looking back over so many years, Vickie seems to have always been in Peggy's corner, even before the Ms. Washington contest.

But she had seen and heard too much of Peggy Sue's machinations to continue to follow her every decree.

Suddenly, Peggy's world had imploded on her. She had no husband, no best friend, no job, and few supporters. Taylor and Mariah were always there for their mother, Jimmie Stackhouse stayed close to his youngest daughter, and Kelvin Thomas, new girlfriend or not, was concerned about his ex-wife.

In the fall of 2008, Russel Douglas's murder was now almost five years in the past, and once her fight with Vickie sputtered to an end, Peggy Sue didn't seem outwardly concerned about the continuing investigation far away on Whidbey Island.

If she hadn't been named more than a "person of interest" after so many years, it didn't seem likely the sheriff's detectives had any kind of evidence—circumstantial or physical—connecting *her* to Douglas's death.

Perhaps Peggy Sue was unaware that the search warrant served on her house in Henderson, Nevada, in 2004 had revealed the operation manual for the Bersa Thunder handgun. Fingerprint experts were able to find Jim Huden's prints on it—but they also found Peggy's.

It wasn't the strongest physical evidence; her prints could be explained away by a shrewd defense attorney who might say she had been dusting the coffee table where the pamphlet rested and unknowingly picked it up. Fingerprints in blood are dynamic physical evidence; these fingerprints didn't begin to reach that level.

If Peggy Thomas had blood on her hands, it was only in a figurative sense.

Jim Huden had long since disappeared. Brenna Douglas had collected what was rumored to be about four hundred thousand dollars in Russ's insurance and left Langley. She bought some expensive vehicles and a house, but didn't stay long in any one place. Brenna had bought a house sometime in 2004, but it was foreclosed upon and sold at auction in August of the same year.

She moved from town to town around the state

of Washington, and eschewed contact with the Island County investigators whenever she could.

PEGGY MAY HAVE BEEN somewhat dismayed in 2009 by the inopportune timing in divorcing Mark Allen. Reportedly, her alimony was a spare twenty-five hundred dollars a month, far less than what she had hoped to get. She did retain a number of assets she had managed to hide from Mark. Conservatively, they added up to more than a million dollars.

But Mark had been on his way up. In the spring of 2009, Mark's horse Mine That Bird won the Kentucky Derby—and was headed for the Triple Crown.

Bird's winning run was the second-largest upset in the 185-year history of the Kentucky Derby!

Had she stayed with Allen, Peggy Sue would certainly have enjoyed the Derby, the fancy clothes and ridiculous hats, mint juleps, and most of all, being in the winner's circle as the wife of a winning owner. It would have been almost like reliving her Ms. Washington days, not to mention the purse that went with the win.

Three books were written about Mine That Bird's courage, and a theatrical movie is still rumored to be in the works.

How Peggy Sue would have thrived in that exciting and inspiring Derby outcome, but she had burned those bridges.

CHAPTER TWENTY-EIGHT

JIMMIE STACKHOUSE'S FAMILY—or rather, families—had known enough upheaval and tragedy to make their lives seem like a convoluted soap opera. As adults, Lana, Brenda, and Rhonda were more concerned with their husbands and children than they were about the Sturm und Drang of their half sister Peggy Sue's life. She was nothing like they were, even though they shared the same father.

And Jimmie's first three daughters were still trying to cope with their own loss at the hands of a vicious sex killer. Fourteen years before, they had found answers to many of their questions about Mary Ellen Stackhouse. That helped a lot, but they still bore scars—particularly Brenda.

Brenda had had profound post-traumatic stress disorder for all of her life. She still screamed in her sleep and suffered terrible nightmares.

Her sisters worried about her, but weren't sure

how to help. They, too, were survivors of a homicide victim, but Lana and Rhonda were able to deal with the pain more effectively.

In October 1995, Rhonda, who was a superior court clerk in Boundary County, Idaho, was watching television with the rest of the court staff as they waited to hear the verdict in the O. J. Simpson murder trial.

As reporters did a summary of how Nicole Simpson had perished, Rhonda realized that that was probably how her mother had died.

"The details on the Simpson case made me sick," she recalls. "And then O.J. was acquitted. I wondered if whoever killed my mother was still in prison—or if he was wandering around free."

Rhonda and her sisters were consumed with the need to know the things they had never learned about Mary Ellen Stackhouse. Would they feel better or worse if they found out what had really happened?

They decided that it was worth the chance. Rhonda began to surf the Internet, looking for her mother's name. She found a link there to the *San Jose Mercury News*, and a column called "Ask Andy Bruno."

It had been such a long time—more than thirty years—but Rhonda wrote to Bruno, wondering if anyone on the paper had any information about a crime so far in the past.

Bruno headed for the microfiche for newspapers in the sixties, and found an article written by Ed Pope.

"He still works here," he told Rhonda. "He wrote the original story about your mother's death."

Rhonda says, "I talked to Pope, read the newspaper coverage from 1963, and I had proof that my mother had existed."

FOR THE FIRST TIME, Lana, Rhonda, and Brenda saw the article that dominated the front page of the *San Jose Mercury News* on June 5, 1963. The headline was seven inches wide and stretched across the top of the page: HUNT SEX FIEND WHO KILLED MOTHER OF 6.

They recognized their mother's picture from seeing it in an old album. She was a lovely dark-haired woman wearing a cashmere sweater and a double string of pearls. The woman in the photo was years younger when she'd died than they were now.

A smaller headline said: CHILDREN FIND BODY OF VICTIM, YOUNG WOMAN BEATEN, KNIFED.

And there they all were, lined up on their back patio steps, squinting toward a photographer for the *Mercury News*. They had never seen a picture of themselves at that age; there were photos later—but not in 1963, not any they had seen.

Tommy, 8, Mike, 7, Robby, 18 months, Lana, 5, Rhonda, 2, and Brenda, 4.

Their brothers and Lana half smiled, although they clearly had little idea of what had happened to their world. Robby, in Lana's small arms, was crying, and Rhonda and Brenda had identical expressions of shock and suspicion.

It seemed a transgression of their privacy to line them up that way, six little kids whose mother had been violently raped and murdered only twenty-four hours earlier.

Rhonda wondered who had allowed them to be thrust into the strobe light of the photographer's camera. Probably not their father; Jimmie was on his way home from Tennessee at that point. Perhaps one of the neighbors whom the paper said was taking care of them? Those neighbors' quotes in the paper showed that they, too, were in shock. In the end, she knew it was the newspaper's cameramen who had snuck up through the neighbors' yards to get photos.

None of the trio of sisters remembered that particular moment on that particular day.

Thirty-two years later, it hurt to read the details about the very questions they had been afraid to ask. But there was also the beginning of cleansing. Until they read that newspaper article, the three sisters had all felt an amorphous terror, something waiting in the shadows that they couldn't see clearly, something that frightened them. Of them all, Brenda had blocked any memory of her mother's leaving.

She seemed to be doing all right as they set out to learn more and to honor Mary Ellen in whatever way they could.

There were things printed that would not have been allowed in the media of the twenty-first century, things revealed that could have interfered with a murder probe. Fortunately, in their mother's case, they hadn't.

Deputy Coroner Richard Mayne told reporters that Mary Ellen had received "at least seven severe blows on the back of the head resulting in the basal skull fracture."

He added that a Cutco steak knife, taken from her own kitchen, had been used to stab her in the throat, severing her trachea while she was still alive. Her slacks were ripped from her body and dangled from her ankles. Her flower-print blouse was "in disarray."

Investigating officers had located a cast-off blood spot on the wall, and another stain on the living room chair. Although she had perished from exsanguination, all of her blood drained from her body, the red rug beneath her had absorbed that blood, disguising the scene so that her children weren't aware of how grisly it was.

There were remarkably few signs of a struggle. Mary Ellen's cup of coffee was still precariously balanced on the arm of the chair.

AS THEY READ THE newspaper articles, Lana, Brenda, and Rhonda knew that they had to go back to San Jose. Most of all, they had to visit their mother's grave, to be with her in any way they could. And they could not just glean what they could from old newspapers; they needed to look into her killer's eyes. Maybe they could say something to him that would make him know what anguish he had caused.

When they learned that Gilbert Thompson, who was forty-seven in 1995, was about to have another parole hearing, their minds were made up.

"We needed some kind of closure, even though we knew there could never be *true* closure," Rhonda said. "This would be our therapy."

Their half sisters—Sue and Peggy Sue—met the trio at Sea-Tac Airport in Seattle as they landed there after a flight from Idaho and waited to catch a plane to San Jose. Sue and Peggy Sue, of course, had no blood bond with Mary Ellen Stackhouse; Doris Matz was their mother.

Lana, Brenda, and Rhonda boarded the plane headed for a place they scarcely remembered.

They found the funeral home that had overseen their mother's funeral services, and learned that she was buried in Golden Gate Cemetery in San Bruno. They went there first and pored over the huge registry, hoping they could find Mary Ellen's grave.

"We found it quickly," Rhonda said. "It was just off the main road. I had brought a wreath all the way from Bonners Ferry, and I carried it to my mother's grave."

They knelt beside the headstone and posed for pictures. They traced the names and dates from the grave marker with onionskin paper.

And then they poured some of Rob's ashes on his mother's grave.

They gasped as they saw the steel pins mixed in with his cremains. These were put in to brace Robby's broken bones after he'd been run over by the bus so many years before.

So many losses. So many tears.

They were shocked to learn that Gilbert Thompson had not been in prison over all the years since his conviction. In the late seventies, the state of California released a number of prisoners on parole. Correctional facilities had become more and more crowded, and even some "lifers" were being considered for parole. "Rehabilitation" was the magic word and life didn't mean life literally.

William P. Hoffman, chief assistant district attorney of Santa Clara County, was appalled when his office was notified in the summer of 1977 that the California Men's Colony was about to "set" Gilbert Richard Thompson's term.

"When I prosecuted Mr. Thompson, Judge Callahan sentenced him to life in the state penitentiary. I most respectfully suggest to you that this is the proper term, and this is the term which ought to be set.

"Mr. Thompson has a severe disability," Hoffman wrote sarcastically. "He thinks about knifing women and girls and having intercourse with them. Unfortunately, he doesn't just *think* about it, he *does* it.

"Releasing people like Thompson into society

is something like releasing an elephant in a china shop. It is completely predictable that other innocent people are going to be killed and, in the analogous case, a lot of china is going to be broken."

Hoffman offered to furnish those making a parole decision with eight-by-ten color copies of Gilbert Thompson's "handiwork" to help them understand what he had been found guilty of thus far.

His warning did no good. Gilbert Thompson, then in his early thirties, had been released on parole after only fourteen years. He lasted just forty-three days before he grabbed a woman in a mall parking lot in broad daylight. She screamed and clung to her steering wheel as he threatened her with a knife and tried to wrestle her out of her car.

It took nine bystanders to pull him off the terrified victim. Clearly, Gilbert Thompson was not a candidate for rehabilitation and he never would be.

He went back to the San Luis Obispo prison, but remained eligible for parole every five years. In prison, he earned a college degree, and although his college professor knew of his record, *she married him*!

When that didn't work out, he began to court her mother.

BRENDA, RHONDA, AND LANA drove next to San Luis Obispo to attend Gilbert Thompson's 1995 parole hearing. Exhausted, they stayed in a small motel there. In the morning, they would finally see the man who had stolen their mother from them.

He was there, monitored by two guards. The room was almost empty except for themselves and the three parole officers who sat at a table facing the prisoner.

The charges against Thompson were read, and they heard their mother's name—Mary Ellen Stackhouse—as the victim. It somehow made her more alive to them. She wasn't just a name on a headstone or a blurred memory.

"That's when my grief really started," Rhonda says. "We finally had proof that our mother had existed, and that she was a victim of murder!

"My mother was *real*!"

The sisters had decided to let Rhonda make their statement opposing any parole for Gilbert Thompson. When she began to speak, he averted his eyes.

"*You* look at me," she said angrily.

Thompson looked up briefly.

"There was no one there behind his eyes," she recalled. "They were just blank."

The female member of the parole board warned Rhonda, "You cannot speak directly to the offender."

The parole board put Gilbert Thompson through the mill, demanding that he answer embarrassing questions. He finally admitted that he had gone home after he murdered Mary Ellen Stackhouse and masturbated in his garage, still excited because he had realized his fantasy.

The prisoner whined that it wasn't fair—that the whole case had been "sensationalized," turning everyone against him.

"Mr. Thompson," the woman on the parole board spoke again. "How could anyone do *more* to sensationalize this story? *You* did that."

Mary Ellen's daughters' cheeks were wet with tears, but they were resolute, strong even in their grief. Lana spoke, too, her words sharp as actual blows as they blasted Gilbert Thompson. These were not helpless little toddlers anymore; these were strong women.

It took only a few hours for the decision to come down. Parole was denied.

When the sisters were led to a private room, the parole board members smiled at them. "Ladies, that was all done for you—because *he's* not going anywhere."

Lana, Brenda, and Rhonda drove back to San Jose, passing acres and acres of orange and lemon groves. It was a beautiful day, a wonderful drive, and they felt that an oppressive weight had finally been lifted off their shoulders and their hearts.

But there was something more the three sisters needed to do.

Rhonda recalled, "We had gone to the funeral home, to our mother's grave, and to her killer's parole hearing, but that wasn't enough.

"I said, 'I want to go back to the house. We're here in San Jose . . .' We found our old house. I started up that front walk, with Lana and Brenda behind me, and I knocked on the door.

"When a woman answered, I said, 'Hi, we used to live here when we were little'—and she suddenly burst into tears, and said, 'I *knew* you would come back someday.'"

Gloria Perez invited them in, leading them to the living room where their mother had been murdered so long ago. The furniture and the carpet were different, of course, and yet they had some recall of being in this room a very long time ago.

Gloria, who looked to be about fifty, explained that she had raised five children there.

"She told us, 'We didn't know what was wrong with the house,'" Rhonda recalled.

"My husband kept saying, 'I'm not gonna stay here—there's something wrong. I don't know what it is—but I'm not going to stay here,'" Gloria told them.

"And then he left me and moved out. I kept seeing shadows in the house. I've lived here nineteen years, but we weren't the first buyer after your family left. Realtors didn't have to tell house buyers about the history of houses back in those days.

"We used to hear footsteps. The kids would hear them, too, and I'd tell them it was just the heater thumping. One time, I heard a noise in the kitchen, and I said, 'I'm not scaring you and I don't want you scaring me.' But I'm sure she isn't really here to scare me."

Gloria told them that one night about eleven,

there was a knock on the door and they found a woman standing there, holding a rosary and a cross. The woman said, "You need to get out of this house!"

Gloria, startled, had gasped, "What? Why?"

"Someone was murdered here. Something evil happened here."

"I told her to stop," Perez said, "because she was frightening my children. She looked at me with sad eyes and then she turned around and left. She just came out of nowhere that night. I had never seen her before—and I never saw her again."

Gloria Perez said she went next door the next morning and talked to her neighbor Madeline Cassen to see if she had any idea what the woman was talking about. Of course she did. Madeline was the same next-door neighbor the Stackhouse children had run to when they found their mother murdered in 1963. Madeline was the pretty young woman with the puffy blond hair. She was in her sixties now, but she hadn't forgotten anything about that ghastly morning in June.

"Apparently, we'd somehow gotten dressed," Rhonda recalled. "I don't know if that's true or not—all I can remember are the pajamas that our mother made for us. But we were good little soldiers and we marched over to Madeline's. Our mother taught us to be that way."

Gloria Perez said Madeline Cassen told her about what had happened there in the early summer of 1963.

That could explain the shadows, her husband's refusal to live in the house, and her own strange feelings of anxiety. Finally, she told Lana, Brenda, and Rhonda that she had contacted a priest and asked to have her house blessed.

"After that, we weren't afraid any longer."

There was no way to find out who the mysterious woman with the rosary was. Another of the neighbors from the sixties? Someone a little deranged who had read the newspaper articles about Mary Ellen's murder? Some member of her killer's family?

Or could it have been the ghost of Mary Ellen herself, her spirit somehow back from the other side? That, of course, was far-fetched, but the sisters were learning how caring and loving their mother had been in life. In some way that was impossible to explain, could she have been watching out for the new family that replaced her own in the house of shadows?

Gloria's daughter wasn't there when the Stackhouse sisters visited, but later she wrote to them.

> When I heard you were all here, I couldn't believe it. My mom gets so emotional about your mom, you, and your family. There's a connection. When I was little, and I was afraid, I would talk to your mom sometimes. I just knew she would look after me—us—and she wouldn't let anything happen to us because of what hap-

*pened to her. Our house was unhappy for
so many years. It wasn't because of Mary
Ellen, but because of what happened to her.*

Gloria's daughter wanted to stay in touch, and
Rhonda sent her and her mother a photo of Mary
Ellen.

"All these years," Gloria told *Mercury News* reporter Ed Pope, "I've wondered what happened to
those kids. And now I've seen her [Mary Ellen's]
face, I feel complete. Maybe now that her kids
have been here, she can rest."

What they had learned so far was oddly com-
forting to Lana, Brenda, and Rhonda. They realized that there were still people who cared about
their mother, and had never forgotten her.

It was as if long-locked floodgates were opening.

"My first email to the *Mercury News* column
'Action Line,'" Rhonda said, "drew so many responses from people who had known my father
or my mother."

Rhonda wrote to everyone who was involved—
the DA, detectives.

The "Dear Action Line" column received many
responses from the Stackhouses' neighbors and
friends who had lived in San Jose in the early
sixties.

"Our children played together," one began. "We
didn't know what happened to you. You were just
gone."

Through the following years, Rhonda and her

sisters heard from people who were able to fill in some of their early history. This mattered a great deal to them.

In 2002, Lana Galbraith and one of her cousins returned to San Jose to witness yet another parole hearing for Gilbert Thompson. He was close to fifty now and had been turned down for all his petitions to have his sentence reduced. Prison psychologists still considered him dangerous, particularly after his one early release where he attacked a woman only weeks later.

Thompson looked up as Lana and her cousin entered the room, grimaced, and asked to leave the room. Remembering how he had been castigated and shamed before, he was ready to withdraw his plea for parole rather than face his victim's family again.

Gilbert Thompson died at the California Men's Colony prison shortly before Christmas in 2004.

Jimmie Stackhouse's first three daughters heard from their San Jose neighbors and their mother's friends occasionally over the next eight years. As late as 2012, Rhonda Vogl received an email from a woman who worked for a university in Kansas. She had come close to living the same nightmare the Stackhouse children endured.

"Every once in a while, I've done a search on the Internet for Gilbert Thompson," Cathleen Wilkinson wrote. "And I found the story about how you and your sisters confronted him—"

Cathleen explained that her own mother had

been attacked and beaten by Thompson a few months before he murdered Mary Ellen Stackhouse. The assault had happened at the Fort Ord military base.

"My mom was on her way to walk to work, which was probably a couple of miles away across a wide open field [with a] dense shrub area. Every day, she took our German shepherd with her so they could both get some exercise. On the one and only day that she did not take our dog, a 'soldier' came out of the trees and came up behind her. When she turned around to see who it was, he hit her in the head with a huge wooden two-by-four, knocking her to the ground. He drug [sic] her back to the trees, strangling her so badly that she was fading in and out of consciousness. I remember her telling me that she'd always heard people say that when someone was dying, they could hear music. She said she could hear music and was seeing white horses coming to pick her up."

Although her mother had died recently, Cathleen wrote that she sensed her mom had always felt guilty that her testimony wasn't enough to get Thompson convicted before he could creep into Mary Ellen's home.

Rhonda and Cathleen exchanged many emails and calls. Facing the ugly past together helped the heretofore strangers cope with it.

That is so often true; survivors of victims can understand and empathize with what more fortunate people can't begin to understand. There is

shock, grief, tragic acceptance after losing someone to murder—but there really is no closure. It
is a concept that is alien to survivors. They *do* go
on, but they never forget the time when their lives
were forced into a different direction, when everything changed.

PART EIGHT

Arrest and
Punishment

CHAPTER TWENTY-NINE

AS TIME PASSED, MARK PLUMBERG of the Island County Sheriff's Office never gave up on tracking down Jim Huden or knowing where Peggy Sue Thomas was. While he handled day-by-day assignments, Plumberg kept the missing suspect in the back of his mind, and worked on possible leads and theories whenever he could. Island County didn't have that many detectives and they were kept busy with more current cases.

Plumberg didn't believe that Jim Huden had committed suicide as Jean Huden sometimes hinted. Unless he was in the Atlantic Ocean or the Gulf of Mexico, it was probably a lot easier to keep a few steps ahead of the investigators who were tracking him than it was to commit suicide without having your body discovered over seven years.

It was, however, quite possible that the wanted man had somehow managed to get out of the country. If Jim had had help, it would have been achievable.

Often it seemed that it would take the next thing to a miracle to find Jim Huden.

The year 2011 was to be a watershed in the long-unsolved murder of Russel Douglas. As the Island County detectives had long suspected, Jim Huden's wife, Jean, had known where he was since late 2004, but she had gone to great effort to keep that information to herself.

But Jean continued to have a drug problem, and a very long rap sheet that listed more than twenty drug and larceny arrests. In the spring of 2011, she was arrested again on drug charges, and she faced a long prison sentence in Florida if she was convicted.

She had a choice. Authorities in Florida were aware of the Washington investigators' continuing search for Jim. Jean was offered a deal: if she would reveal where her husband was, she was likely to get a much-reduced sentence on her own criminal charges. If she didn't, she could go away for years.

Jean wouldn't be able to help Jim if she was in prison, but most of all, she valued her freedom. Her only chance to avoid prison was to divulge where Jim was—*if he was still alive*—and to agree to cooperate when he went on trial for murder.

In the end, Jean caved in. She admitted that she did know where her missing husband was.

"He's in Mexico," she said quietly. "He's earning a living down there teaching guitar.

"They call him 'Maestro Jim,'" she said.

JIM'S BLAZING AFFAIR WITH Peggy Sue hadn't lasted much longer after Russ Douglas was murdered. Perhaps they were stalked by the terrible memory of what he—or *they*—had done near the empty cottage on Wahl Road on December 26, 2003. When they looked at each other, they must have seen Russ's image caught forever in the pupils of their eyes.

They very well may have stopped trusting one another. One of them, it turned out, had vowed to protect the other, no matter what. And the other would do whatever was necessary to stay free and avoid prison.

Following their peripatetic trip to see friends around western Washington on the day Russ died, Peggy Sue and Jim had driven straight through to a motel near Peggy's house in Nevada. Vickie had just moved in, and they undoubtedly wanted to gather themselves and get some rest before they joined her in Peggy's home.

Jim stayed with Peggy for only a little over a month. Probably she was a constant reminder of the dead man in the yellow Tracker. Perhaps Jim was frightened that the Island County investigators would rapidly focus on both of them. It would be wiser for them to separate, at least until the homicide investigation slowed down.

Jim Huden was never known to be cruel or violent; the close friends with whom he had grown up insisted, "That's just not Jim Huden. He's a good guy."

When Mark Plumberg and Mike Beech had come to his house in Florida seven months later at the end of summer in 2004, it was obvious that Jim *knew* why they were there.

And he had seemed to be resigned to whatever fate had in store for him. He may have been in shock after the unannounced visit, and that was why he disappeared for a few days in September. But he had come back to Jean.

Jean Huden recalled that near Christmas 2004, she and Jim were in a beachfront hotel in Florida when he told her he was leaving. He had learned that the murder gun had been found, and was traced to him. He was so depressed that Jean was afraid he was going to commit suicide. She begged him not to go, but she later admitted to Mark Plumberg that he'd walked off and simply disappeared into the dark night.

"I'm so worried that his body may be out there someplace," she said then—but she was lying.

At that time, Jean didn't say that Jim had confessed to her the shooting of Russel Douglas, or that she had overheard a phone conversation he had with Peggy Thomas.

Now, Jean said that Jim had never told her what Peggy knew about the murder, but she did say, "I heard him tell Peggy on the phone that he had killed a guy but not to worry because she would never see him again."

Was he deliberately raising his voice in that phone conversation so that Jean would believe Peggy had no part in the death of Douglas?

Jean finally admitted that she and Peggy Sue Thomas had indeed been in touch with one another, and that sometime in 2004 Peggy had actually come to Punta Gorda where the threesome talked. Later, afraid to talk on the phone about Russ Douglas's murder, Jean Huden had traveled to the Las Vegas area once or twice to meet with Peggy. And Peggy had joined with Jean to provide money for Jim to live in Mexico.

At one point, Jean said that she and Peggy could have been "best friends" if they had met under other circumstances.

She admitted that Jim had managed to cross the border into Mexico as Hurricane Charley roared into Florida.

By avoiding telephone calls to her home or *from* the house where she lived in Punta Gorda, Jean had evaded phone records that might link her to Jim or to any messenger between them. Jean Huden said she had succeeded in getting money to Jim using a Mexican friend as an in-between emissary.

Even though he had openly carried on an affair with Peggy Sue Thomas, Jean still loved him, and she confessed that she had visited him in Mexico several times over the past seven years while he was a fugitive. She believed that at some point, she could join him there.

She knew what he had done the day after Christmas 2003 because he had confessed to her. He had told her that he planned to kill Russ with the help of Peggy Sue.

The motive?

"Jim told me that Russ Douglas was an abusive husband and father."

That wasn't true, although either Peggy Sue or Brenna Douglas might have convinced Jim Huden of that.

Still, Mark Plumberg and Mike Beech didn't believe that Jim Huden had suddenly decided to shoot a man he didn't even know. Nor was Jim familiar with the death site on Wahl Road, but they discovered that Peggy Thomas was. The estate right next door to the driveway where Russ died was owned by a woman named Cindy Francisco. And Cindy Francisco was a good friend of Peggy Sue's. It was Cindy who had gone with Peggy Sue to China City where they heckled the comedians. In fact, Peggy had lived in the Francisco mansion for about six months at one time. She knew the properties along Wahl Road very well indeed.

It almost seemed as if Peggy Thomas had played Jim Huden like a marionette, pulling just the right strings to get him to do whatever she wanted.

Even so, Huden had free will and he could have refused to be involved in a deadly scenario. A warrant for Jim Huden's arrest was prepared, along with a request for his extradition from Mexico. According to Jean, Huden could be found in Vera Cruz and she gave directions that were passed on to federal marshals.

Jim Huden was arrested in Vera Cruz on June 9, 2011, by Mexican authorities who had the power to detain violators who were in the country illegally. Then he was turned over to Deputy U.S. Marshal Raymond Fleck, a fifteen-year veteran who specialized in the capture of fugitives. Fleck had retrieved offenders from Canada, Ireland, Costa Rica, and Belize, as well as Mexico.

Vera Cruz is a thriving port city on the Gulf of Mexico with more than a half million population. It had been a wise location for Huden to hide. There were many expatriates living quiet lives out of the mainstream there.

Jim waived extradition and the marshal handcuffed him and escorted him across the border into the United States.

Jim was extremely tan, he had grown a mustache, and his long hair was bleached blond by the sun. It was just as thick as it had been in high school so many years earlier. He was lean and well muscled and seemed to be in good health.

He was transported to the Island County Jail. On July 9, 2011, Jim Huden pleaded not guilty to the charge of first-degree murder. His bail was set at ten million dollars. There was no way he could come up with 10 percent of that. He had no property and he surely hadn't made a fortune as an Anglo guitar teacher in Vera Cruz.

Although Peggy had always said that Jim was the one who left Dick Deposit's house to buy "smokes" on December 26 almost eight years earlier, and she had kept the receipt, the investigators and Prosecuting Attorney Greg Banks felt that it was Peggy Sue who had bought the Swisher Sweets cigars and saved the receipt. He believed that Jim was on his way to shoot Russ at the time.

She needed that small proof to establish where she and Jim Huden were while she was buying them. Banks felt that that might have the opposite effect on jurors.

Who saves a receipt for a pack of smokes for a year?

No one saw the couple at Dick Deposit's house on December 26 and Deposit himself couldn't be sure if the beds had been made when he visited his property. The couple hadn't turned in the house key to him, and Dean and Cathy Hatt were sure Peggy hadn't stopped by to give them the key.

A warrant was issued for the arrest of Peggy Sue Stackhouse Harris Thomas Allen.

PEGGY SUE WAS UNAWARE of what was about to come down. After almost eight years, she probably felt her connection to Russ Douglas's murder was a thing of the past. Now, on July 9, 2011—exactly a month after Jim Huden's arrest—Peggy Sue was spending some time away from her limo driving, and relaxing on her houseboat, *Off the Hook,* that was anchored on Navajo Lake in New Mexico.

The San Juan County Sheriff's Office in New Mexico had had her under surveillance since they traced her to the half-million-dollar houseboat. She didn't know that the sheriff's detectives were watching her from a neighbor's boat.

Fearing that she might resist arrest or run if she had forewarning, the San Juan County sheriff's men asked the Pine River Visitor's Center to notify Peggy Sue Thomas that there was a package waiting for her there.

It was a trick, of course. There was no package. How ironic. Russel Douglas had gone to meet his killer, expecting to find a package—a gift for his wife, Brenna. And he had been shot between the eyes.

And now Peggy Sue walked blithely into an ambush, too, expecting to find a present someone had sent her. Instead, when she showed up at the Pine River center, Peggy Sue was surprised to be surrounded by officers. Told she was under arrest for first-degree murder, she was obviously shocked—but she remained calm as she was handcuffed and taken to jail.

Her glory days seemed to have come to a sudden, bone-jolting stop. Peggy had continued to drive limos in Las Vegas after her divorce from Mark Allen, and earned a healthy living, interspersing her work schedule with vacations on her plush houseboat. She may have felt that she'd gotten away free. She may have been planning the next move she would make to re-create herself.

She knew Jim was in jail, charged with first-degree murder, but she had been confident he would never do anything to hurt her. Now she wasn't so sure.

After a few weeks in the San Juan County Jail in New Mexico, Peggy Thomas waived extradition and, dressed in baggy orange jail coveralls, she rode a prison bus for four days on her way back to Whidbey Island.

Peggy's bail was, like Jim Huden's, set in the millions, although hers was half his: five million dollars at her arraignment in Island County. That was rapidly reduced to a tenth of that. Even though her original bail was slashed, very few prisoners have five hundred thousand dollars to put up.

Peggy Sue's attorney, Craig Platt, argued that she was not an escape risk, and convinced Superior Court Judge Alan Hancock to accept a property bond in lieu of keeping her in jail. Her mother, Doris Matz, put up her home in Langley, with a market value of $231,924, and Peggy put up one of her houses—her Las Vegas home—worth $331,320.

She was released on bail in early September 2011 with the stipulation that she would live with her mother and wear a GPS device on her ankle that would allow law enforcement to track her movements so they would know where she was at all times.

That living situation didn't last long.

CHAPTER THIRTY

THE NEWS OF PEGGY SUE'S and Jim Huden's arrests on first-degree murder charges galvanized the residents of Whidbey Island. The *South Whidbey Record* had headline stories every week on the shocking case, and the *Everett Herald* and the *Seattle Weekly* weren't far behind. The eight-year-old murder investigation drew national attention, and docudrama shows such as *Dateline* and *48 Hours* sent first scouts out to see what the case of the beauty queen, Buck Naked and the X-hibitionists, and the unlikely murder victim was all about.

Russel Douglas's name was hardly mentioned in headlines about his murder; Peggy Sue was still the star, as it was usually referred to as "the Drop-Dead Gorgeous" case.

Two trials seemed imminent and they promised, quite literally, sex, drugs, and rock and roll.

After each article in the Whidbey Island papers, there were dozens of comments and opinions.

The first six children fathered by Jimmie Stackhouse had been through the rumors and fallout of violent murder before. Tom and Mike were living far away, Robby was long dead, Lana and Rhonda were living in Idaho, but Brenda was living in her daughter's home in Marysville, Washington, just north of Everett, a short drive and ferry ride to Whidbey Island. She could not avoid the gossip and the media blitz and all of it disturbed her a great deal.

Of all the trio of sisters, Brenda Stackhouse Gard could be the most fun and the most outrageous. She was smart and pretty, and loyal to a fault. It was sometimes hard to picture *that* Brenda as the woman who cried out in fear as she slept.

Ever since June 1963, when Mary Ellen Stackhouse was murdered in San Jose, Brenda was the child, teenager, and then the woman who suffered the most post-traumatic stress. She had seemed to do a lot better after she and her two sisters went back to San Jose and confronted Gilbert Thompson, but even so, Brenda continued to suffer from nightmares.

Brenda had stayed in touch with Rhonda, but she hadn't spoken with her older sister, Lana, in years. When she saw a message on Twitter from Lana—who was writing a book about their mother and seeking information about Gilbert Thompson—Brenda wrote back within a few hours.

"Lana, where are you?" she responded. "This is your sister Brenda. I haven't heard from you in years. I was looking up Gilbert Thompson online and found this. E-mail me. Love, Brenda."

With Peggy Sue's arrest and the media publicity, Brenda became angry and depressed. She responded to the numerous posts that appeared in the *South Whidbey Record,* asking readers not to lump her whole family into her half sister's alleged crimes. In her posts, Brenda alternately sounded combative or crushed by the hoopla surrounding Peggy's coming trial.

Peggy Sue Thomas was originally scheduled to go to trial before Jim Huden, and the date set first was September 24, 2011.

Jean Huden would be a strong witness for the prosecution, and so would Bill Hill. Jim had reportedly confessed to both these Florida witnesses that he had shot Russ Douglas after Peggy Sue had lured him to Wahl Road on the pretense of giving him a present for his wife, Brenna.

What few knew was that Brenda, Peggy's own half sister, was the rumored secret witness who would testify for the prosecution.

Her testimony might be the most damning to Peggy.

Sometime in 2003, when Brenda was considering a divorce from her second husband, Flint Gard, she had an odd and disquieting phone call from Peggy Sue and Jim Huden. Peggy Sue had offered to help Brenda get rid of Flint, and then she put Jim on the phone.

Jim had offered to "take Flint out," and, with

dawning horror, Brenda had understood what they meant. They were suggesting that they would murder Gard so she wouldn't have to go through all the hassles of divorce.

"No!" Brenda responded. "No—he's my son's father. I wouldn't think of doing something like that—"

Brenda had revealed this conversation to Mark Plumberg in October 2006, and it was part of the thick case file on Russ Douglas's murder, although few people were aware of the bizarre offer to kill Brenda's estranged husband.

Brenda would have other things to add when she testified at the upcoming trial.

But September 2011 was a desperate time for Brenda Gard. She dreaded testifying. She and her sisters had done their best to keep the family together, although that became impossible when Doris, their stepmother, played favorites with her own biological children.

There had been some good times with Peggy Sue, especially when she was little. Enough good times that Lana, Brenda, and Rhonda had tried to stay close to her. And she *had* let Brenda live with her in Las Vegas. Of course, Brenda was scared to death of Peggy and some of the scenarios she came up with. When she left Peggy's house in Nevada, she packed her bags secretly and snuck out in the middle of the night.

Once she was out of Peggy's house and not so frightened of her plots and bossy ways, Brenda was able to look back and feel grateful that Peggy had given her a place to stay.

In the early fall of 2011, Brenda was living alone in her daughter's empty house in Marysville, Washington. And that was supposed to be only a temporary situation because her daughter, Heather, needed to put it on the market.

Brenda had had a half dozen careers. She was a trained dental hygienist, a bartender, a cocktail waitress, and she had a real estate license.

After her divorce from Flint Gard, she lived off and on with Bill Lindquist, and he knew all too well about the nightmares that caused her to cry out in terror. She had never been free of them since the morning their mother was murdered.

In that bleak autumn of 2011, even Brenda's best friend said it was very difficult to be close to her. "There's just too much negativity," she explained.

And then Bill Lindquist left. As much as he cared for Brenda, he told her, "I can't watch you kill yourself any longer."

Brenda needed to have her medications—antidepressants—evaluated. The ones she was taking were causing her to tremble, and at the same time, energized her to the point that her sleep was interrupted, and she was up all hours bleaching her kitchen counters and the toilet, dusting where there was no dust.

Brenda's tenuous hold on her life began to slip as the world seemed to crash in on her. Rhonda would have rushed over from Idaho to help her cope, and her daughter, who loved her devotedly, would have, too, but they didn't realize that Brenda had finally hit bottom.

Prospective suicides often hurt so much emotionally that they cannot think about what their loss will do to those who love them. Somewhere in her troubled mind, Brenda knew that it would be Heather who found her, but she couldn't worry about that.

She was in too much pain.

On September 18, 2011, Brenda went to the garage and looped a rope over a beam, and then around her neck. Hanging doesn't require a long drop.

Brenda Stackhouse Gard simply stepped off the rear bumper of her Mustang that was parked in the silent garage.

When Heather found her mother there, she called her Aunt Rhonda and Rhonda Vogl rushed to Marysville as soon as she could get there.

It was one more tragedy for the family that had endured so many over the past five decades.

Brenda had grown a thick outer shell during that time, but those who loved her knew that despite her sometimes raucous sense of humor and her feistiness, she had never lost her vulnerable and tender center. As the elements of her life that gave her a modicum of safety slipped away, Brenda found herself sadly alone. Her two marriages were over, her children were grown up enough not to need her any longer, and her financial picture was bleak. She was mortified that Peggy Sue had brought shame to her family, and feared they would all be painted with the same brush.

Even so, her suicide was a terrible shock.

"How could someone as vivacious and full of life as Brenda hang herself in her daughter's garage, knowing Heather would find her?" Rhonda asked.

"She just stepped off the back fender of her Mustang and hung herself. She had put all of her files out, and told us what she wanted done. It rocked my world. Our family was fractured—and it had been for such a long time. Losing Brenda may have brought us together a little bit. But only time would tell."

Brenda was to have been a witness for the state in Peggy's trial—an event set to start in only four days. Brenda's death notice was only a short column in the Whidbey Island papers: PEGGY THOMAS'S RELATIVE DECEASED. There was no mention of her having been on the witness list for the upcoming trial.

Peggy Sue's trial was quickly postponed for four weeks, although no reason was given. Peggy's day in court was to begin on October 24. That would be a wondrous season in Coupeville as yellow and scarlet leaves fluttered on the trees that lined streets where beautifully restored old houses abounded.

Tourists would flock to bed-and-breakfasts and

stroll through shops before the end of the season. Once the fierce winds blustered off the Sound, Whidbey Island wouldn't be nearly as welcoming.

It didn't matter for reporters, writers, and television docudrama teams. All of us booked reservations, guessing how long Peggy Sue's trial might last. Most thought it would be two—possibly three—weeks.

ABC's *Dateline* was rumored to be following the strange murder of Russel Douglas, and so was *48 Hours*. Whatever verdict was handed down by her jury, Peggy Thomas's fate would undoubtedly be determined by Thanksgiving.

But no one could have foreseen just how long it was going to take for either Jim Huden's or Peggy Sue Thomas's trials to actually take place.

I made and canceled many hotel reservations, packed and unpacked, and often wondered if I would *ever* actually write this book.

CHAPTER THIRTY-ONE

ON OCTOBER 3, 2011, defense attorney Craig Platt presented the court with an amazing request. He explained that his client, Peggy Sue, needed time and the freedom to travel because she had so many loose ends to tie up. Forcing her into a premature trial without letting her take care of her affairs would be unfair.

Michael Moynihan—a visiting judge from Bellingham, Washington—was sitting in for Judge Alan Hancock. Moynihan had retired from the bench, although he occasionally took over the reins from superior court judges when they took time off.

Moynihan pondered Platt's reasons for asking that Peggy Sue be allowed to travel to at least five states over the following two weeks to visit her several properties and for personal reasons!

Island County prosecutor Greg Banks listened, astounded, as Platt ticked off the errands the defendant had to see to before the end of October.

Peggy's attorney said she needed money to pay for her defense. She and her mother, Doris, had already put up two of their properties for her bail bond. In order to liquidate more of her assets, she found herself forced to sell outright one of her other houses—the one she had purchased in Roswell, New Mexico, after her divorce from Mark Allen.

Platt said that Peggy Sue also had to clean out another New Mexico residence and bring her possessions back to Nevada. She needed to get her winter clothing, she had to winterize her houseboat, and see that her lawn and garden in Henderson, Nevada, met the standards of the homeowners' association in her gated community. If she didn't do that, Craig Platt said, she would be fined by the association.

There were so many things the accused murderer needed to tend to. Peggy Sue had her own dentist in Nevada and her teeth needed attention. Almost as important, she wanted to get her car and bring it up to Whidbey Island so she could run errands, seek employment, and attend court.

Platt added that Peggy Sue also needed to retrieve items, including photographs, to use in her defense on the first-degree murder charges.

And then there was the tragedy of her half sister Brenda's suicide. The Stackhouse family would gather in Idaho for her services. She wanted to go to Brenda's funeral in Bonners Ferry.

Greg Banks was against it. Why did Peggy want

to go to Brenda's funeral when she knew Brenda was going to testify against her in her upcoming trial?

Not surprisingly, Island County prosecuting attorney Greg Banks opposed Platt's other requests. He pointed out to Judge Moynihan that Peggy had *not* been released on her own personal recognizance, and she shouldn't be treated as if she was. She was being monitored constantly through the tracking device on her ankle. Banks said he considered Peggy Thomas an escape risk, nonetheless.

Several of the areas she wanted to visit would be ideal jump-off spots, the prosecutor said, where she could slip across the U.S. border if she wanted to.

"It sounds to me like just about everything she's asking to do could be done by others, by family members or hired contractors," he continued in his arguments to prevent the defendant from leaving Whidbey Island.

"She wants to travel to New Mexico and Nevada to visit her two daughters, mow the lawn at her Nevada residence, take care of some of her other real estate, and pack up some stuff and move it."

The prosecutor didn't see why Peggy herself needed to go to Nevada to cut her grass or winterize her houses. Couldn't she hire someone to do it?

"We *do* have dentists in Washington," Banks told Judge Moynihan. "And they *do* sell clothing in Washington as well."

The GPS anklet that semihobbled Peggy Thomas was far from foolproof. It would not work in areas outside certain cell phone ranges. If the person wearing the device wandered outside the coverage of AT&T towers, transmission would stop and no one could track where she was. Nor would the GPS activate on airplanes. And Peggy Sue was asking to go to Bonners Ferry, a Canadian border town in Idaho, and to Nevada, New Mexico, Washington State outside of Whidbey Island, and Utah.

Much of Peggy Sue's travel would be in regions where there were dead spots for cell phone transmission. And she would also be flying much of the time.

Platt countered that his client had every reason to return for her trial. There was the property bond that she didn't want to forfeit, and there was her sincere intention "to appear in court and defend herself zealously."

To the prosecutor's dismay, Judge Moynihan granted Peggy Sue's request to travel America, albeit with a GPS device that would sound an alarm on Whidbey Island if she attempted to pry it off.

She was required, of course, to give Greg Banks's office a detailed itinerary of her travels, right down to times, dates, flight times. She also said she would be glad to check in with local law-enforcement agencies wherever she went.

Craig Platt had extolled Peggy Sue's many virtues and reliability to Judge Moynihan, but it didn't do much to ease Banks's mind.

Media outlets all over America and in Great Britain found Peggy's travel arrangements after being charged with murder in the first degree so unusual that her case made headlines again in many newspapers and television programs.

WHILE PEGGY SUE WAS gone on her bizarre trip to get her world and wardrobe in order before her trial, it would be fair to say that Island County prosecuting attorney Greg Banks had some anxiety, wondering if she would come back or end up in another country. He knew how charismatic and engaging she could be, how chameleon-like. Although she was an almost Amazonian-size woman, Peggy could appear very feminine, even demure. She was many things to many people.

Banks worried that if she took off her tracking anklet in a dead zone in the New Mexican desert, Peggy Sue could be long gone before they realized it.

But she did show up at the places she had intended to visit. She was there at Brenda Gard's memorial service in Bonners Ferry, Idaho. Along with her many half siblings and family members, she watched the slide show of Brenda's life, a life ended too soon, and seemed as saddened as the rest of the mourners.

As Brenda's lovely face flashed on the screen in still pictures and home movies, it seemed impossible that she should be gone at only the age of fifty-two.

No one was sure why Brenda had taken her own life. It could have been the long-delayed result of her mother's murder, it could be that she had lost her two marriages and felt very alone, and it could also be because of guilt she felt over the prospect of testifying against her own half sister. Despite the differences among Doris's and Jimmie's kids, they had always tried to be loyal to each other, protecting their joint family against the outside world.

There were even those who suspected that Brenda had not died by her own hand—but that someone else had wanted to take her out of the picture. Autopsy findings did not validate that. In the case of hanging, forensic experts can determine which way a rope or cord has frayed and then see the difference between someone dropping from a height, and someone who has been unconscious and *hoisted* up over a beam of some sort by a killer standing behind him or her. The petechiae (small burst blood vessels) in the deceased's eyes and face usually occur in both cases.

For whatever reason, Brenda was gone.

CHAPTER THIRTY-TWO

THE FALL OF 2011 was not the happiest time of Greg Banks's career. One of his prime suspects was flying—somewhere—around America, the second was locked in the Island County Jail, unable to make bail, and the victim's widow—a woman who rumor said was part of a murder plot—had yet to be charged with anything.

Greg Banks grew up in upstate New York and Connecticut, and graduated from the University of Connecticut with a degree in engineering in 1985. At the time, there were few engineering jobs in that area. Banks had a brother living in Portland, Oregon, who encouraged him to come west and consider moving there.

In many ways the Northwest and New England are vastly different, but Banks liked the lifestyle he found in Oregon and Washington—ocean beaches, mountains, and skiing. The Pacific Ocean was an easy drive from the cities on the west side of the

Cascades, and Banks and his wife appreciated the casual friendliness of the people they met.

He ended up being hired by the Boeing Company as an engineer, and later took a job with a software company. By 1990, Greg Banks realized that his career as an engineer wasn't where he was meant to be, and he entered law school, graduating with a law degree in 1993.

Banks worked as a deputy prosecutor at the King County Prosecutor's Office in Seattle, and then in Island County. And he knew that the law was where he fit in.

Banks is a brilliant attorney, much respected in Island County and among other prosecutors in Washington State. He is a kind man who thinks always of the victims and the survivors of crime. He understands the pain that families who have lost loved ones to murder feel, and he often consults with them before he makes major decisions on how to prosecute defendants. If and when he feels that accepting a plea bargain rather than going to trial is the wiser choice, he will consult not only with the detectives on the case, but with the victims' survivors to assess how they feel before he makes the final decision.

Either way, Banks goes with what he thinks is right and that justice will be done. In the death of Russ Douglas, Greg Banks had worked with the investigators throughout the probe. He knew every twist and turn of the frustrating case.

Banks's family grew to include three children

ranging in age from late teens to midtwenties. While they were growing up, he coached a lot of soccer. Like Detective Mark Plumberg, with whom he has worked so many years on the Russel Douglas case, Greg Banks is an avid vegetable gardener, a pastime that many islanders share. And he is also an athlete who runs, swims, and bikes.

Banks has had so many challenging and tense cases during his tenure in office that he *needs* the healthy pursuits he practices.

There is the case of a young man who killed *both* his grandfathers. He left the first crime scene and drove to the second house where he repeated his killing spree.

In 1997, Jack Pearson, sixty-seven, lived with a woman friend, Linda Miley, fifty-eight, after he had invited her to move into his home. It seemed to work out well for about six years. But when he suddenly kicked her out, leaving her a note, "Don't drag your feet . . . just get out of here!" she was enraged.

Miley did not leave quietly. Instead, she bludgeoned Pearson in the head and then shot him five times in the chest. She ran to their neighbors and told them that a burglar had broken in and killed Jack. Later, she claimed that Pearson had raped her and she had no choice but to fight back in her own defense.

In her 2008 trial, Linda Miley's attorney argued that she suffered from a dissociative mental disorder that prevented her from having the capacity to plan and carry out a premeditated murder.

She made a lengthy statement claiming that she had been tricked by an investigator to admit things that weren't true while she was under the influence of her medication. She insisted that evidence had been lost that would have made the jury come back with an innocent verdict.

Found guilty of second-degree murder, Linda Miley faced a sentence of from fifteen years and three months to twenty-three years and four months. Greg Banks asked for the higher limits.

And Judge Alan Hancock agreed. He sentenced Linda Miley to twenty-one years in prison.

A sadder case was filed against a Whidbey Island teenager whose fifteen-year-old girlfriend disappeared suddenly. He finally admitted that he had killed her and buried her in his grandfather's mulch pile. Her body had deteriorated so much that it was no longer possible to tell if she had been pregnant when she died.

Like the "grotesques" in Sherwood Anderson's classic novel, *Winesburg, Ohio,* Whidbey Island has its share of bizarre crimes, just as other small counties and towns across America, crimes that involve residents who heretofore seemed normal and harmless.

Huey Ford, sixty-five, had one best friend: Mahlon "Lonnie" Gane Jr., fifty-five. They seemed an unlikely pair; Lonnie was black and mobile, and Huey was Caucasian and used a wheelchair, but they became truly close friends. Lonnie couldn't do enough for Huey. He once drove Huey all the way to Louisiana and back so his disabled friend could visit his relatives and see once more where he had grown up.

Such a friendship is hard to find, especially for lonely older men. But one summer, the two began to argue, and the arguments turned into a feud.

Huey Ford was very proud of his lawn but it wasn't looking good, bare and yellowing in many areas, and nothing like the green velvet perfection he had come to expect since Lonnie began helping him.

Huey suspected that Lonnie was deliberately poisoning his grass, although he wouldn't say why. He found that just downright mean. They fought for weeks as Huey accused and Lonnie denied. And the grass continued to look peckish.

Because he was disabled and needed his wheelchair to get around, Huey Ford took extra precautions to protect himself; there was always a .38 hidden beneath one of his legs.

One day in July 2005, Lonnie Gane went over to visit Huey in his house on Camano Island. He brought with him a .45 caliber handgun that he had borrowed earlier from Huey.

They began to argue about the grass again, and Gane threw a pillow at Huey Ford who responded with a racial slur. It was so unlike both of them, but it escalated the fight.

Huey pulled his .38 from its hiding place under his leg and fired two shots at his best friend's legs. Lonnie made a grab for the .45 off a table where it rested, but Huey hit it out of his hand. Then Lonnie punched Huey in the face and knocked him out of his wheelchair onto the ground.

The two longtime buddies rolled over and over on the ground. If they had taken a moment to think how ridiculous it was to get so angry over a patch of grass, they surely would have stopped, laughed, and shook hands.

But they were both mad. Huey Ford managed to reach the .45 and gain control of it. He fired blindly but still managed to hit Lonnie in the back of his head.

Even so, Lonnie continued to fight him, and Huey didn't think he was hit. Huey fired again and his gun jammed. He could hear Lonnie gasping, "I'm dying—I'm dying. Let me go . . ."

It should have been over at that point, but Huey reached for his .38 and shot Lonnie two more times.

Lonnie Gane wasn't moving any longer. Huey Ford reloaded his gun. He told Island County Detective Sue Quandt later that he did that because he intended to shoot himself afterward.

But he changed his mind and called 911. He told them he had shot his friend. When EMTs arrived, they found that Lonnie was beyond saving.

Huey Ford pleaded guilty to second-degree murder and was sentenced to fifteen years in prison. He died there in October 2011.

"We never expected him to get out of prison," Greg Banks said when he heard that Ford was dead. "But it happened sooner than we thought."

As the prosecuting attorney of Island County, Greg Banks had been to trial or overseen complicated plea bargains multiple times—but he had never seen a case as demanding as the investigation into Russ Douglas's death in the silent woods.

There was a plethora of circumstantial evidence, very little physical evidence, and virtually no clear motivation that sparked this Christmas homicide. Banks hoped that Peggy Sue Thomas's trial would unearth some of the long-buried secrets behind Douglas's death.

ONE MORE THORN IN Greg Banks's side in 2011 was a local editor/reporter, Brian Kelly of the *South Whidbey Record,* who had obtained many of the sheriff's follow-up reports. Under the Freedom of Information Act, it was legal for Kelly to get the records. Most reporters, however, understand that the release of too much information in the media *before* trial can seriously impact both the prosecution and the defense. Journalists, including myself, adhere to a kind of gentleman's agreement to withhold certain details until a case has been adjudicated. We don't want to hamper either side.

Kelly felt no such constraint. Beginning in the first week of September 2011, the reporter wrote headline stories about the Russ Douglas murder. Greg Banks had been closemouthed about the widow—Brenna Douglas—as the investigation continued. Now, Kelly's first story announced that Brenna had been the third suspect in Russ's murder ever since 2005, but the prosecutor and sheriff had chosen not to inform the public. He also wrote some searing articles about his perceived belief that county officials were involved in political wars that muddied the waters and resulted in too many mistakes in the Douglas case.

Of course there was information published that Greg Banks, Mark Plumberg, and Mike Beech had attempted to keep private until Peggy Sue Thomas and Jim Huden went on trial. Her attorney would have access to that through the rights of discovery—but everyone living on the island didn't need to know that now.

The prosecution team was not pleased with Brian Kelly's premature reporting.

In the twenties and thirties—long before television and the Internet offered virtually instant news—newspaper reporters were sometimes infamous for their outrageous tactics. But the era of Ben Hecht was long gone. Hecht, born at the end of the nineteenth century, was a popular journalist/ reporter for the *Chicago Daily News*. He went on to write successful Broadway plays and scripts for Hollywood movies. In his book, *A Child of the Century*, Hecht wrote of the aggressive maneuvers reporters of the day employed to get exclusives before their rivals did. This included buying witnesses too many drinks, approaching the bereaved widows and families for interviews—often even before the police did—and even crawling through the windows of funeral parlors to get pictures of the recently deceased.

Some of Brian Kelly's reporting smacked of the Hecht school of journalism. But, then again, he was an investigative reporter and it probably went against his every instinct to wait until the cases actually went to trial.

Prosecutor Greg Banks and lead detective Mark Plumberg were working hard to prepare for Peggy Sue's trial now only weeks away, and Kelly's continuing "breaking news" and revelations about things they had struggled to keep in-house wore on their nerves.

It was surely going to be much more difficult to find prospective jurors who hadn't already read too many details in the media—including the specifics of the hefty insurance payoffs Brenna Douglas had collected after Russ died.

IN TRUTH, BRENNA DIDN'T receive nearly as much from the insurance companies as gossip said. She had quite a long struggle with their underwriters, particularly when she refused to have a chunk of the money put in a trust fund for her two children, Jack and Hannah.

Once she had her insurance payoff, she had spent most of it quickly, but not wisely. She put money down on a house—not Peggy Sue's house—but the one she chose was foreclosed upon in less than a year. She bought an expensive SUV, and any number of items that chipped away at her bank balance.

CHAPTER THIRTY-THREE

BY OCTOBER 2011, TO almost everyone's surprise, Peggy Sue Thomas had crossed off all the items on her to-do list: she had attended her half sister Brenda's memorial service in Idaho, winterized all her properties, bought new clothes suitable for a fall trial, and collected documents for her attorney.

And then she came home to Whidbey Island!

Peggy still wore her tracking anklet, and a few of her relatives commented that they could hear it when it went off. She would have to wear it throughout her trial. She was semifree on bail, but she remained in a kind of purgatory.

On Halloween—October 31, 2011—Peggy was arraigned and formally charged with first-degree murder. To no one's surprise, she pled not guilty.

Who would go to trial first? Peggy Sue Thomas and Jim Huden began a kind of musical chairs with their trial dates.

The holiday season was almost upon them. Ten Thanksgivings and Christmases had come and gone since Russel Douglas died. Newcomers to Whidbey Island didn't even know who he was. The case had lain fallow ever since Jim Huden went into hiding. Predictably, neither of their attorneys wanted Peggy Sue Thomas and Jim Huden to be tried jointly.

Initially, Jim was supposed to go first, followed by Peggy Sue. He was expected to take the defendant's seat in court on November 27, 2011.

I made reservations at a motel in Langley and packed my bags. And then I unpacked them.

Huden's trial was switched with that of Joshua Lambert, the homeless high school dropout who was accused of killing both of his grandfathers on the same day.

On January 6, 2012, Judge Vickie Churchill granted attorney Peter Simpson's request to release him as Jim Huden's defense attorney. Matthew Montoya was chosen to replace him. Montoya immediately asked for a trial delay because he needed time to go through stacks of sheriff's follow-up reports and legal documents.

Judge Churchill granted his request, and Jim Huden's trial was now set for March 13, 2012.

Peggy Sue would face a jury after that. Her trial would begin on May 1.

But once again, the scheduling changed. None of this was a surprise; for a relatively small county with few prosecutors, three separate murder trials were going to demand a lot of juggling of dates and staff.

I kept making hotel reservations and canceling them. I finally just kept my bag packed. At some point, there would be a trial, although no one could say absolutely which of the two defendants would go first.

And then, once more, Jim's and Peggy Sue's trial dates were reversed. Prosecutor Greg Banks said it really didn't make much difference which of them went first—that they would basically be trying the same case twice.

In the end, it was Jim who went on trial in Superior Court Judge Vickie Churchill's courtroom in Coupeville on Tuesday, July 10, 2012.

Courtroom 2 in the law and justice center had three long benches and shorter benches on opposite sides of the aisle. There were no windows beyond two small panes of glass in the door, making the courtroom isolated from the world outside.

Prosecuting attorney Greg Banks would speak for the state, with his assistant Michelle Graff and Detective Mark Plumberg beside him at the state's table. Michelle could put her finger on whatever documents Banks might need, and Banks expected to call and recall Plumberg to the witness stand for the prosecution.

Matthew Montoya and his paralegal, Glenda Ward, sat beside Jim Huden at the defense table. The bailiff was Ron Roberts, and the court reporter was Karen Shipley.

Huden was clean shaven, his ponytail pulled back and cinched neatly. And compared to photos taken of him just after he was extradited from Mexico, he looked healthier and well rested. He wore a dark gray suit with a navy blue tie and shirt. The expression on his face was almost impossible to read.

The jury pool began with seventy-five potential jurors, and they filled the benches and sixteen folding chairs brought in to accommodate them. These possible jurors had to be winnowed down to twelve people, with two alternates—in case any of the sitting jurors became ill or had to withdraw for other reasons.

Judge Churchill addressed the jury panel, explaining the jury instructions, and they were given questionnaires to fill out. Nine prospective jurors were dismissed for cause; most of them had already made up their minds that Jim Huden was guilty.

There were soon others who appeared to know more than a little about the well-publicized case. Three said they had been influenced by "media bias," one was dismissed for an illness in his family, and one had gone to high school with the defendant.

Clearly, the jury selection would be a long and tedious process. One by one, possibles were eliminated. Judge Churchill read over the questionnaires and saw that many had issues of anxiety and depression, spinal pain, and family responsibility.

As was to be expected, several juror candidates stepped down because they knew Banks and Churchill, or other members of the legal cast.

Hearing a list of witnesses expected to testify, the smaller panel didn't seem to recognize them. Nor did anyone feel they had bias or prejudice that would flaw their fairness in rendering a verdict.

Greg Banks asked when they felt murder might be justified. Several answered in self-defense or time of war. Vigilantism? All said never.

"What about the killing of a rapist or serial child rapist?"

Overwhelmingly the panel believed that the justice system should handle it.

But could they all deal with graphic and grisly photos? More dropped out. Five responded that they watched violent television shows, and could view the photos without becoming upset.

Matthew Montoya asked more questions. "If you were required at this point to say what you believe?"

All answered "innocent."

The day was inching by and it was after three. The courtroom had become progressively more muggy and warm and it was difficult for many to keep their eyes open. This is the curse of summer trials.

Greg Banks asked several members of the panel if they knew the difference between "reasonable doubt" and "beyond the shadow of a doubt." This was a hard one, and none of those questioned could give a clear-cut answer.

Montoya asked how the panel would evaluate the credibility of a person or a scenario.

"By a person's actions, eye contact, body language, intuition, and demeanor," one prospective juror answered. Court adjourned at 4:10 that first day of trial. They had eliminated only twenty-seven members of the panel.

On Wednesday, cameramen from *Dateline* were busy setting up their gear and rearranging benches to be sure they got good shots of the participants.

Greg Banks told the forty-eight remaining members of the jury panel that there was an "extra chair" in the courtroom. He referred to "someone else who might be involved, but would not be called to testify."

The only logical person would have to be Peggy Sue Thomas, now charged with first-degree murder, and long considered a prime suspect in Russel Douglas's murder. She still wore the tracking anklet on her leg. Brenna Douglas was also a likely contender, but she *was* on the witness list.

And there was an empty witness chair, which would never be filled, one that the state had hoped would be occupied by Brenda Gard. Brenda had cooperated fully with the prosecution team, and they had expected her to make a compelling witness—probably *the* strongest witness—against Jim Huden, first—and then against her own half sister Peggy Sue. She had been prepared to testify that Jim and Peggy had offered to kill her estranged husband for her.

But Brenda had been dead for almost ten months. Mark Plumberg had called the Snohomish County Sheriff's Office within minutes of learning Brenda had died to tell detectives there that her "suicide" might be not be as it seemed. There were likely suspects who might well have wanted Brenda out of the picture.

In the end, the preparations she had left, her note, her financial records, other important documents, and her state of mind had convinced both counties' detectives and medical examiners that Brenda had died by her own hand.

The possibility that someone might have murdered her just didn't hold up, considering physical and circumstantial evidence.

One prospective juror said that any missing witness would not be an issue for him, and others agreed. It would have been foolhardy for Peggy Sue to show up in the courtroom with the tracking device on her ankle. Moreover, all eyes would have been on her, and most spectators would consciously or unconsciously link her to Jim Huden and a plot to kill Russ Douglas. Anything she said would, indeed, tend to incriminate her.

A man's future depended on an impartial jury, and both Banks and Montoya were asking questions that many laymen wouldn't have thought of, striving to dismiss those who might not qualify.

Greg Banks asked: "If you received a confession of a serious crime by a good friend or relative, would you report it to the authorities?"

"It would depend on the facts," one said.

Several knew Wahl Road very well.

Three had higher degrees and were confident they could evaluate physical evidence.

Four said they had had good experiences with police.

Matthew Montoya asked several panel members: "Who do you trust?"

"My wife."

"My wife and my dad."

"I don't trust anyone—been burned too many times."

The mostly middle-aged panel, which had begun with more men than women, was growing smaller and smaller.

By late morning on the second day, the accepted jurors and alternates were seated.

Judge Churchill gave her instructions to the jury and adjourned the session for lunch. At 1:30, Greg Banks would give his opening remarks, and the trial itself would begin.

CHAPTER THIRTY-FOUR

AS JIM HUDEN'S TRIAL began in earnest on Wednesday, July 11, 2012, there was room for many court watchers to sit. Russel Douglas's family and friends sat in the front row of the gallery, and many of Huden's longtime friends were there to support him. Doris Matz, Peggy Sue's mother, was there—but not Peggy Sue herself. Doris sat far back in the corner of the gallery, well out of camera range.

Shirley Hickman, whom I've known for almost fifty years and who lives on Whidbey Island, was there to help me and would be there every day to take notes and observe the body language of the defendant, the attorneys, witnesses—and the jury.

The *South Whidbey Record* would be there each day, too, but they were no longer represented by Brian Kelly. Reporters Jessie Stensland and Ben Watanabe would spell each other, covering what was probably the most newsworthy trial Island County had seen in a decade or more.

Every time the door opened, heads craned, mostly to see if Peggy Sue might walk in.

Anyone who was listed as a possible witness waited in the hall outside the courtroom so they could not hear others' testimony. Once they finished and were excused, they could come in and observe—if they wanted to.

Prosecuting attorney Greg Banks began his opening remarks by saying that Russel Douglas's death was not just murder; it was "an assassination." He told the jury that the evidence would show that Jim Huden and his "accomplice" had deliberately lured Douglas to the cottage driveway off Wahl Road.

"The defendant didn't know the deceased," he said. "Yet Jim Huden opened the victim's car door, looked him in the face, and shot him."

Banks promised that he would provide jurors with a "framework" to help them in their deliberations.

He gave them an overview of the whole case, and told them who the players were and what was happening in their lives over Christmas 2003.

As the prosecutor referred to lead detective Mark Plumberg—who sat beside him every day at the prosecution table, and was available to testify or assist Banks throughout the trial—he said that as hard as the investigators worked, the case remained fallow from December 26, 2003, to July 2004, when Detective Sergeant Mike Beech began to receive phone calls from a man in Port Charlotte, Florida, who eventually revealed he was Bill Hill, a former member of Buck Naked and the X-hibitionists.

"Mr. Hill will testify, and he will tell you that the defendant confessed a killing in this county. He told Mr. Hill that when he pulled the trigger, it gave him a rush."

Banks offered a possible motive for murder. Jim had detested his stepfather for the domestic violence with which he ruled his family when Huden was just a boy. Jim might well have carried a need for revenge most of his life. A witness for the state would explain that when he testified.

Banks explained how a dissemination of facts about the search for the murder gun had led the detectives to retired Oregon law officer Keith Ogden, who had been holding on to it for Huden.

(When I interviewed Greg Banks and Mark Plumberg later, they said that finding that gun and linking it to Jim Huden had turned a probable cold case into a winner. If Huden hadn't wanted to someday sell that gun and get his money back—*if* he'd simply thrown it off a ferry that first day—he might have walked away free and clear.)

But, of course, the .380 Bersa had become a vital piece of physical evidence that eventually trapped Jim Huden. They had almost enough to arrest him in late August 2004, but by then Huden had disappeared in the midst of a hurricane.

Matt Montoya, whose brevity became familiar to the gallery, spent only two or three minutes in his opening remarks. He asked the jurors to view the "facts" critically, repeated that two or three times, and reminded them to be sure that the prosecuting attorney met the burden of proof.

BRENNA DOUGLAS WAS THE first witness for the state. Brenna had remained on Whidbey Island until about 2011 when she moved to Ellensburg on the promise of a job there. That hadn't worked out, and she now lived in Ferndale, Washington— not far from Bellingham.

Brenna was a large woman, but attractive. Her body was stiff as she took the witness chair, and she seemed nervous.

Greg Banks asked her easy questions first. Her address and her profession.

"How do you know Russel Douglas?"

"My husband."

"When did he die?"

"December 2003."

"Where did you meet him?"

"Coupeville High School."

"When were you married?"

"June 1994."

"Do you have children?"

"Two. Jack and Hannah."

"What was your marital status in December 2003?"

"Separated—but married."

Banks moved closer to the more interesting facts. Brenna explained that she had been doing hair since 1989, and she and Russ bought Just B's and opened their salon in January 2003. It had four chairs and three were rented to other stylists.

Banks held out a photo of Peggy Sue Thomas, and Brenna identified her. She explained that Peggy rented a chair at Just B's, and when she moved to Las Vegas, Brenna and Russ Douglas had rented her house in Langley.

"Did you keep in touch with her after she moved?"

"By phone, we did."

"Have you ever visited Las Vegas?"

"Once."

Brenna agreed that she had discussed her separation from Russ with Peggy Sue, who was separating from Kelvin Thomas at about the same time.

"Do *you* know Jim Huden?"

"I met him once. I didn't really know him."

Asked to identify the defendant in the courtroom, Brenna pointed to Jim at the defense table.

Banks asked her about the Christmas holiday nine years before. Would Brenna paint her late husband with as black a brush as she had to detectives? No. She spoke cautiously and with no apparent vitriol. She testified that she had known Russ was involved with someone who lived off-island.

"But he did come over to spend time with his family?"

"Yes."

"Did he pay child support?"

"Yes, he did."

As she recalled, Russ had stayed at their family home in Langley—Peggy Sue's house—from December 23 to December 26. They had had a traditional Christmas with family and guests coming over, presents, and holiday food. The morning after Christmas, Russ told her that he needed to run some errands.

Brenna looked at the picture of a yellow GEO Tracker, and identified it as Russ's vehicle.

"When did he return? *Did* he return?"

"He never came back. I didn't know what to think. I thought our reconciliation was working well . . . I was worried, angry, confused . . ."

Brenna said that when Russ didn't come home as the night wore on, she grew angry. "And then the detectives knocked on my door in the middle of the night to tell me what had happened."

Banks changed the subject. "Did you see Peggy Thomas over the holidays?"

"She worked a couple of days in the salon."

"Regarding Russel, prior to your separation, you had a restraining order against him," Banks pressed. "What was the situation at home?"

"Well, he had a girlfriend on the side, and there was physical and verbal abuse toward me and our kids."

"What happened to that restraining order?"

"It was withdrawn."

"You *did* discuss the situation with Russel with Peggy Thomas, didn't you?"

"Yes—we did talk about it."

Matt Montoya cross-examined Brenna.

"Did you receive a gift of money from Peggy?"

"Yes."

"And you discussed Russel's abuse with Peggy and with others?"

"Yes."

"While separated from Russel in April or May of 2003, how was their relationship?"

"It was amicable."

The defense attorney often repeated the same questions that prosecutor Banks had asked, and it seemed counterproductive to Jim Huden's case. Montoya's cross-examinations thus far had lasted no more than five minutes.

"Do you recall what your husband was wearing on the morning of December 26?"

"Shorts—and some kind of top."

"Witness excused," Montoya said.

Next to testify were the residents who lived along Wahl Road and had seen the yellow car parked for so long with its door open in the cold rain, and those who finally saw the body and called the sheriff. And then there was the usual parade of the officers who responded to the crime scene, the coroner, and a number of criminologists from the Washington State Patrol who explained ballistics, DNA testing, and fingerprints that had helped to build the case against Jim Huden.

Greg Banks, Mark Plumberg, and the rest of the sheriff's investigative team had worked so hard for so long to bring some kind of justice to Russel Douglas, now long dead. Banks was building a strong foundation, one he hoped would be so solid that nothing could tear it down.

With each day of trial, the testimony grew in intensity and one got the feeling that the strongest witnesses were yet to come.

July is almost always one month when north-westerners can count on sunny and rainless days. But now, the night sky burst open with a series of frightening electrical storms. Chain lightning streaked shards of blue and white across the dark sky and hailstones as big as golf balls pounded down on windows and skylights, waking sleeping citizens in Coupeville and other island towns.

Jurors and those who had become familiar faces in the courtroom often had to run through wind-driven rain sluicing down the building's exterior walls as the storm didn't let up in daylight, either.

Inside Judge Vickie Churchill's domain, there was another kind of storm building; without win-dows, no one could see or hear the raging lightning and thunder outside. Still, there was a heaviness here. When someone's cell phone rang, spectators jumped in surprise. Peggy Sue's mother, Doris, had forgotten to turn off the ringer on her phone. She fumbled with it quickly and the sound stopped. Judge Churchill chose to wait until the end of the day to chastise her for what is considered a blatant interruption in a court of law.

JEAN HUDEN'S NAME WAS not on the witness list, but William Hill's of Port Charlotte, Florida, was. Jean was still married to Jim, and couldn't testify against him because of the state's marital disqualification law. She could, however, testify against Peggy Sue Thomas when her trial began in a few months. Detectives had interviewed Jean, who now admitted that both Jim and Peggy had told her they plotted to kill Russ. She also revealed that Peggy had traveled to Punta Gorda and come to the house Jean shared with Jim.

Peggy had confided they just needed to figure out "how to get Russel to where they needed him to be and take care of it."

Bill Hill was scheduled to testify on a most inopportune date: Friday the thirteenth. It would be agonizing for him to face Jim Huden and the jurors and seal Jim's fate.

Hill was a retired air force officer, a man of late middle age whose haircut was a spiky crew cut. He was one of the "X-hibitionists" in the band that Jim Huden headed, but he hardly resembled an aging rock star!

Bill Hill testified that he and Jim were driving along the Gulf Coast from Punta Gorda to Sarasota when Huden blurted out that he had shot and killed a man back in Washington State. As the man he considered his best friend gave details on Russ Douglas's murder, Hill had said he had difficulty believing him. This wasn't the Jim Huden that he had come to know.

But Jim told Bill Hill that he went up to the yellow Tracker and shot Russ Douglas point-blank in the face from about six inches away.

Jim had confided that his stepfather used to beat him and his mother, saying: "I always hated that man with a passion, and I wanted to find someone who was like him and get revenge."

Jim told Hill that Peggy Sue, his mistress at the time, had convinced him that Russel Douglas was an abusive husband and father, and Huden had finally found the ideal target.

"I didn't know what to do," Hill testified. "I waited a couple of months before I contacted the authorities here [Whidbey Island]. I wasn't sure whether I was gonna spill the beans or not."

"Why was that?" Greg Banks asked.

"Partly out of fear, I guess. And loyalty," Bill Hill finally said, fighting back his own emotions. "He's my best friend."

The witness said he and Jim were such good friends that he had flown to Las Vegas and walked Jean down the aisle when Jim and Jean got married.

"When did you talk to him last?" Banks asked.

Bill Hill recalled having lunch with Jim Huden sometime in 2004. Hill complained about his boss, and Jim had asked him: "Do you want your boss to be *taken care of*?"

Hill demurred, and Huden said: "Well, I've done it once. I could do it again."

The "best friends" never saw each other again until this moment in a courtroom in Coupeville, Washington.

On Monday, July 16, a witness who had not been in the news much took the witness stand. Cindy Francisco was the woman who once lived in the lavish estate next door to the murder site.

"What is your current residence?" Greg Banks asked.

"On Saratoga Road in Langley."

"How long have you lived on Whidbey Island?"

"Since 1990, except for two years when I was in Las Vegas and Colorado."

"How do you know the defendant?"

Cindy said she had met Jim Huden through her good friend Peggy Sue Thomas, whom she had known for a decade. At Banks's direction, she pointed out Huden at the defense table. She said she had not seen him for "many years."

Cindy Francisco said she had met Peggy Sue at a hair salon in Langley. "We were good friends, close at that time."

She agreed that she had once lived on Wahl Road but thought that had to be almost ten years ago.

"Had Peggy Thomas spent time there?"

"Yes, she and her two girls once stayed with me for a few weeks."

"Was Jim Huden ever there?"

"No."

"Was Russel ever there?"

"Once—to pick up some plants I was getting rid of."

The witness said she had traveled with Peggy, once to Florida, where she met Jim Huden.

"Did you ever spend time in Las Vegas with Peggy?"

"No."

Dick Deposit was the next witness. He answered questions about his connection to Whidbey Island.

"I grew up here."

"How long have you known Jim Huden?"

"Since fourth grade . . . I consider him a best friend."

Deposit explained that he had met Peggy Sue at "Sweet Sue" Mahoney's wedding. He recalled that Peggy and Jim had "become an item" in the summer of either 2002 or 2003.

Deposit owned a vacation home in the Useless Bay Colony and he testified that Jim and Peggy had stayed there several times when they visited the island.

"When was the last time?" Banks asked.

"They arrived the week before Christmas 2003, and left the twenty-third or twenty-fourth."

Deposit said he'd left his key with the Hatts, who lived next door.

The retired CPA said that the last time he had heard from either Jim Huden or Peggy Sue was on December 26 when they called to say that they had forgotten to return the key on the twenty-third, but they had just dropped it off, and they were currently on their way to visit Bill Marlow, and then to drive south to Longview to have dinner with friends.

"Have you had any contact since then?"

"No."

"Any attempts [on your part]?"

"No."

Matt Montoya's cross-examination questions continued to take only a few minutes. As before, he seemed to be asking the same questions that Banks had.

Even though the next few witnesses were testifying for the prosecution, it was obvious that this was difficult for them. They had all considered Jim Huden a good and close friend for many years.

Still, Bill Marlow had to tell the truth. He testified that neither Jim nor Peggy had visited him around midday on December 26, 2003. He agreed that Jim "consumed alcohol" and had been drinking his favorite Crown Royal whiskey more heavily than he did the last time Marlow had seen him earlier in 2003.

The next witness was Richard Early, one of the people Peggy Sue and Jim said they had dinner with the day after Christmas. And that, Early said, was true. The couple had joined their group in Longview late, and left after appetizers, but they *were* there.

Early looked at exhibit number 93, a copy of the receipt from the restaurant that he had signed at 7:41 P.M. on December 26, 2003.

"How did Jim appear that evening?" Banks asked.

"He looked like he'd been drinking heavily."

"Was he driving?"

"Probably Peggy drove."

CHAPTER THIRTY-FIVE

THERE WAS PROBABLY NOTHING more important in the case against Jim Huden than the gun that was lost—and then found. In most cases, guns can be traced back to the day they came off the assembly line in the gun factory. It wasn't necessary to go all the way back with the .380 Bersa that had killed Russel Douglas in an instant, but Prosecutor Greg Banks and the sheriff's detectives knew its history through three owners.

Exhibit number 95 could well be the key to the entire case.

Martin Snytsheuvel, who was the manager of an Internet company and lived in Las Vegas, bought that gun in 2003. It wasn't what he wanted, so he asked his father to place an ad in hopes of selling or trading it.

Around the same time, Jim Huden had asked his friend Keith Ogden, the retired Oregon law-enforcement officer, if he had a gun that Jim could buy. Ogden told him no.

He asked Jim why he wanted a gun, and Huden said that he wanted to shoot the pigeons that were becoming a nuisance around Peggy Sue's pool in Henderson.

Jim called soon after to say he had purchased a gun and he asked Ogden if he would show him how to use it. Ogden said he would if Jim Huden would come to his house.

"Have you ever been to Jim's residence?" Banks asked.

"Yes."

"Does it have a pool?"

"Yes. He brought the gun—a Bersa—over to my house. I showed him how it worked—broke it down to show him how to clean it and how to fire it."

Huden said he needed some way to silence the noise it made because he and Peggy lived in an up-scale residential area in Henderson.

"I taped a one-quart plastic bottle over the muzzle and shot once. Then we tried it with a pillow," Ogden testified. "That made it very quiet."

Jim Huden was obviously an amateur with a gun, but Ogden hadn't been concerned that he now owned one. Jim and Peggy Sue *did* have a pool and they *did* live in an exclusive neighbor-hood where gunfire wouldn't be condoned. Ogden explained how the investigators from the Island County Sheriff's Office had located the slugs and casings in the ground. Both he and his wife, Donna, had witnessed that.

The murder gun itself was probably worth between $250 and $300. But Jim Huden hadn't been able to simply throw it away where no one would find it; he didn't want to lose that much money.

Detective Bill Farr had taken DNA samples from Huden after he was captured in Mexico—but it was impossible to match those to the gun.

Mark Plumberg had obtained DNA from Peggy Thomas in February 2004, and he rolled the defendant's fingerprints in May 2012.

Peggy's DNA wasn't helpful, either, although top criminalists from the Washington State Crime Lab, Margaret Barber and Lisa Collins, worked on microscopic evidence analysis that might link their bodily fluids, hairs, and fibers.

Kathy Geil, of the Washington State Patrol firearms exam team, had hit a bonanza and she testified that the bullet found in Russ Douglas's head had tool marks identical to the bullet dug up in Keith Ogden's backyard—where he and Jim had fired it long ago.

Jill Arwine of the WSP Latent Prints Unit in Olympia, Washington, had found something almost as valuable. Arwine, who has testified well over fifty times as an expert witness, gave the jurors a fast lesson in how to lift latent prints from both a hard surface and a soft surface such as paper. She also explained AFIS: Automated Fingerprint Identification System, which includes a massive volume of fingerprints.

"Did you process a .380 casing?" Banks asked.

"Yes."

"Did you find any prints?"

"No."

"Did you find any prints on the car [the yellow Tracker]?"

"Yes."

"Did you do a comparison of the prints?"

"Yes—they belonged to Russel Douglas."

Arwine had also found fingerprints belonging to Brenna Douglas, but that wasn't significant. Brenna had long since told detectives that she often drove Russ's car.

Greg Banks asked her if she had been provided other items to test.

"Yes—a gun and a gun manual, magazine, and paperwork."

"Were you able to obtain prints from the gun?"

"No."

"How about the manual?"

"Yes, I processed each page and I made digital images of the prints found."

"Were you able to compare images, and if so, to whom?"

"Yes—James Huden and Peggy Thomas: exhibit 92 belongs to Peggy Thomas, and exhibits 99 and 100 belong to Huden. There were nineteen prints identified—thirteen belong to Huden, and one on page fourteen of the manual belongs to Peggy Thomas."

*   *   *

JIM DIDN'T BLINK. THROUGHOUT his trial, Huden had maintained a stoic presence. He occasionally wrote something on the yellow legal pad in front of him, or whispered briefly to Matt Montoya, but he didn't make eye contact with anyone else in the courtroom.

The spectators behind the rail kept their hopes up that he would testify in his own defense. That, however, is a very risky endeavor. Once a defendant testifies, he opens himself up to cross-examination by the opposing attorneys. Prosecuting Attorney Greg Banks is a shrewd lawyer, and throughout the trial, he caught every inference or odd statement that the defense made. He would have a field day jousting with Jim Huden.

And what excuse would Huden have for the many times he had been in the wrong place at the wrong time? Although he and Peggy Sue Thomas had been seen (or not seen) by people who could validate where they showed up on the day of Russ Douglas's murder, there appeared to be too many connections that led back to Huden. Banks had shown the link between the bullet in the victim's head to the gun that the defendant owned. How could that be if Huden had no involvement in the homicide?

CHAPTER THIRTY-SIX

MATTHEW MONTOYA HAD A witness for the defense that he was counting on. Dr. Jon Nordby's fee to conduct tests on the way human blood drips, pools, spatters, and is otherwise emptied from a body after death by gunshot was well over thirty-five thousand dollars.

I have known Nordby for more than thirty years. When I first met him, he was working as an assistant to the Pierce County, Washington, medical examiner. A Scandinavian originally from Minnesota, Nordby is tall with thick blond hair, now turning to gray, and a "walrus mustache." There is no question that he is very intelligent—so smart, in fact, that he sometimes has difficulty communicating his expertise to laymen.

Nordby heads Final Analysis Forensics, and gives his areas of expertise as: "Medical-legal death investigations; blood stain patterns; trace evidence analysis; crime-scene processing and investigation; reconstruction of crime scenes; ballistics; firearms and gunshot residue testing."

He has written or contributed to three textbooks on forensic techniques. Dr. Nordby, however, is not a medical doctor, but holds a PhD.

On July 19, 2012, Dr. Nordby took the witness stand. His testimony on blood spatter to come was so esoteric that he took it upon himself to give the jurors some education in the way blood behaves. He spoke of forward spatter, back spatter, impact spatter, and two kinds of sprays. And then there were stains: drip, swipe, wipe, soaking, wicking, saturation, transference.

Although Jon Nordby knew well what he was discussing, most of the jurors had trouble following his testimony.

The gist of the hours he spent testifying was that he did not acknowledge that Russel Douglas had been shot while he sat behind the wheel of his car. Nordby suggested that the blood patterns were inconsistent with that conclusion.

If he was shot *outside* the Tracker, how would that be significant in this case? Russ weighed about two hundred pounds, and after he was shot, he would have been, quite literally, dead weight and very difficult to lift and put back behind the wheel.

Detective Mark Plumberg felt that an attempt to move Douglas was possible, because of the slight shift of blood in his hand, but if that succeeded, the blood movement on the victim's shirt and hand would have been far more noticeable.

And where was this line of testimony going? Since the gun wasn't there, there wasn't any chance that Russ's death had been a suicide.

As Greg Banks cross-examined Nordby, he began by quietly questioning the witness to suggest that his education and experience were not those of a true forensic expert.

"Are you a medical pathologist?"

"No."

"Do you have a medical degree or a medical residency?"

"No."

"What was your bachelor's degree in?"

"Arts and philosophy."

"Your master's?"

"Philosophy and math."

"PhD?"

"Philosophy."

After a break for lunch, the cross-examination continued and the courtroom was filled with thoughts and scenarios involving blood for the rest of the afternoon.

To offer a movie parallel to the back spatter in the actual murder, Dr. Nordby even brought in a gunshot scene from the film *Pulp Fiction* starring John Travolta and Samuel Jackson, explaining that Travolta was "drenched in blood," while Jackson had simulated brain matter on him after the shots were fired.

Greg Banks suggested that the hefty witness fee had relevance to possible bias on Dr. Nordby's part. He asked him what his fees were for his testimony on behalf of Jim Huden's defense.

"Thirty thousand dollars. That's three thousand dollars per day—in court at five hundred dollars an hour. In general, I charge two hundred and fifty dollars an hour, plus travel."

Asked by Matthew Montoya why he hadn't read narratives about the homicide, Dr. Nordby said he hadn't wanted to taint his own impression.

"Why did you include information about *Pulp Fiction* [the movie] in your report?"

"To mention a current example—that back spatter is a natural phenomenon."

The afternoon lengthened and Nordby apologized that tests on another case had been inserted by mistake into the appendix of his long report on the Douglas case.

The jurors were tired, and some of them complained that they hadn't been able to hear some of Jon Nordby's testimony. In the end, the day hadn't gone well for the defense.

There was another witness subpoenaed by Montoya that afternoon. He was Ron Young, one of Jim Huden's oldest friends. Young said he had seen Jim about three times during the Christmas holidays in 2003. The last time was on the twenty-sixth.

"Morning or afternoon?" Montoya asked.

"Between noon and one."

"Was he by himself?"

"No, he was with Peggy Sue Thomas."

"No more questions."

On Friday, July 20, 2012, Banks recalled Detective Mark Plumberg to the stand. The tall investigator went over the circumstances of his videotaping Jim Huden in Punta Gorda in the late summer of 2004. He, Mike Beech, and the Florida officer were present at the time.

After some editing (to remove about eight minutes of tape where Huden sat alone waiting for the interview to begin), Matt Montoya reviewed the tape and agreed that the jury could see it. It was shown to both the jury and the gallery.

It was, of course, a damning tape, where Jim had been advised of his Miranda rights and he freely admitted going to Whidbey Island with Peggy at Christmas, and discussed the present he delivered "to Mark's apartment" during that time.

Greg Banks again questioned the county coroner, Robert Bishop, to help the jury understand blood back spatter. Bishop had been the Island County coroner for decades. When Banks asked him how much experience he had in evaluating fatal gunshot wounds to the head, Bishop answered: "Ninety-two fatal gunshot to the head cases [specifically], and over five thousand deaths since I became coroner."

"What is your opinion as to where the victim was shot [inside the car versus outside]?"

"I feel very strongly he was shot where he was found, considering evidence of blood drainage as the victim was positioned in the car, lack of blood over bottom of the driver's-side door frame, position of feet, no bunching of pants around the knees—which appears when a body has been moved—*and* the tiny shards of shattered sunglasses."

Bishop's testimony negated virtually all of Dr. Jon Nordby's scientific conclusions. Indeed, Nordby's ponderous and lengthy time on the witness stand had obviously annoyed some of the jurors as they struggled to keep up with *his* theories.

CHAPTER THIRTY-SEVEN

EVERYONE INVOLVED HAD EXPECTED Jim Huden's trial to last at least two weeks. But then the gallery had hoped to hear from both Jim and Peggy Sue. Most of the testimony so far had shown that everywhere that Jim went in late 2003 and early 2004, Peggy Sue went, too.

No longer.

Jim had never made so much as a move toward the witness chair, and no one had seen Peggy Sue anywhere near the Island County courtroom. Had they testified, the trial would certainly have been much longer. As it was, there had been only eight days of testimony when the opposing attorneys rose to make their final statements. Judge Vickie Churchill would then give the jury instructions for their deliberation.

Judge Churchill advised the jury on that Friday morning that they would need to agree that four elements of the case before them had been proven in order to find James Huden guilty of first-degree, aggravated murder:

1. That Russel Douglas was indeed deceased.

2. That the incident occurred in the state of Washington.

3. That James Huden was involved in the murder of Russel Douglas on December 26, 2003.

4. That Douglas's homicide was premeditated.

Greg Banks began his closing arguments and stressed that all of these essentials had been proven in Huden's trial. Bill Hill's testimony and physical evidence had validated the third element, and circumstantial evidence had substantiated the fourth. The site of Russ Douglas's homicide and the fact that he was deceased left no doubt that number one and number two were correct.

Banks moved to charts and photographs that would help the jurors understand timelines and the trail of the deadly .380 Bersa to and from Washington State and Arizona.

Russ Douglas's face appeared on the screen, along with photos of Bill Hill and Keith Ogden.

"This case is also about heroes," Banks said. "I submit to you that Bill Hill is a hero; he had to choose between loyalty to his best and closest friend, and what his conscience told him."

And so, of course, did Keith Ogden, the former Oregon cop who hadn't hesitated to turn in the .380 when he learned that Washington detectives were looking for it.

"Neither of them were familiar with Whidbey Island or the crime, but they were motivated to testify against Huden because of their consciences.

"Mr. Hill knew there was something up here that he had to make right."

Greg Banks had begun his opening remarks by saying, "Mr. Huden assassinated Russel Douglas; [and now] the evidence is in, and most assuredly, the evidence has shown what I said to be true. And I repeat now that the defendant *did* cold-bloodedly assassinate Mr. Douglas."

The prosecutor had spoken for just under an hour and a half. He obviously knew every facet of the homicide almost nine years earlier and he had reconstructed it flawlessly for the jurors.

Matt Montoya responded for the defense. He scoffed at the state's reasoning and evidence. Montoya used a phrase repeatedly that was difficult to grasp, as he asked the jury to think "critically," and he praised Dr. Nordby's expertise.

"Facts are the enemy of the truth," Montoya said. He asked jurors if the state had *truly* overcome the presumption of Jim Huden's innocence.

Facts are the enemy of the truth.

In what way? I wondered. Perhaps Jon Nordby,

whose PhD in philosophy had led him to teach that subject at Pacific Lutheran University, could explain it.

Montoya said, "No one—*no one* can put Mr. Huden on Whidbey Island on December 26, 2003!"

But what about the sales slip for the cigars that Peggy Sue Thomas had—the one with that same date on it? Peggy Sue had saved it so carefully . . .

What about Jim's and Peggy Sue's story about returning Dick Deposit's house key on that day?

Over and over again, Matt Montoya's point was that nothing Greg Banks said "made sense." Why didn't Huden throw the gun into the Sound, if indeed he had one? Who said that Huden was abused as a child?

Facts are the enemy of the truth.

Montoya had relied on the testimonies of Jon Nordby—indeed, gambling thirty-six thousand dollars on Nordby's fee—and Ron Young, one of Jim Huden's three best friends since their teen years. Young lived in Tukwila, Washington, at least two hours away from Freeland. He had said he saw Huden on December 26, sometime between noon and 1 P.M.

"How could my client have arrived in Longview by five P.M.?"

Very easily. Even driving the speed limit, Longview wasn't much more than two and a half to three hours away from the landing dock of the Mukilteo or Keystone ferries.

That period between noon and 1 P.M. on the
day after Christmas 2003 was vital.

Maybe Montoya's axiom works better
backward.

*The truth is the enemy of the facts. No, that
didn't make sense either . . .*

Montoya was correct. Nothing matched. Jim
and Peggy could not have been two places at once
over the noon hour when experts believed Russel
Douglas was murdered.

"I ask you for a verdict of not guilty," Matt
Montoya finished.

Greg Banks spoke once more.

"Facts are stubborn things—there is no way
they can be avoided. You need to look at the fact
using common sense, while thinking critically.
Don't be distracted by any lack of phone records.
They're not always available and don't always provide evidence. Regarding Ron Young; eight years
later he recalls the time of day he saw Jim Huden
when he'd seen him three or four times since, but
can't recall when.

"The evidence is overwhelming. Focus on the
facts—they are stubborn."

At approximately 1 P.M. on July 20—a Friday—
the jurors retired to deliberate.

It didn't take long. By 11 A.M. on Monday,
July 23, Judge Vickie Churchill's courtroom was
packed. A verdict had been reached. It seemed as
though everyone who had waited for a verdict for
so long was there, with the somewhat surprising

exception of Brenna Douglas, the victim's widow, and their children, Hannah and Jack.

Peggy Sue Thomas wasn't there, either—but that wasn't surprising.

Judge Churchill accepted the slip of paper with the verdict from the jury foreman.

James Huden, fifty-nine, had been found guilty of murder, with aggravating circumstances in that a firearm was the weapon, and the victim was particularly vulnerable. Strapped into his car seat behind the steering wheel, believing he was there to pick up a package for his wife, he had seen a man approaching. Whether he had seen Huden before or if he was a complete stranger, no one might ever know for sure.

Certainly, Russ Douglas had had almost no warning that would prepare him for what was to come.

This was not a movie or television courtroom; there were no outcries or shouts. The room was very quiet, and Jim Huden kept his head down as he heard his fate read aloud.

Russel Douglas's mother, Gail O'Neal, stepfather, Bob, sister, Holly Hunziker, and her husband, Victor, were there. His father, Jim Douglas, was on Skype from Alaska. It was over, at least until Huden's formal sentencing, and as that sunk in, the Douglas family began to cry softly.

Jim Huden would remain in the Island County Jail until the sentencing date Judge Churchill chose. It would take almost exactly a month. Sentencing was set for the afternoon of August 24.

Prosecutor Greg Banks commented that he planned to ask for an "exceptional sentence" for Jim Huden because the murder had been so coldly premeditated. That might mean as much as a thirty-one-year prison sentence—until Huden was ninety years old.

"And even that does not come close to accounting for the malevolence of this crime," Banks added.

SHIRLEY HICKMAN, MY COURTROOM assistant for this book, is married to Lloyd Jackson, and knows many of his and Jim's longtime friends.

"I feel so sorry for Jim's friends: Lloyd, Dick Deposit, Jeff Gaylord, Ron Young, who have known him for so long and can't believe he's capable of such a terrible crime," Shirley told me. "They are all suffering through this ordeal. It's almost as if their youth was a lie, and now someone they trusted and loved is not who they thought he was. Or maybe he was, but something or *someone* influenced him in this tragedy."

JIM HUDEN'S SENTENCING WAS moved ahead a few days, and he was back in court on August 21 at 9 A.M.

Greg Banks categorized Russel Douglas's murder as "the most egregious, atrocious, premeditated crime," and said that Huden deserved no leniency.

Several offers of leniency had been offered to

Jim Huden if he would cooperate and help the prosecutor and investigating detectives understand why Douglas was murdered. They all believed that he had been heavily manipulated by the woman he was passionately in love with at the end of 2003: Peggy Sue.

But Jim had never said anything that might damage her or help to convict her.

His only counteroffer was not one they could even consider. He didn't hint at what he might tell them, but he had offered to cooperate if his prison sentence would be set at only ten years.

Greg Banks pointed out that Russ Douglas's murder was cold-blooded, calculated, and planned well in advance.

"He had many opportunities to change his mind," Banks said, "but he carried through with the planned assassination of someone he *didn't even know*!"

Banks's suggestion for sentencing was eighty years, considering that Russ's two children each faced forty years without a father. He also recommended financial restitution that Jim Huden was responsible for: approximately thirteen thousand dollars for the prosecution costs, thirty-six thousand dollars for Dr. Jon Nordby, and reimbursement to Russel's father, Jim Douglas, for burial expenses.

Jim Douglas and Russ's brother, Matthew, gave their victims' statements through Skype. His stepfather, Bob O'Neal, his mother, Gail, and sister,

Holly, made eye contact with Huden as they spoke of the terrible loss they had suffered because of the coldly motiveless murder.

"I gave him his first hug," Gail O'Neal said, "but I wasn't there to give him his last hug . . . In one split second, you pulled the trigger and you killed Russ. And you changed our lives and futures forever."

Unlike Jim's mien throughout his trial, he did meet their eyes, but he never changed expression.

They all had the same question: "Why? You didn't even know him!"

"He was a good father to his children," Gail O'Neal said. "He was in no way an abuser. You must have listened to someone else and someone needs to own up; someone needs to tell the truth so that this family can put it behind us."

But Jim Huden had no statement to make. Was he protecting someone—or was he hoping to file an appeal for a new trial? His attorney said later that that was why Jim didn't say a word.

Judge Vickie Churchill sentenced him to eighty years, while telling him that everyone needed to know why. "There is something more to this case, and we all know it. Anything else is just crazy."

And of course it was.

After Jim Huden was handcuffed and led from the courtroom, the judge offered her sympathy to Russel Douglas's family, and urged them to move on with their lives in a positive manner, in the hope that would help them in the healing process.

Once again, Brenna Douglas was absent from the courtroom. Greg Banks had told her of the new date and time—but she said she was afraid media crews from around the country would be there and she would be exposed by television coverage.

Brenna had had no choice but to testify six weeks earlier, but she never came back. Her husband had been dead for almost nine years, and it was obvious that Brenna wanted the whole thing to just go away.

But she was still a "person of interest," and she knew it.

CHAPTER THIRTY-EIGHT

IT WASN'T OVER. Peggy Sue Thomas's trial for first-degree murder lay ahead, set for November 2012. One could only hope that some of the mysterious questions in Russ Douglas's strange and lonely death might be answered then.

Peggy Sue seemed to be preparing to look her best for her trial—or for whatever prison sentence she might receive. Undoubtedly, she was shocked by the exceptional eighty-year sentence Jim had received. Since he was almost sixty, that was well over a life sentence for him.

Could she expect the same punishment if a jury found her guilty, too? Surely she considered that.

Peggy's "Thanksgiving trial" was postponed until January 29, 2013.

When she visited her father and stepmother in Idaho over Christmas, her relatives detected a subtle difference in the way she looked—but they couldn't put their finger on what it was.

Nor could Greg Banks or Mark Plumberg. Her sister Rhonda knew; Peggy Sue had had some further plastic surgery, and it was done well. She had had a filler injected into her lips, which made them more cushiony and fuller.

Further, Peggy had some permanent tattooing, particularly around her eyes, lining them exotically, and now had perfect eyebrows, thanks to tattoos. Her lip liner tattoo would last forever, and there was also a soft reddish color there. If she did go to prison and was unable, for whatever reason, to have access to makeup, it wouldn't matter; her makeup was now a part of her.

There was another tattoo, one that Peggy Thomas shared with her two daughters. They weren't little girls now, and whatever else had happened in her life, Peggy's girls had always been there for her. One was in medical school and the other was doing well in college, but they agonized over the thought of their mother going to prison. They loved and trusted Peggy Sue.

So Peggy Sue, Mariah, and Taylor got identical tattoos on their backs: a Bible quote from Proverbs 31 about the virtues of a perfect woman. Thus far, the exact words remain a secret among Peggy and her daughters.

ON FRIDAY, JANUARY 18, 2013, Peggy Sue Thomas and Jim Huden met in person for the first time in nine years. Would this reunion be the culmination of a great love? Many thought that Jim had given up any chance of freedom to protect Peggy. Would he maintain his huge sacrifice for her?

Island County Prosecutor Greg Banks arranged to have Jim Huden brought from prison under heavy guard to the courtroom where Peggy Sue and her attorney, Craig Platt, would also be present. Die-hard romantics expected some longing glances, or perhaps a whispered private word or two.

One of the issues to be discussed at this January hearing a short time before Peggy's trial for first-degree murder was whether Jim Huden would testify against his former lover in *her* murder trial. If he should refuse to do so—citing the Fifth Amendment on the grounds that his testimony could be self-incriminating—the hearsay rule would not then prevent Bill Hill and Jim's wife, Jean Huden, from testifying.

Hill continued to say that Jim Huden had confessed murder to him, and so did Jean Huden. They also believed that Peggy Sue Thomas was an integral part of the plot to shoot Russ Douglas.

A lot was at stake. But romance in the courtroom was not part of the drama. Jim and Peggy avoided each other's eyes. At the most, they might have been casual acquaintances who had known each other briefly many years before.

A meeting earlier that Friday morning had included Huden, Montoya, and Craig Platt. There, Jim Huden insisted that he had *never* implicated Peggy Thomas in any guilty way in Douglas's death. She hadn't lured the victim to Wahl Road with the promise of a Christmas gift for his wife, Brenna Douglas.

Jim did, however, make a number of disparaging comments about Bill Hill's character flaws as he met with Montoya and Platt.

No one could force Huden to testify against Peggy.

When he took the stand, Jim Huden invoked the Fifth Amendment many times, refusing to answer any questions about Peggy. As he repeated the same phrase, Peggy stared at him with hard eyes from across the courtroom. If she was anxious or frightened by what he might say, she didn't show it.

Would he or wouldn't he testify against her in her actual trial?

Not likely.

Greg Banks won a single victory during that hearing. He asked Judge Allen Hancock to add a second charge against Peggy—that she be charged with "conspiracy to commit first-degree murder."

The conspiracy charge would be much more likely for Banks to prove than the first-degree murder case.

The one person who could bring Peggy Sue down—the one person who would undoubtedly convince a jury of her guilt—was Jim Huden. And he had dug his heels in.

Jim Huden had filed an appeal, but he seemed adamant that he would continue to leave the woman he once loved—or perhaps still loved—out of any appeal.

Mark Plumberg had focused on Huden as he answered questions on the witness stand. Huden wore a bright orange prison-issue jumpsuit. Plumberg had detected no acknowledgment on Jim's part that Peggy Sue was even in the room.

"But as he stepped down," Plumberg said, "I saw him wink at Peggy. I don't know if anyone else in the room saw it."

What did it mean? That Jim and Peggy Sue were still partners—silent partners? Was it Jim's way of reassuring her that her dark secrets were safe with him? Or was it a sardonic wink meant to tell her he knew she had betrayed him?

WITH A TRIAL DATE set for January 29, it seemed as though Peggy Sue Thomas was *finally* going to face a jury of her peers. Embarrassed to make and possibly have to cancel a reservation for the fourth time with a motel in Island County, I contacted another hotel. Still, it looked as if this time the trial was a solid go.

And then, three days before Peggy's trial was to begin, I got a phone call from Prosecutor Greg Banks. He and his staff had been very considerate over the prior two years about letting interested parties know when circumstances and trial dates changed suddenly.

This time, the news was truly shocking, and I must admit, disappointing.

"Peggy Sue Thomas is not going to trial," Banks said. "She is going to plead guilty to the lesser charge—first-degree criminal assistance involving first-degree murder."

How could this be?

She had been facing a forty-five-year prison sentence if she was convicted on the murder charge, and she was forty-seven. If she didn't die in prison, Peggy would be ninety-two when she was released. She would be far from "Drop-Dead Gorgeous" by then, her auburn mane gray, her smooth face a mass of wrinkles. And her beloved daughters would probably be grandmothers themselves.

Peggy and her attorney were well aware of Jim's eighty-year sentence. That was twice as much as he had expected in the worst possible scenario. She could not imagine being locked behind bars for the rest of her life.

Was Peggy so afraid of getting as long a sentence as Jim had that she chose to plead guilty? It seemed so.

Shocked, I asked Greg Banks what sentence she might be facing now—with her guilty plea.

"Four years."

"You mean that's the shortest amount?" I asked with a slight sense of confidence. "Surely she will get at least twenty years?"

"No, that's the most she can get under Washington State statutes."

"*Four years? And with an automatic deadly weapon charge adding on five more years?*" I persisted.

"No. Just four years."

Banks and Peggy Sue's attorney, Craig Platt, had been in intense meetings. A trial was risky, and would not have had a foregone conclusion—for either the state or the defense.

Jim Huden had been convicted, yes, but there was solid physical evidence that linked Jim to the deadly ambush murder—the gun, casings, bullets, his fingerprints on many pages of the gun manual. Indeed, he himself had confessed to his wife and his best friend, Bill Hill.

But Peggy was another story. There were no "damned spots" soiling her pretty hands. There was that single fingerprint on the .380 Bersa manual. A good attorney—and Platt was a very skilled lawyer—could certainly raise doubts that she had only touched the manual casually as she stacked magazines or dusted her coffee table.

According to Keith Ogden, the former cop who had turned in Jim's gun, Peggy knew about the gun. She was present when Jim brought the Bersa over to Keith, seeking instructions. But she'd shown no interest in it. Learning how to shoot it was Jim's thing.

Had Jim had anything to gain from Russ Douglas's death? No. Had Peggy had a potential motive? Yes. She and Jim had been living high on the hog, and despite her salary and tips from her limousine driving in Las Vegas, they were close to broke and had maxed out her credit cards.

In 2003, Peggy wanted to sell her house to Brenna Douglas—but Brenna had no money to buy it. If Russ was dead, Brenna expected seven hundred thousand dollars in insurance payoffs.

With part of that, she could buy Peggy's house, and Peggy wouldn't be constantly living over a financial abyss.

If he could present only circumstantial evidence, albeit masses of it, Greg Banks realized that Peggy might possibly win in court. She was facing a murder charge that might not be easily provable, a case that was at some points as fragile and flyaway as dandelion fluff in the wind.

Peggy Thomas was very attractive, most convincing when she wanted to be, charming enough to impress gullible jurors. And she could walk away free and clear, never to be tried again because double jeopardy would attach.

And Banks had lost his most powerful witnesses. Brenda was dead, and Bill Hill was in critical condition in a Florida hospital. There was no way that he could survive a trip across the country and the stress of testifying once more against his best friend. Indeed, he might never be able to take the stand again.

Jean Huden was on the state's witness list, but it would be easy for Craig Platt to convince jurors that she was not a reliable and believable witness. Jean had a long, long criminal background—mostly having to do with illicit drugs. Platt could deconstruct her image with very few questions. As a backup to Bill Hill's testimony, Jean would be valuable to the prosecution. Alone, any power she had as a truth teller would be decimated.

Ironically, both Greg Banks and Craig Platt were eager to see Peggy Sue go on trial. Hers would be a landmark legal event, and it would be a challenge for both of them. Jousting in court at its best.

And still. Banks was well aware of the hundreds, thousands, of hours his office and the Island County Sheriff's crew had put into finding out who *really* spearheaded the plot to destroy Russel Douglas. He and Mark Plumberg both believed that Jim Huden was the shooter. But neither of them felt the cowardly murder had been Jim's idea.

They had long considered that Brenna Douglas had guilty knowledge in the case. And they both believed that the Peggy Sue Thomas they had come to know well was the most likely suspect to set the murder plan in motion.

She had approached several people in sticky situations and offered Jim up as an assassin who would take care of their "problems." It was almost as if she had her own "bucket list," and setting up and getting away with murder was high on that list. That may have been one of her motivations; the other was money.

Peggy had sought big-time money for as long as anyone could remember.

If the state's case against the lovely redhead should fall short, no one in the prosecutor's or sheriff's office could deal with watching her walk away with no punishment at all. Banks had discussed the plea bargain with Russ Douglas's family, and they had agreed, somewhat grudgingly, to the only way they could be certain that Peggy Thomas served prison time.

Craig Platt, on the other hand, had seen the massive coverage and speculation in the media and among the residents of Island County. Peggy Thomas had few supporters, other than her mother and father, her half sister Sue Mahoney, her two daughters, and her ex-husband, Kelvin. She wasn't a famous beauty queen any longer; she was infamous and notorious as an accused murderer.

Depending on how she impressed a jury—or not—she could be facing a very long prison term.

And so, for their own reasons, Banks and Platt agreed to a plea bargain from Peggy. With her personality, she wouldn't be getting off easy. A woman who had become bored married to a billionaire after only a few months would not be happy locked in a cell with a thin mattress and no privacy, eating bland prison food, and wearing a drab uniform while she scrubbed floors and did dishes or some other onerous prison assignment.

Most of all, she would hate having someone control everything she did for forty-eight months.

And so there was no trial for Peggy Sue Thomas. There was only a sentencing, set ironically for the day after Valentine's Day 2013.

FEBRUARY 15 IN COUPEVILLE, WASHINGTON, was one of those late winter days in the Northwest where the day dawns inexplicably with azure blue, cloudless skies, and sunshine beams down on every street, every budding crocus. It was a perfect day and the historic houses built in the 1800s looked brand-new again.

Courtroom number 2 in the Island County Justice Center opened early that morning so video cameras could be placed to focus on Peggy Sue Thomas. Reporters and still photographers—not jurors—now found spots in the jury box.

There had been a few court days during all the trials and hearings concerning Peggy Sue Thomas and Jim Huden when the courtroom in Coupeville had many empty seats—but not now. While the long benches on the left side of the courtroom filled up quickly, and those on the right were reserved for Peggy Sue's family and friends, court house employees stood against the back wall.

I wondered if Peggy Thomas had looked out the windows of the vehicle bringing her here and realized that she was about to be separated from the world she knew, shut off from true fresh air for sixteen seasons to come.

She had been free on bail until she got to court. When she walked in with her daughters, Peggy looked great, with her thick hair falling below her shoulders, and bangs swept to one side of her forehead. Her makeup, of course, was tattooed on.

She wore a beige unconstructed jacket with large buttons over a gray top and dark slacks.

Peggy Sue took her place at the defense table next to her attorney, Craig Platt. Kelvin Thomas and her daughters, Taylor and Mariah, sat in the row behind her. Doris Matz wasn't there. Whether she was ill or simply could not bear hearing her precious daughter sentenced to prison, no one knew.

Kelvin had Peggy Sue's back—as he always had. He would be the sole parent to their two daughters over the next four years. That wasn't unusual; Kelvin had always shared raising the girls. That was one thing she wouldn't have to worry about while she was in prison. If they needed someone to turn to, they had their dad.

THIS WAS ONE OF the strangest sentencing events I've ever observed. Greg Banks told the court that Peggy Thomas was prepared to plead guilty to rendering criminal assistance in the first degree, explaining that this was the same terminology that was used in other jurisdictions as a defendant "knowingly being an accessory after the fact of a crime."

Platt gave Judge Allen Hancock about twenty letters written in support of Peggy's character.

Everyone involved, in whatever way, in the long-unsolved murder of Russ Douglas was in this courtroom. Everyone—except for Russ, of course, and Peggy Sue's mother, Doris—and Jim Huden and Brenna Douglas.

During a break, I found myself standing in the central aisle next to Mark Plumberg, who was standing within inches of Peggy Sue and her daughters. She didn't acknowledge Plumberg—or me—as she seemed to clasp every minute with her girls she could get. So much would change in the next four years, but Peggy would be on the inside looking out as Mariah and Taylor became mature women.

I wondered if she was finally accepting the truth about what she threw away because of Russ Douglas's murder.

Russel Douglas's family appeared to feel more enmity toward Peggy than they had toward Jim Huden. Jim Douglas was once again in the courtroom via Skype and he said he was speaking for both himself and his son Matt.

"This was a cold and premeditated act," he said. "I hope she won't hurt anyone else. Her short sentence is a travesty. She lured Russ to his murder, and Jim Huden is also a victim. This isn't justice, but it does bring finality. You used your feminine wiles with utter callousness. You're not a victim [of anything]. You are a predator."

Bob O'Neal, Russ's stepfather, stood about eight feet away from Peggy. "You took my son, a part of my life. I don't believe your apologies. You played them as you've played people all your life. You sullied my son's reputation."

As she faced the rage and bitterness of her victim's family, Peggy Sue looked at them without expression. The pupils in her eyes seemed huge; it was quite possible that she had taken tranquilizers before her sentencing.

Peggy Sue, at last, was scared.

Gail O'Neal was next. She demanded that Peggy look at her as she spoke. Peggy looked up from time to time, but mostly focused on the floor.

"Russ and Brenna had a tragic mess of a marriage," Gail said. "They both played mind games with each other. The kids were pawns. Russ wasn't perfect—but you have the key to all the answers. I *beg* you to tell what happened. You have nothing left to lose. If you ever get the guts to tell, please call me."

And then, oddly, Craig Platt rose and began a PowerPoint presentation designed to show Peggy Sue's innocence!

Perhaps he felt compelled to give what should have been his final arguments in a trial that never happened. Those used to the ground rules of a trial were baffled as the slide show continued.

Didn't Platt understand that that train had left the station? There was no trial, and the sentencing was no place for argument now. Still, Peggy's attorney continued to extol her as a great mother, with no criminal record. "She is a credit to her community and she's not a headline grabber. Three times she was released to travel. Three times, she came back."

Given a few more minutes, Platt might have likened Peggy Sue to the Virgin Mary.

He gave Jim Huden short shrift—calling him a "nut head" and a "complete loser."

Greg Banks had had enough. He reminded Judge Hancock that Russ Douglas's friends and family had been suffering for nine years with too many unanswered questions. "We see through a glass darkly. James Huden learned about Russ from either Brenna Douglas or Peggy Sue Thomas."

Judge Hancock carried on the plea that Peggy

Thomas tell what she knew. It was so clearly the decent thing to do.

"It makes no sense that both Jim and Russ should be in the same place [at the time of the murder]. *Why?* There was no motive at all," the judge said. "Peggy Thomas has it within her to alleviate this family's suffering. If she is so kind, caring, and compassionate [as Craig Platt had characterized her], then she will tell."

But Peggy Sue said nothing.

It was time for Judge Hancock to read her sentence.

"You will serve forty-eight months in prison— that's as much as I can give you."

The judge then listed what she would be required to pay:

> $217 in court costs
> $500 for the Washington State Victims
>   Compensation Fund
> $100 for collection of fines

The courtroom throbbed with silence for what seemed like a long time. And then Peggy Sue Thomas stood up and submitted to a body search by Deputy Bill Becker. She was taller and heavier than he was. Satisfied that she had no contraband, he locked her hands behind her back with handcuffs and led her out of the courtroom.

Her daughters cried quietly.

Epilogue

PEGGY SUE WILL SERVE her time in the Washington Correction Center for Women in Purdy—not far from the soaring Tacoma Narrows Bridge. As prisons go, it is neither a hellhole nor a country club, and is actually quite livable.

Ironically there *was* a country club less than a mile down the road from the women's prison—the Canterwood Golf and Country Club—but Peggy Sue Thomas wouldn't be using those posh facilities. That lifestyle was gone for her—at least for four years.

After being the center of a great deal of media attention for several years, Peggy Sue Thomas has actually dropped out of the headlines and television news flashes. She is yesterday's news.

How she will fare in prison is anybody's guess. She has always been adept at befriending women who initially find her caring and considerate. She has had several "best friends forever" in the past, although none of those friendships have ended happily.

Prison will be one place where having a close female friend, a kind of "second lieutenant," is important. If Peggy wants to find a close buddy, she will be able to accomplish that easily.

I can see Peggy being an inmate like Martha Stewart was. She is highly intelligent, inventive, and fun to be around. And she is a take-charge personality who enjoys being the center of attention. She is quite likely to be one of the most popular inmates at Purdy. Or the most hated.

Will she miss male companionship? Possibly not. Men have been a means to an end—usually wealth—for Peggy Sue Thomas, and I suspect she doesn't really *like* them. She is so attractive that she is likely to get mail from men on the outside who will be eager to send her money for extras and treats from the prison commissary. But she already has family who will try to make her as comfortable as possible. Kelvin Thomas, her second husband, will undoubtedly continue to stand behind her. If her mother, Doris, is in good health, she will see that Peggy Sue gets everything she wants—given the constrictions of incarceration.

Mariah and Taylor will visit her as often as they can.

And Peggy does have scores of former limousine clients who may get in touch with her when they learn that she is spending the next four years behind bars.

Will she see a ghost in her cell when the lights are dimmed? Probably not. Peggy Sue appeared to forget Russel Douglas within a week or so of his murder. It is Jim Huden who has been haunted by the image of the man in his gun sight.

I think the lack of freedom to come and go may be the worst punishment for Peggy Thomas. I have never been *sent* to prison, but I have visited any number of felons there. Although I am inside for only a few hours, I dread the sound of iron doors clanging shut behind me. Even when Peggy Sue was a murder suspect, she was allowed to travel with that heavy GPS chained to her ankle.

And now she can't do that.

Jim Huden has filed an appeal, but he still hasn't said anything linking his former lover to the death of Russ Douglas.

I discussed Huden's stubborn loyalty to Peggy Sue with Mark Plumberg.

"How could Jim Huden have become so obsessed with Peggy that he committed a murder for her?" I asked. "And then he accepted an eighty-year sentence to protect her when she doesn't seem to care about him at all?"

"I've thought about that a lot," Mark said. "I think that Jim really loved Peggy, and that his protecting her and not 'ratting' out either Peggy or Brenna is, perhaps, the only nobility he has left."

Mark Plumberg would like nothing better than to talk to Jim Huden. "But I can't right now because Jim has filed an appeal. I hope that someday we may have a conversation."

The Island County detective would also like to talk in depth to Brenna Douglas. She had no choice but to testify in Huden's trial, but whenever investigators attempt to talk to her, she refuses to say anything more about her husband's murder. They visited her once more after Peggy Sue was sentenced, but she refused to answer their questions.

As things stand now, there isn't any physical evidence to link Brenna to the plot to kill Russ.

And that is ironic, because in the end, Brenna has been the only one who benefited financially from the murder. The insurance money is long gone. Brenna has moved frequently since she left Whidbey Island. She has not remarried, although Russel's mother thinks she is currently dating someone. Brenna has gained a lot of weight over the past decade.

Not surprisingly, the Stackhouse family has not survived all the tragedies intact. "We've been torn apart," Rhonda Vogl says. "Our mother is gone, Robby's gone, Brenda's gone—and no one really gets along with each other anymore. I was invited to Peggy's wedding to Mark Allen, but I had no idea who he was or when she had met him. Nothing. I didn't attend the ceremony.

"Those members of our family who are left just aren't close."

Jimmie Stackhouse has had to rebuild his magnificent Idaho log home twice because it was destroyed by fire on two separate occasions.

IN THE SOMETIMES EERIE way that my choices for book titles turn out to seem more than coincidental, it happened again. More than two decades after Rhonda lectured Peggy about lying, and long before I met or talked to any of its principal characters, I chose *Practice to Deceive* as the title for this book.

When I first interviewed Rhonda Stackhouse Vogl, she asked what my book would be called. When I told her, an odd expression flickered across her face.

Later, she sent me an email: "I was a little shocked," she wrote. "That sounded so familiar, but I couldn't place it. And then I remembered that night when Peggy Sue wanted me to lie and give her an alibi for her sneaky date. I wouldn't do it, and I told her, 'Oh what tangled webs we weave when first we practice to deceive.'

"It didn't make much of an impression on her. She snuck out anyway. She usually did what she wanted to do."

And, indeed, what a tangled web *was* woven when those without conscience practiced to deceive.

ACKNOWLEDGMENTS

I MIGHT NEVER HAVE HEARD of this strange and complicated story were it not for my longtime friend Shirley Hickman. She happened to mention it over lunch a few years ago, and handed me a short newspaper clipping.

"Have you heard about this?" she asked. "My husband went to school with this man, and now his friend has been charged with murder. You might want to look into it."

I get about four thousand suggestions every year—mostly from strangers—and the mass of them won't work for me for one reason or another. Shirley and her husband, Lloyd Jackson, live on an island in Puget Sound, and I had been attending a trial in another part of the state. Indeed, I had never heard of the cases she mentioned. But I certainly looked into it.

So, first and foremost, I thank Shirley Hickman. She kept me apprised of what was happening on her island, and often attended hearings and trials with me.

Even though I try to do intense research for every book I write, there is no way I could unearth the stories beneath the stories without the help and co-operation of law enforcement officials, homicide detectives, prosecuting attorneys, and numerous witnesses who add to my files about what led up to astounding tragedies. This story turned out to be one of the most wide-ranging series of events that I have ever written.

Some of the officials, detectives, and acquain-tances of the principals I interviewed prefer not to be named, and others tell me it's okay.

And there are always my friends who boost me up when I think I can't write one more paragraph. They have no idea how much they help me.

I will begin with those citizens of Whidbey Is-land, Washington, who patiently answered ques-tions and provided me with documents under the public information statute and with their own per-sonal stories:

Island County Prosecuting Attorney Greg Banks, his paralegal and assistant, Michelle Graff, and Is-land County Sheriff Mark C. Brown and Detective Mark Plumberg, and numerous officers on staff there, who all helped me immeasurably. Court Re-porter Karen Shipley, Judge Vickie Churchill, Judge Alan Hancock, and Deputy Bill Becker.

Although I know it was difficult for them, I ap-preciated the memories—spoken and written— of the victims' family members: Jim Douglas, Gail O'Neal, Bob O'Neal, Holly Hunsicker, Victor Hunsicker, Rhonda and Mitch Vogl, and Lana Galbraith, who will soon publish her own book on her family. I truly believe that family members who have been lost to accidents, homicide, and suicide would have spoken with me—if only they could.

Lloyd Jackson and Vickie Boyer shared the history of those who were accused, information that few will know until they read this book. I also thank Angela Vosburg, Cathy and Dean Hatt, and Jennifer McCormick of Whidbey Island, and Keith and Donna Ogden of New Mexico. There are many others who prefer not to be named here. There are also individuals who refused to be interviewed for their own reasons.

As always, I thank my very first reader, Gerry Hay, and my second reader, Kate Jewell.

All of the Jolly Matron Society members, and the Semi-Boeing Union Meeting friends: Carol Lovall and Donna Anders. Kathleen and Jeff Huget, Laura, Rebecca, and Matthew Harris, Leslie and Glenn Scott, Andy Rule, Mike, Marie, Holland, and Gray Rule, and Bruce, Machel, Olivia, Tyra, and Logan Sherles. Captain Dan Jones, Cindy Wilkinson, John P. Kelly, and Barb Thompson.

The *South Whidbey Record*, especially reporters Jessica Stensland and Ben Watanabe.

To my literary agents of forty years: Joan and Joe Foley of the Foley Agency, and my theatrical agent, Ron Bernstein, vice president of International Creative Management Partners.

I am grateful to have been associated with Simon & Schuster/Gallery Books for decades, and for the capable and intelligent team who take my manuscripts from first draft to a real, live book: my perceptive and tactful editor, Mitchell Ivers; my publisher, Louise Burke; Natasha Simons, Mitchell's assistant, who does a yeoman's job as she enters editorial changes and helps me create the photo sections—one of the most difficult parts of what we do! My publicist at Gallery: Jean Anne Rose, production editor Carly Sommerstein, production manager Larry Pekarek, managing editor Kevin McCahill, copy editor Faren Bachelis, art director Lisa Litwack, and book designer Lewelin Polanco.